Indigenous Healing as Paradox

KRISTA MAXWELL

Indigenous Healing as Paradox

Re-Membering and Biopolitics in the Settler Colony

UNIVERSITY *of* **ALBERTA** PRESS

PUBLISHED BY

University of Alberta Press
1-16 Rutherford Library South
11204 89 Avenue NW
Edmonton, Alberta, Canada T6G 2J4
amiskwaciwâskahikan | Treaty 6 |
Métis Territory
ualbertapress.ca | uapress@ualberta.ca

Copyright © 2025 Krista Maxwell

LIBRARY AND ARCHIVES CANADA
CATALOGUING IN PUBLICATION

Title: Indigenous healing as paradox :
    re-membering and biopolitics in the
    settler colony / Krista Maxwell.
Names: Maxwell, Krista, author.
Description: Includes bibliographical
    references and index.
Identifiers: Canadiana (print) 20240357868 |
    Canadiana (ebook) 20240357957 |
    ISBN 9781772125740 (softcover) |
    ISBN 9781772127898 (EPUB) |
    ISBN 9781772127904 (PDF)
Subjects: LCSH: Indigenous peoples—
    Canada—Social conditions. |
    LCSH: Indigenous peoples—
    Health and hygiene—Canada. |
    LCSH: Biopolitics—Canada. |
    LCSH: Social medicine—Canada. |
    LCSH: Canada—Ethnic relations.
Classification: LCC E98.S67 M39 2024 |
    DDC 305.897/071—dc23

First edition, first printing, 2025.
First printed and bound in Canada by
Houghton Boston Printers, Saskatoon,
Saskatchewan.
Copyediting and proofreading by
Joanne Muzak.
Indexing by Stephen Ullstrom.

This publication is licensed under a
Creative Commons licence, Attribution–
Noncommercial–No Derivative Works 4.0
International: see www.creativecommons.
org. The text may be reproduced for noncommercial purposes, provided that credit
is given to the original author. To obtain
permission for uses beyond those outlined
in the Creative Commons licence, please
contact University of Alberta Press.

University of Alberta Press supports
copyright. Copyright fuels creativity,
encourages diverse voices, promotes free
speech, and creates a vibrant culture.
Thank you for buying an authorized
edition of this book and for complying
with the copyright laws by not reproducing, scanning, or distributing any part
of it in any form without permission.
You are supporting writers and allowing
University of Alberta Press to continue to
publish books for every reader.

University of Alberta Press is committed
to protecting our natural environment.
As part of our efforts, this book is printed
on Enviro Paper: it contains 100%
post-consumer recycled fibres and is
acid- and chlorine-free.

GPSR: Easy Access System Europe |
Mustamäe tee 50, 10621 Tallinn, Estonia |
gpsr.requests@easproject.com

This book has been published with the
help of a grant from the Federation for the
Humanities and Social Sciences, through
the Awards to Scholarly Publications
Program, using funds provided by the
Social Sciences and Humanities Research
Council of Canada.

University of Alberta Press gratefully
acknowledges the support received for its
publishing program from the Government
of Canada, the Canada Council for the
Arts, and the Government of Alberta
through the Alberta Media Fund.

Contents

vii	Preface
xiii	Acknowledgements
xxi	Artist Statement
1	**Introduction:** Indigenous Re-Membering and Biopolitics in the Liberal Settler Colony
45	**1** | Giizhiiganang and Anishinaabe Re-Membering, 1965–1980
75	**2** | Re-Membering and Biopolitics in Urban Ontario, 1973–1980s
101	**3** | "Family Violence Is Weakening Our Nations": Indigenous Women, Political Dismemberment, and Family Healing, 1972–1990

129	**4	Biopolitical Tactics under Neoliberal Settler Colonialism:** Healing as Public Discourse, 1990–2015
167	**Conclusion:** Towards an Indigenized Politics of Life
179	Appendix: Methods and Sources
183	Notes
213	References
251	Index

Preface

THIS BOOK has a long and convoluted history. I could simply locate its origins in the early 2000s, when I began doctoral research with an initial goal of understanding how and why "Aboriginal mental health" was becoming a ubiquitous discourse in Canada. Instead, I offer a more personal and rigorous account of how it came to be, one that includes my coming to terms with individual and familial complicity in settler colonialism as beneficiaries of Indigenous dispossession.

I was born in the province of Nova Scotia, a descendant through my father of Scottish and Irish settlers who crossed the Atlantic in the late eighteenth century to claim their free portions of Mi'kmaq territory. My English and Danish maternal grandparents immigrated with their young children in 1946, settling in Edmonton in the Treaty 6 territory of the Cree, Anishinaabeg, Saulteaux, Nakota, and Blackfoot, and the prairie homeland of the Métis. Growing up during the 1970s in socially conservative Halifax, the observant, questioning (some would say difficult) child of a single mother, I developed an early political consciousness and curiosity about the everyday social exclusion and discrimination that I witnessed: sexism and misogyny, class hierarchy, homophobia, and racialized segregation of members of the oldest Black community in Canada. But I had little awareness of the ongoing presence of the Mi'kmaq whose land my ancestors had stolen, or the history of their violent dispossession, including a mid-eighteenth-century bounty policy rewarding settlers who killed Mi'kmaq under British governor Cornwallis. (At the time of writing, Cornwallis Street in downtown Halifax has been renamed to honour the Mi'kmaw activist Nora Bernard, with substantial support from Haligonians.)

In the early 1980s, a Mi'kmaw woman came to speak to my grade-eleven social studies class. I was disturbed by her account of her people's historical dispossession and ongoing struggles, shocked and angry that this was the first time I had heard about this history, and horrified by the rudeness, even hostility, displayed by some students. I started asking questions about this hidden history and clearly ongoing but mostly latent conflict, to which the adults around me were unable to respond meaningfully. A few years later, while attending the North American Anarchist Gathering in Toronto, I happened upon a copy of Jeannette Armstrong's *Slash* in the Toronto Women's Bookstore. By this time, I'd lived in London, England, for several years, where I was active in the squatting and anti-apartheid movements, pirate radio, and anarchist feminist organizing. I remained ignorant about Indigenous experiences in Canada. Reading *Slash* helped me to understand a little better what I'd witnessed in that social studies class. And with my growing understanding of international history and politics (from living in a city whose diversity reflects its imperial history, more so than my A-level studies), I began to connect Indigenous dispossession in Canada with world histories of imperialism. But it wasn't until I returned to Canada, more than a decade later, that I figured out how to start learning more about these connections.

My first job as a returning Canadian after many years of living and working in England and Nigeria was coordinator of a diversity training program for employees at a large mental health research and treatment facility in Toronto, Southern Ontario. There I observed an awkward dance around Indigeneity and "diversity." I was told that the trainers should briefly acknowledge Indigenous Peoples during our day-long mandatory diversity workshop, which took a vaguely intersectional approach, but weren't to discuss Indigenous issues in any substantive way, lest we subsume Indigeneity within the diversity paradigm. Being enfolded within multiculturalism is a long-standing concern of Indigenous people, and particularly acute in Southern Ontario, where ethnically diverse cities are sites of long histories of anti-racist organizing, including around mental health, by non-Indigenous racialized groups. But this concern was inadequately addressed by the institutional arrangement, which included a separate course addressing Indigenous perspectives on mental health (not mandatory and with less administrative support, and therefore attended by only a small proportion of staff), while the universally required diversity training all but rendered Indigenous Peoples invisible. Meanwhile, the diversity training team was directed to start delivering workshops to mental health and addictions workers at various sites around the large province of Ontario. Prospective participants in the north of the province, where Indigenous people make up a much larger proportion of the population, told us in no uncertain terms that training on diversity with minimal attention to Indigenous experience would be absurd in their social and workplace contexts. But our team of (mostly racialized and/or queer) trainers were ill equipped to respond.

After leaving this job, my enduring interest in the Indigeneity-diversity friction and consciousness of my own ongoing ignorance about Indigenous experience and Canadian settler colonialism led me to volunteer to write research proposals for the Aboriginal Services team led by Anishinaabe social worker Dr. Peter Menzies and including Cree Elder Vern Harper. Peter and Vern introduced me to the recent history and institutional politics of Indigenous well-being in Toronto, which became the starting point for my PhD research. Early on, I realized that my academic training and prior experience of collaborative research with racialized and otherwise marginalized groups did not sufficiently equip me to work in respectful and rigorous ways with Indigenous people in the context of ongoing Canadian settler colonialism. This was a humbling realization to have in my late thirties, following a successful early career as a researcher in public health and medical anthropology with a focus on race and health equity. Quite simply, my long-standing interest in colonialism and health informed by work in "postcolonial" settings (with Black communities in Britain, and in Nigeria, a former British colony) had not prepared me to understand the particularities of Canadian settler colonialism as continuing in the present, what that meant for Indigenous experience, and the entailments for settler scholars.

The doctoral research initially inspired by my curiosity about the friction between Indigeneity and diversity training in the mental health sector involved learning from dozens of people, mostly Indigenous, including providers of health and social services, Elders, and policymakers. My initial geographic focus, in part due to family obligations, was close to home: three Southern Ontario cities—Hamilton, Ottawa, and Toronto—each home to a significant Indigenous population. During my final year of doctoral research, I met an Anishinaabe Elder from Naongashiing (Big Island) First Nation in Treaty 3 territory, Joseph Morrison (Bigwekinang). Although Joseph lived outside of Kenora, in November 2009 he was in Hamilton for a powwow, part of the veterans' contingent, so I took the bus to Hamilton to meet him, my seven-year-old son in tow. During our initial conversation in a hotel restaurant, Joseph spoke frankly and at length about personal and family histories of residential school attendance, alcohol abuse, interpersonal violence, community leadership, and social and political organizing in Kenora and Treaty 3 territory, and shared his critical analysis of contemporary relations between Indigenous people, Canadian society, and the settler state. Joseph's extensive expertise reflected his rich life experiences as a long-serving justice of the peace, in the Friendship Centre movement at local, provincial, and national levels, military service, as well as Anishinaabe spiritual and linguistic knowledge. We met again twice during his visits to Toronto over the ensuing year, and Joseph shared more detailed accounts of his personal and family histories. I shared with him historical documents about the Kenora Waystation where Joseph's father, Giizhiiganang (Don Morrison), had worked as a counsellor, retrieved from the Centre for Addiction and Mental Health Archives in Toronto.

Joseph's oral history considerably enriched my PhD thesis, but I felt my analysis hadn't done justice to the histories he shared. Our conversations left me reflecting on the many artificial separations and binaries that organize and constrict public and academic conversations about Indigenous healing and well-being: health/politics, reserve/urban, status/non-status, resurgence/reconciliation. Joseph's accounts challenged these binaries, for instance by revealing how Indigenous healing histories are profoundly intertwined across urban and reserve settings, the significant roles played by non-status individuals in shaping Indigenous social and political life, and the entangled histories of Red Power direct action and more conciliatory advocacy for services for Indigenous communities. Joseph also impressed upon me that the urban centres of Northern Ontario are sites of more overt racism and interpersonal violence compared with the urbanized, ethnically diverse, and socially liberal south of the province, a very different social and political context for healing discourse and practice. After defending my thesis in January 2011, I resolved to learn more about these interconnections and how regional diversity shaped Indigenous experiences by visiting Treaty 3 territory and speaking with more Anishinaabeg. This meant a shift from focusing mainly on urban Indigenous experience in the south to a more integrated consideration of urban and reserve experiences inclusive of the north.

Further research and learning over more than a decade after finishing my PhD deepened my understanding of Indigenous histories and ongoing experiences of settler colonialism in many subtle and profound ways, which I've tried to express throughout the book. This process has involved long-term relationships with several Anishinaabeg in Treaty 3 territory and a series of conversations spanning many years. I travelled to Treaty 3 territory for the first time in the spring of 2011. There I attended a ceremony at the Morningstar rehab centre, named for Joseph's late father, Don, about whom I'd already heard and read, listened as Joseph and others sang with Waakebiness, the Drum Don had built in the early 1960s; and met Joseph's beloved wife, Mary Alice Smith. I returned frequently over the subsequent decade, stayed for weeks at a time with households at Wauzhusk Onigum and Wabaseemoong First Nations whose members I came to consider friends, visited other reserves, and attended social and political events.[1] After listening to accounts shared by the Anishinaabe women I met in Treaty 3, I became committed to learning more about the history of Indigenous women's organizing against gendered and interpersonal violence, and to explore the connections between their work and the shifting politics of Indigenous healing.

Expanding my political and historical consciousness as a returned British Canadian white settler has also included reflection on how to practice and situate my research in the context of historical and contemporary relations between Indigenous Peoples and the academy. After being hired into an anthropology department in 2013, I realized I needed to start to redress my ignorance about the colonial history of North American anthropology: how, in Audra Simpson's characteristically pithy quip, "Indigenous elimination holds hands with disciplinary formation" (2014, 67).[2] Reading and teaching about how the production of anthropological knowledge about Indigenous people through typically exploitative, unethical, and dehumanizing research practices was not only foundational to the discipline, but in many ways enabled the expansion of the Canadian and US settler states, has deepened my awareness of what is at stake in navigating research relations with Indigenous Peoples. Burgeoning work by Indigenous scholars addressing the ethics and politics of research methodologies and representation has also been extremely helpful. I take seriously my responsibilities for ongoing learning from interlocutors and colleagues about how to forge more genuinely reciprocal research relations, challenging disciplinary and institutional complicity in continuing settler colonialism, and sharing my experiences with students and supervisees. This book represents some of my first steps on this path.

Acknowledgements

THIS BOOK WAS POSSIBLE because of the kindness of knowledgeable people who entrusted me with their histories. I hope the analysis I offer validates your trust, and that by encouraging readers to think carefully and critically about Indigenous healing amidst contemporary settler colonialism, this book will be a fitting tribute to my many teachers.

The late Joseph Morrison's importance to my thinking cannot be overstated. Joseph (Bigwekinang) encouraged me to think more deeply about how Indigenous lives in urban and reserve settings are intertwined and how experiences in Northern cities are patterned differently from those in the south. Joe, I'm so sorry you won't see this book come to fruition. Joseph's widow, Mary Alice Smith, has been a generous and patient supporter of this work over many years, willing to talk through ideas, provide helpful comment on drafts, and suggest people who might answer outstanding questions. Chi miigwech to

Mary Alice and the Morrison family for allowing me access to material in your family archive that has helped me to tell Giizhiiganang's story in more detail.

Marlene Pierre's oral history contribution and critical analysis have also been central to the development of this book, enabling me to provide a richer account of Indigenous women's social histories in Northern Ontario, their foundational contributions to healing in public discourse and programs, and the failure of more recent service developments to reach particularly those in remote reserves and rural communities. Chi miigwech, Marlene, for making the time to help me while working on your own book, which I look forward to reading very soon. Another important contributor was the late Adolphus Cameron, my friend, teacher, and primary collaborator on an ongoing research project with Wabaseemoong Independent Nations. Adolphus died in the summer of 2023, a tremendous loss for his family and community. Chi miigwech, Adolphus for all that you patiently taught me about Anishinaabe family, community, and political life, and for sharing your account of Giizhiiganang's life-changing role in your sobriety. Also in Treaty 3 territory, the "Old Guy" from Naicatchewinin and Charles Copenace generously shared extensive oral history and reflections on healing that have significantly enriched this book. The late Madeline Skead taught me about the importance of ceremony, reciprocity, and humility to research relations, on one memorable occasion by assigning me extensive laundry duties over a powwow weekend when we could monopolize the washer and dryer. Chi miigwech to Mary Equay Letander for your trust and generosity over many years, including permission to use your powerful story of that challenging interaction with your sister and the nurse to introduce this book. Chi miigwech to Anita Cameron and Tina Armstrong at Waasegiizhig Nanaandawe'iyewigamig, and visiting Healer Kathy Bird, for your generosity in speaking with me about your experiences of providing primary health care in Treaty 3 territory.

Visits to Treaty 3 territory have been foundational for many of the ideas expressed in this book and would have been impossible (and much less enjoyable) without the help of Anishinaabe friends there.

Miigwech to Cindy Piche and Harold Piche, Dorothy Cameron, Linda Cameron, and Cindy Cameron and Adolphus Cameron for providing welcoming homes away from home, to Beverly Williamson for your willingness to meet and talk through half-formed ideas over meals in Kenora and Toronto, to Bev and Cindy for sharing your childhood memories of powwows, and to Janine Seymour for the rides, putting me up in Winnipeg, critical feedback, and sharing your extensive insights. Debbie Lipscombe, administrator at Grand Council Treaty #3, provided invaluable guidance during my early visits. I am grateful to Andy White for sharing oral history about the early Lake of the Woods powwows, and to Randy White for enabling my conversation with Andy. Anita Cameron and Miigwaans Cameron provided helpful feedback on draft chapters and contributed to the final review of the manuscript, and Dorothy Cameron (Taajii) shared her expertise in Anishinaabemowin to assist with translating important terms.

Thanks also to the white Kenorans who were willing to share difficult histories but asked to remain anonymous.

My doctoral research feels like a long time ago now, but I've not forgotten the generosity of all of those in Toronto, Ottawa, Hamilton, and surrounding territories who contributed to my early understanding of the issues discussed in this book: Friendship Centre, Aboriginal Health Access Centre and shelter managers and frontline workers, Elders, physicians and psychiatrists, policymakers, and others with expertise in Indigenous healing. I'm particularly thankful to those who were willing to engage in ongoing communication and share oral histories over multiple meetings. Sylvia Maracle was exceptionally helpful in not only sharing extensive oral history and analytical commentaries on Indigenous healing histories but introducing me to other important long-term participants in the Friendship Centre movement. Leslie Saunders and Joe Hester provided invaluable insights into the intersections of healing with services for addictions, mental illness, and homelessness in Toronto. Castille Troy very kindly queried my early preoccupation with "mental health" in a way that set me on a more meaningful path, and introduced me to the many challenges of managing women's shelter services in ways consistent with Indigenous values. Corene Cheeseman shared personal insights into significant historical shifts in the services offered by Friendship Centres. Contributions by Mike DeGagné and Jonathan Dewar of the former Aboriginal Healing Foundation were particularly valuable to my developing analysis of the federal government's increasing involvement in healing. The late Elders Lillian McGregor and Vern Harper were willing to meet on many occasions and remained patient and good humoured in the face of my endless, often naive, and sometimes irrelevant questions. I'm grateful to Dr. Peter Menzies for allowing me to volunteer with his team, and to him and Jeff D'Hondt for their support in the early stages of what became this project. Many thanks also to Irene Lindsay, Al Garman, Bradford Morse, and a white Ottawa-based physician who opted to remain anonymous for your valuable contributions to my learning. The late Grafton Antone, Elder and Knowledge Keeper at First Nations House, University of Toronto, provided guidance and encouragement in the early stages of my PhD research. Archivist John Court at the CAMH Archives provided friendly assistance and advice on multiple occasions during my doctoral research, and current archivist Jaqueline Edwards has been helpful in tracking down missing information.

At the University of Toronto, I am grateful for colleagues who have seen me through some challenging years as I struggled to prioritize work on this manuscript amidst many competing responsibilities and a succession of major life events. Jesook Song and Katie Kilroy-Marac have provided stalwart support ranging from feedback on often very underdeveloped writing, to practical advice about navigating the challenges of academic work. Shiho Satsuka and Sarah Hillewaert were thoughtful readers of early draft chapters and providers of much-needed encouragement. Alejandro Paz has been a supportive colleague and friend since my postdoc days at University of Toronto Scarborough Campus, and Naisargi Davé was a helpful mentor during my early years in the Department of Anthropology. I've appreciated the opportunity to develop my analysis through conversations with undergraduate students in Indigenous Health Histories and Canadian Settler Colonialism (ANT458) and graduate students in Anthropology and Indigenous

Studies (ANT6060). I'm grateful for the assistance of talented graduate research assistants Antony Zelenka, Laura Beach, and Ness Maloney. Special thanks to Sarah Spaner, who has provided highly skilled research and editing assistance at multiple junctures over the years.

Mary Jane Logan McCallum, whose academic work powerfully models Indigenous-centred historical analysis, has provided important inspiration and guidance since we first met at a graduate event on Indigenous health many years ago. As academic workloads expand, I am particularly appreciative of the two anonymous reviewers who made time for close readings of my manuscript and provided knowledgeable, detailed comments, which have helped me to considerably strengthen this work. Several colleagues provided timely and helpful guidance and feedback in the late stages of writing. A heartfelt thank you to Valerie Lambert for your inspiring visit to Toronto at just the right moment, and insightful comments on draft sections of the manuscript. Many thanks to Andrea Muehlebach, Michelle Elleray, and Maureen Matthews for your careful readings and constructive suggestions. Chi miigwech to Karen Pheasant and Maya Ode'amik Chacaby for advice on Indigenous style.

The doctoral research that informs some of this book was supervised by historian of medicine Anne-Emanuelle Birn, who fostered my interest in archival research and whose graduate course on the history of international health deepened my understanding of the interrelationship between health, imperialism, and political economy. Bonnie McElhinny was a supportive co-supervisor, and supervisory committee member Cornelia Wieman provided valuable guidance during the early stages of my PhD. James Waldram was a stimulating and rigorous external examiner and kindly provided extensive notes on my thesis. My time as a PhD student was significantly enhanced by the friendship and collegiality of Jeannie Samuel, Amrita Daftary, and Wendy McGuire. A heartfelt thank you to Kari Dehli for rigorous graduate training in Foucaultian biopolitics and your willingness to again engage with my work many years later.

The analysis presented in this book has benefitted from several workshop and conference presentations and discussions, including

Rethinking Historical Trauma in North American Aboriginal Contexts at McGill University in 2012, organized by Laurence Kirmayer, Joseph P. Gone, and Joshua Moses; the Manitoba–Northern Ontario–Minnesota–Saskatchewan History of Medicine Conference at the University of Winnipeg in 2017, hosted by Mary Jane Logan McCallum; and Native American and Indigenous Studies Association meetings in 2016 and 2017. Funding for the research on which this book is based is from the Social Science and Humanities Research Council and the Network for Aboriginal Mental Health Research; the former has also contributed to open access publishing costs. Some of the content in chapter 4 was originally published in a journal article in *Comparative Studies in Society and History*.

It has been a pleasure to work with Mat Buntin, patient and professional acquisitions editor at University of Alberta Press, and kind, meticulous copy editor Joanne Muzak. I'm grateful to members of the University of Alberta Press Committee for valuable guidance on final revisions. Many thanks also to staff at University of Alberta Press, including production editor Duncan Turner, designer Alan Brownoff, and associate director Cathie Crooks for your contributions to bringing this project to fruition. My sincere thanks to Department of Anthropology chair Holly Wardlow for support in accessing additional funds towards open access publishing costs. I am grateful to librarian Grant Hurley at the University of Toronto, who provided thorough and timely help with tracing an obscure missing citation.

Thanks to Algonquin sculptor, curator, and fellow Parkdalian Robin Tinney for the introduction to Thunder Bay–based Anishinaabe artist Giziizikwe (Deanna Therriault) and her work. Chi miigwech to Deanna for permission to use her stunning painting *Windigo Eats the Sun* on the cover, and for our conversations that affirmed the alignment of your work with this book.

Finally, I'm grateful to those in my life outside of the university who have helped me to be well during the difficult years that coincided with this research and writing: close friends, family members, and the various healers I regularly rely on. Topsy, Gail, Leila, Neil, Vinita, Helen, Tricia, Anne, Michelle, and Debbie have stuck by me for decades despite my tedious preoccupation with work. My autistic friends and cousins in Canada and the UK and the Asperfemme/Good Company group have been important sources of support as I've navigated a mid-life autism diagnosis. My late aunt Dinah Murray, public intellectual, linguist, and groundbreaking critical autism studies scholar, was a long-standing champion of my intellectual work whose absence I have felt keenly while finishing this book. Intergenerational family relations help to keep me grounded: my mother, Linnet, gently persists in encouraging work-life balance (especially through knitting!) and my son, Sesu, has witnessed the long trajectory of this research and writing through most of his life with good humour and patience while growing into a thoughtful reader and critical thinker.

Artist Statement

THIS IS A PERSONAL PIECE. This image is a representation of my metaphorical state of being when my depression and anxiety get to be too much. My spirit name is Giziizikwe/Sun Woman, and the Windigo represents my struggle with mental illness that can steal my shine and blot out the light, devouring my spirit, my mind, and my body. The spirit and intent is to convey the impermanence of cloudy days. My style is neotraditional Woodlands: everything is connected and speaks to the circle, the cycle, and the way everything comes back around. Those little dots are circles, the sun is a circle, Windigo is part of the bigger circle. That circle in the belly is the soul and spirit of me and Windigo. That symbol is also the pictographic representation of the Great Spirit, Our Creator, and speaks to how we are all the light and dark and part of the whole. I use red in this series of works because red is the east on the Anishinabek Medicine Wheel, representing new beginnings, fire, and earth, something we all need more of.

Giziizikwe (Deanna Therriault)
On "Windigo Eats the Sun," the artwork that appears on the front cover.

Introduction

Indigenous Re-Membering and Biopolitics in the Liberal Settler Colony

MARY EQUAY LETANDER (née Henry) brought the white nurse to her sister's home on the reserve, hoping that her sister and brother-in-law would agree to participate in an interview. The nurse was researching Anishinaabe experiences of diabetes, and Mary was working for her as an interpreter. As they stood at the doorway, Mary's sister asked her in Anishinaabemowin, "How much is she paying you to help them destroy us?" Many years later, Mary shared this story with me, a white medical anthropologist, while working with me as an interpreter of Wabaseemoong Elders' oral histories. She offered this narrative as part of her ongoing effort to educate me about some Anishinaabeg's well-founded suspicions of well-intentioned white visitors to Northern reserve communities. Mary's sister's question also conveys an awareness that in liberal settler societies such as Canada, Indigenous well-being is a paradox. I argue that the seemingly irreconcilable perspectives of Mary and her sister on the Canadian health care system—working towards their People's well-being, or their deliberate destruction—are both accurate. Together, they make up the paradox of Indigenous health and healing under conditions of ongoing settler colonialism.

Paradox can be useful, socially and politically, because it enables "management of normative oppositions" (Carr 2023, 193). Several scholars offer similar analyses of a fundamental tension between collective Indigenous well-being, on the one hand, and the governance of a settler-colonial nation enabled by Indigenous dispossession on the other. Anthropologist Robert Paine's (1977) ethnography reveals the moral intractability of the Canadian welfare state's attempts to serve Indigenous "others" while colonial relations continue. Paine describes the imposition of foreign models and methods of well-being on Inuit lifeways by a racialized hierarchy of workers as "welfare colonialism." In a comparative discussion of Indigenous health histories across settler-colonial settings, historian of medicine Warwick Anderson (2007) points to common patterns of settler state investments in Indigenous health as part of intensified efforts at assimilation, alternating with policy aligned with Indigenous self-determination over health that works to legitimate state neglect through systemic underfunding. Anthropologist Lisa Stevenson (2014) points to the radical disjuncture between state actors' perceptions of providing "care" to Inuit through public health interventions, while Inuit themselves experience these same interventions as expressions of indifference, even murderous intent. Naming Indigenous healing as a paradox helps to make visible how and why it has become a dense site for relations of power, encompassing but also obscuring competing, even contradictory, paradigms for explaining and responding to Indigenous social suffering.

This book centres Indigenous social and political actors who have navigated this paradox with interventions and practices described in recent decades as "healing." Since the 1990s, "Indigenous healing" has become a part of public discourse in Canada and other settler-colonial settings, most notably Australia, through reconciliation politics: approaches to navigating purportedly past state violence that have emerged under neoliberalism (Corntassel and Holder 2008; Henderson and Wakeham 2013; Sundar 2004). Contemporary Indigenous healing is both continuous and discontinuous with Indigenous people's long histories of medical and ceremonial practices, some predating European invasion of Turtle Island, others more recently innovated in response to new forms of suffering in the wake of settler colonialism. Building on existing scholarship in anthropology (Myerhoff 1982), colonial studies (Ngũgĩ 2009), and Indigenous studies (Cariou 2007; Grande and McCarty 2018; Jeffries 2015), I use the concept of "re-membering" to convey how the resurrection of suppressed Indigenous knowledge and practice enables social repair, reconstituting collective social bodies—families, communities, nations—by restoring connections among their members. The following chapters show how, from the 1960s, community organizers and advocates like Mary attempted—with some success—to bridge older healing histories and contemporary practices to counter colonial social dismemberment of their people through tactical engagements with the agents and institutions of the Canadian welfare state. Such tactics have enabled access to resources and the development of programs to promote and protect Indigenous lives, including re-membering, but are not without risks, because vibrant Indigenous societies and polities continue to threaten the settler-colonial status quo.

Settler colonialism describes the political and socio-cultural formations of nation-states such as Canada whose existence is predicated on the dispossession of the pre-existing, self-governing Peoples whose lands they seek to occupy and exploit. Settler-colonial theory provides an important corrective to postcolonial theory, influential in humanities and social science scholarship from the 1990s, by distinguishing sites where colonizers "come to stay" from extractive or franchise colonies (Wolfe 2006).[1] The latter colonies became formally independent of European rule during the middle decades of the twentieth century, but settler colonialism continues in the present. In former British colonies of Canada, the United States, Aotearoa New Zealand, and Australia, the foundational and enduring approach to legitimating illegitimate settler claims to territory has been the attempted "elimination of the Native" (Wolfe 2006, 388).[2] But these settler states have by and large failed in this quest: Indigenous Peoples endure and assert sovereignty as distinct societies and polities (A. Simpson 2014). Attempts at "elimination" have included mass killings by state and non-state actors, but also the deliberate destruction of Indigenous societies by excising their members through legislation and welfare interventions. Such excisions—what I describe in this book as social and political dismemberment—have occurred through a diverse range of state interventions and non-interventions, some glossed as "care" and "protection," aligning with Mary's sister's suspicion that an ostensibly benevolent research project on Indigenous diabetes could be eliminatory in its effects. As I've argued with reference to "settler humanitarianism" (Maxwell 2017), settler state interventions may claim to be healing or caring and simultaneously work to disrupt Indigenous subjectivities and undermine kinship-based social and political systems. In the liberal settler colony, such interventions may not be readily distinguishable as either "welfare" or "genocide" (van Krieken 2004). This ambivalence endures in the reckless (mis)treatment of Indigenous life by welfare state actors and institutions (W. Anderson 2007; Stevenson 2012, 2014). Health professionals' racist neglect and abuse of Indigenous patients causing preventable deaths is just one illustration of the complex interplay of biopolitics and necropolitics—the politics of life, and the politics of death—in Canadian public services (McCallum and Perry 2018).[3] These practices are part of the larger, ongoing social and political dismemberment of Indigenous Peoples authorized by the Canadian settler state that unsurprisingly fuel Indigenous suspicions of state actors such as nurses (and anthropologists). Understanding Indigenous agency around healing in this fraught context requires a conceptualization of power more nuanced than its simple equation with domination. As I elaborate later in this introduction, biopolitics affords a useful theoretical framework for analyzing the paradox of Indigenous health and healing because it can encompass the simultaneity of state actors and institutions working to make Indigenous people live in ways intended to dismember their societies, and spaces for Indigenous agency and tactics aimed at re-membering, including engagements with the settler state.

I've asserted that Indigenous healing in the settler colony is a paradox because collective Indigenous health and well-being are incommensurable with dominant systems and cultures. This tension has intensified since Indigenous healing entered Canadian public discourse in the 1990s. As I show in the following chapters, the contemporary social and political salience of healing is at the interface of long histories of Indigenous grassroots organizing and more recent global political shifts under neoliberalism. The latter have undermined principles that had long supported marginalized groups to make claims on public resources—citizenship rights, equity, and solidarity—inspiring advocates to instead cultivate new, morally inflected claims to public resources grounded in innocence (e.g., "child poverty," displacing simply "poverty") and particular experiences of suffering, often linked to victimhood and trauma (Chen 2003; Fassin and Rechtman 2009; Ticktin 2011). In this context, "Indigenous healing" has become a highly malleable metaphor, what linguists describe as a floating signifier: a phrase that commentators can readily invoke to describe all kinds of phenomena with often limited commonality, including some antithetical to earlier Indigenous meanings, and dominant actors can readily manipulate to perpetuate the settler-colonial status quo.[4] Analyzing Indigenous healing as metaphor and public discourse is not meant to detract from the material, social, and spiritual importance of healing as practice to Indigenous people, demonstrated by an extensive literature spanning Indigenous social history, anthropology, social work, Indigenous health, psychology, and Indigenous studies.[5] But while ethnographic and other empirically grounded accounts acknowledge the historical context of settler colonialism as essential for making sense of contemporary Indigenous healing, this work less often considers how healing discourse, policy, and practice become entangled in ongoing relations of power.

The malleability of Indigenous healing is linked to its power as a signifier for benevolent transformation that presumes universal agreement on the causes of Indigenous social suffering and its remedies, while conveying a moral urgency to intervene. A brief detour through some examples of how "healing" has been invoked in Canadian media demonstrates widely divergent understandings of afflictions to be remedied, interventions needed, and what recovery entails. In 2010 a headline in the conservative newspaper the *National Post* asked, "Can property rights heal reserves?" (Ivison 2020). The ensuing article summarizes the arguments of right-wing political scientist Tom Flanagan in his book *Beyond the Indian Act* (co-authored by Christopher Alcantara and Andre Le Dressay): poverty on reserves is an affliction, privatization of reserve property is medicine, and recovery entails eradication of collective Indigenous rights and full participation in the neoliberal capitalist economy.[6] More recently, the idea that public apologies by political and religious leaders can be "healing" has become prominent in reconciliation politics and, despite widespread dissatisfaction with apologies issued by successive Canadian prime ministers, endures at the time of writing. The persistence of this belief is illustrated by residential school Survivors' calls for Queen Elizabeth II, in her role as symbolic head of the Anglican Church, to apologize for residential schools (Stefanovich 2022). In yet another divergent illustration, in 2021 disgruntled workers at the Ottawa-based Wabano Centre for Aboriginal Health complained that this organization itself "really needs to heal," suggesting that institutions with mandates for healing are not immune from affliction: in this case, alleged financial and human resources mismanagement (Miller 2021). Meanwhile, in some grassroots, clinical, and academic conversations, "healing" refers particularly to individual and collective treatment for addictions and mental illness, and preventing and responding to suicide and family violence, often accompanied by claims about how interventions are continuous with traditional practices (Kirmayer and Valaskakis 2009). But the presumption that healing is coterminous with health care disregards Indigenous ontologies, reflecting an ethnocentric bias amplified by the increasing biomedicalization of many aspects of life, enabled particularly by the expanding terrain of "mental health," which encompasses a vast range of "difficult" behaviours, relationships, and emotions (Kleinman 2012; Oldani 2009). In contrast, some

Indigenous legal studies scholars understand healing as coterminous with justice and predicated on the resurrection of legal systems, a perspective shared by some grassroots proponents of healing, as discussed in chapter 3 (Borrows 2010; Friedland 2018). And scholars and activists whose work is grounded in Indigenous understandings of the interdependence of human health and well-being with that of the land, water, and other-than-human beings also often use the language of healing (Kuppers and Noodin 2021; Wiebe 2014; Women's Earth Alliance and Native Youth Sexual Health Network 2016).

Some proponents of Indigenous healing likely concur with historian Kim Anderson's (2011) assessment of healing as interdependent with decolonization,[7] but I argue that it's important to consider how, like decolonization, healing has become a widely circulating metaphor with an unstable, ambiguous meaning in the context of ongoing settler colonialism.[8] The Canadian state's incursions into Indigenous healing since the 1990s complicate the assumption of alignment with decolonization. Indeed, dominant political actors including successive prime ministers have mobilized Indigenous healing discourse to claim new roles for the settler state in Indigenous lives and reassert its moral legitimacy (Maxwell 2017). As I'll discuss in chapter 4, some state interventions purported to be healing may actually constitute new modes of biopolitical dismemberment.[9] Further, settler state actors can wield healing as "a prerequisite to self-determination": a requirement that Indigenous Peoples demonstrate individual and collective recovery from experiences of colonization prior to fully assuming the mantle of self-determination (Million 2013, 105). Invocations of incapacity and need for healing show continuities with older liberal discourse urging uplift, modernization, and integration into settler society: both locate the causes of Indigenous social suffering within deficient, premodern families and communities, rather than ongoing settler-colonial dispossession.[10] Such understandings of healing contain an embedded expectation of acceptance of the settler-colonial status quo, including state authority to determine the timeline for indefinitely deferred Indigenous political autonomy (Irlbacher-Fox 2009). In this way, Indigenous healing discourse can work to actively disavow an understanding of Canadian colonialism as a *contemporary* phenomenon and instead misrepresent it as past event, most often signified by the Indian residential school system. As Maureen Matthews and colleagues (2023) observe, while Indigenous histories of residential schools provide a powerful and resonant context for understanding contemporary social suffering, the ascent of this now ubiquitous narrative situating these histories as its singular cause obscures continuing experiences of settler colonialism.[11] At the same time, because the language of healing carries a moral urgency—as noted, one reason why it's gained traction concurrently with the neoliberal retrenchment of public services—this discourse can work to divert attention from such egregious misrepresentations of settler colonialism, as critics risk accusations of lacking sympathy for residential school Survivors and the myriad injustices of that system.

I first began to appreciate the significance of histories of Indigenous tactical engagement with the settler state for understanding contemporary healing politics during conversation with Sylvia Maracle, then the long-time executive director of the Ontario Federation of Indigenous Friendship Centres. Sylvia has been an important actor at the interface between politics and healing in Ontario over many decades, and I was fortunate to meet with her early on during doctoral research (2005–2010) that was the formal starting point for this book. Earlier research experiences had inspired my long-standing interest in health care systems as potential sites for both social and political transformation and reassertion of the status quo.[12] I began my PhD project with an interest in understanding the emergence of "Aboriginal mental health" in Canadian policy since the 1990s (the medicalized counterpart of increasingly ubiquitous healing discourse). I was motivated by a commitment to "studying up": making dominant structures, institutions, and political actors the focus of my analysis, a purposeful departure from the anthropological tradition of studying the less powerful, particularly those deemed distant to one's own social and cultural location (Nader 1972).

But Sylvia introduced a different perspective by emphasizing the social and political significance of Indigenous community organizing in response to pressing health and social issues, such as alcohol abuse and interpersonal violence, the initiation of which she traced to the late 1960s. I realized that in my eagerness to avoid repeating the traditional ethnographic objectification of the "other," I risked committing another form of representational violence by rendering important Indigenous histories invisible. Over time, as I learned from Indigenous Elders, policymakers, health professionals, and community leaders, I came to understand more deeply how denying Indigenous presence is fundamental to maintaining the dominant social and political order of settler colonies such as Canada, and solidified my ethical and political commitment to centre Indigenous agency in my work. This awareness helped me to grasp that to analyze the complex multiple, sometimes contradictory meanings and implications of Indigenous healing in the context of ongoing settler colonialism, and particularly to align my intended critical analysis of the settler state's engagement with "Indigenous healing" with Indigenous Peoples' ongoing sovereignty struggles, would require careful accounting for the latter's much longer history of organizing in pursuit of individual and collective well-being. This analysis also requires a socially grounded conceptual framework flexible enough to attend to the many tensions, ambivalences, and contradictions inherent to Indigenous experiences of settler colonialism as encompassing both "wreckage and opportunity" (Deloria 2004, 7).

The remainder of this introduction is in three sections. In the first, I elaborate on the concepts of re-membering and biopolitics and show how they are relevant to a critical analysis of Indigenous healing in the settler-colonial context. I discuss the literature on Indigenous health histories from the late nineteenth through the late twentieth centuries not only as background to the following chapters but also to demonstrate certain continuities and discontinuities: how Indigenous people have long navigated settler-colonial structures to pursue individual and collective well-being, and how Canadian settler colonialism changes over time, despite the enduring goal of Indigenous "elimination," with implications for Indigenous tactics. In the second section, I provide a more extended discussion of biopolitics in the liberal settler colony, including its coexistence with sovereign power and necropolitics (state-authorized killing or letting die), its role in complicating the presumed opposition of resurgence and reconciliation politics, and how its multiple overlapping meanings allow conceptual space for Indigenous political agency. The final section provides a brief account of the research methodology and scope of the book, including summaries of the following chapters.

Re-Membering and Biopolitical Tactics in Indigenous Health Histories

My commitment to centring Indigenous agency and social actions while querying the assumption that "healing" has a singular, stable meaning led me to the concept of re-membering.[13] Re-membering provides a more precise descriptor for Indigenous actors' deliberate, everyday practices countering the colonial dismemberment of their societies: remembering (reinvigorating or resurrecting) knowledge previously suppressed or fallen into disuse under assimilatory social pressures, in order to re-member (restore membership) to Indigenous societies by reasserting social and spiritual roles, relationships, and responsibilities. Re-membering conveys the social and political significance of grassroots work of repairing and restoring kinship and other social and spiritual relations, as well as continuities between late twentieth- and early twenty-first-century practices and older ceremonial and medical traditions. With this usage I'm building on work in Indigenous studies, anthropology, and colonial studies that uses the concept of re-membering to link remembering as collective, social process to social rejuvenation and repair in (post)colonial and other settings of massive loss and disruption (Grande and McCarty 2018; Jeffries 2015; Myerhoff 1982; Ngũgĩ 2009). Ngũgĩ wa Thiong'o (2009) emphasizes that the idea of re-membering is predicated on the mutual interdependence of what we remember and therefore know about the world, and how we relate to one another. In other words, knowledge and social relationships are mutually constituted: practices of recovering and sharing Indigenous knowledge are both *embedded* in social contexts and actively *reshape* social relationships. This is an important awareness to bring to conversations about Indigenous resurgence, which don't always fully acknowledge that the process of remembering and re-enacting Indigenous ways of being is itself inherently social as well as political, and shaped by the locations of its proponents (L. Simpson 2018; Snyder, Napoleon, and Borrows 2015).[14] Re-membering conveys that remembering (and forgetting) are inherently social, political, and moral practices closely linked to individual and collective identities, a perspective shared with the larger literature on the anthropology and politics of memory (Kilroy-Marac 2019; Antze and Lambek 1996). A similar analysis is offered by Warren Cariou in his account of "membering," defined as "a communitarian kind of memory," to describe Métis practices of oral transmission via storytelling and song that enhance social cohesion (2007, 195).

Indigenous health histories from the late nineteenth and early twentieth centuries show how societies survived through adapting pre-contact medical and ceremonial practices to the conditions of settler colonialism, innovating new, distinctly Indigenous modes of healing that often included tactical engagements with colonial actors and institutions. I characterize Indigenous actions to advance collective well-being as "tactical" where they reflect social actors' careful reading of concurrent political contexts, notwithstanding the constraints of dominant systems, and may or may not subvert the workings of settler-colonial power. In Michel de Certeau's (1984) analysis, *tactics* describes limited, situational challenges to dominant relations of power, which aren't truly autonomous and may not have sustainable effects, but nevertheless represent a form of social and political agency with potential to disrupt the established order. De Certeau distinguishes strategies and tactics, using the example of pedestrians who walk the city and choose their paths to suit their own needs (tactics) and whose actions are not completely determined by the powerful, who literally structured the city in a specific way to enable social control (strategies). But my analysis builds on anthropologists' challenges to de Certeau's distinction between tactics and strategy (Kyriakides 2018; Napolitano and Pratten 2007). Theodoros Kyriakides's emphasis on how tactics entail the purposeful formation of social and political relations in a given context is particularly relevant to Indigenous maneuvering for health and healing. His characterization of the tactics of a Cypriot patients' group as centrally concerned with "render(ing) visible to public and governmental perception" the inherently *political* nature of health and illness could equally apply to the Indigenous biopolitical tactics discussed in this book (2018, 471). My analysis is informed by this critique of de Certeau's assumptions that tactics are both disconnected from strategy and necessarily entail resistance to dominant modes of institutional power. As Kyriakides observes, the "tactical subject" may aim "to embed itself in apparatuses of power rather than detach itself from them" and may pursue "political connection" more so than "the reversal of power" (473). I use the concept of tactics to emphasize the creativity, improvisations, and accomplishments of Indigenous political actors harnessing welfare-state resources to meet the needs of their people, amidst but not necessarily against constraints. This analysis counters misrepresentations of settler state power as uniformly repressive and the erasure of Indigenous agency sometimes effected by settler-colonial theory (Kauanui 2016; Lambert 2022; Macoun and Strakosch 2013). In contrast, attending to Indigenous biopolitical agency substantiates the assertion that Indigenous sociality and politics are partially constrained by, but crucially also exceed, an agonistic relationship with the settler state (de la Cadena 2015; Konishi 2019; Moreton-Robinson 2015).

Nineteenth-century Indigenous political leaders held the British Crown (later, by extension, the nascent Canadian state) responsible for providing health care under the terms of signed treaties, and understood that the settler state controls biomedical knowledge and practices often highly effective at treating illnesses linked to colonization, such as some forms of infectious disease. Thus, Indigenous leaders have advocated for their peoples' access to quality biomedical health care since at least the late nineteenth century, illustrated by insistence on the inclusion of a "medicine chest" clause in treaties signed from 1876 onwards, demands for state and missionary treatment for "white" infectious diseases such as smallpox and syphilis, and both advocacy for and direct funding of "Indian hospitals," established near or on reserves from the 1920s (Barkwell 1982; Kelm 1998; Lux 2016). Indigenous people also tactically engaged with Christian proselytizing interventions to enable the survival and well-being of their Peoples amidst the settler-colonial onslaught in the late nineteenth and early twentieth centuries.[15] In this period, missionaries were both the main providers of biomedical health care to Indigenous people and the colonial actors leading the attempted social dismemberment of Indigenous societies, most famously through residential schools but also through health care and other interventions intended to reshape individual subjectivities and intimate, gendered, and intergenerational relations to conform with Christian norms and values.

Indigenous social histories show how women engaged tactically with missionaries to incorporate different ways of knowing and doing to "extend" rather than displace their prior knowledge and practice, thus sustaining their distinct societies (de la Cadena 2015, xxii).[16] Missionaries intended to mould "backwards" Indigenous women according to Eurocentric Christian ideas about feminine domestic labour, but these forward-looking women used missionary interventions to expand their repertoire for crafts-making and income generation, tactics to withstand the colonial environmental devastation undermining long-standing livelihoods. Blackfoot and Peigan women helped their communities to endure the decimation of the bison and other plains animal resources by attending sewing and knitting classes, where they acquired new materials and techniques for domestic industry, enhancing both care for their communities (by producing clothing and blankets) and their capacity to earn income (by selling their skilled crafts to settlers) (Burnett 2010).[17] To the dismay of Indian Affairs officials, Indigenous women also continued pre-contact practices of processing hides and crafting moccasins whenever materials were available, demonstrating that rather than abandoning traditional industry, their interactions with missionaries enlarged their range of skills and media (Burnett 2010). Indigenous people also made tactical use of missionary health care while continuing their own medical practices (Kelm 1998).[18] Siksika women, for instance, attended maternity services at the Catholic-run Blood Indian Hospital for winter births during the 1920s and 1930s, so that they and their children could benefit from the hospital's heat and running water (Lux 2016). During the warmer months, they continued to favour their own midwives.

In contexts of colonialism and globalization, medical anthropologists use the concept of medical pluralism to describe the coexistence of multiple health care systems without privileging Euro-American biomedicine, emphasizing that all health care is inherently social and cultural.[19] Medical pluralism describes the coexistence in space and time of such distinct health care systems, each with their own ontology (understanding of the nature of reality) and epistemology (ways of generating knowledge about that reality), such as the Catholic hospitals and Indigenous midwives alternately used by Siksika women.[20] Historian Mary-Ellen Kelm (1998) uses medical pluralism to describe the coexistence of health care systems navigated by First Nations in British Columbia during the early decades of the twentieth century. Sto:lo, Tsimshian, Kwagiulth, and other Healers continued to practice in parallel with state and missionary biomedical practitioners, who were sometimes sought out for treatment of "white" infectious disease. Some Indigenous people who converted to Christianity accepted missionaries' condemnation of their own healing systems; others incorporated Christian values and practices into their own worldview in syncretic fashion (Fiddler and Stevens 1985; Kelm 1998). Ideally, anthropological concepts such as medical pluralism and syncretism both respect Indigenous knowledge systems and emphasize dynamic Indigenous engagements with modernity, avoiding the problematic reduction of Indigenous cultures to that which was practiced prior to European invasion. Indigenous healing practices were not reserved for treating illnesses predating colonization: plant- and animal-based medicines and ceremony were adapted and innovated to address new afflictions, particularly where biomedical interventions failed (Kelm 1998). Brenda Child's (2014) history of the Ojibwe Jingle Dress Dance illustrates both the continuity of spiritual practices in the early twentieth century and Indigenous people's capacity to respond to and ameliorate new challenges to well-being: in this case, the devastation of the influenza pandemic of 1918–1919, to which the colonial biomedical system offered no satisfactory response. In a contemporaneous demonstration of re-membering, Lakota youth returning from boarding schools (the United States' equivalent to residential schools) led a robust "dance renaissance" resurrecting traditional forms of dancing, drumming, and singing in opposition to colonial prohibition and reintegrating themselves into their families and nation (Troutman 2007). As John Troutman (2007) argues, their actions embodied protest at assimilation and containment, and extended long-standing, context-specific social and spiritual meanings attached to music and dance spanning expression of multilayered identities, communication with other-than-human kin, and entertainment.

As an analytic concept, medical pluralism helpfully emphasizes the coevalness of Indigenous and colonial health care as the backdrop to re-membering and tactical engagements with the settler state. But the concept is problematic in its neglect of wider social and political contexts and relations of power. It has been critiqued for misrepresenting Indigenous and other non-biomedical systems as static and timeless, while biomedical systems may be misrepresented as beyond tradition and culture (Crandon-Malamud 1991).[21] The concept has also been applied in ways that fail to reflect the wider significance of healing systems beyond therapeutic effects—for instance, for kinship (Berry 2010; Janzen 1978), territorial and spiritual relations—and thus failing to convey the complexity of Indigenous ontologies of well-being (Matthews et al. 2023; Watts 2016). To analyze social histories of Indigenous re-membering and tactics engaging the settler state requires more attention to how relations of power shape actors' navigations of coexisting ontologies and systems for health and well-being.

Thus, I turn to Michel Foucault's concept of biopolitics to analyze Indigenous experiences of re-membering amidst ongoing social dismemberment: specifically, how, under liberal settler colonialism, subjugation coexists with possibilities for tactical maneuvers. Biopolitical theory is particularly relevant to this analysis because it recognizes that the workings of power, including state power, are historically contingent and uneven. Settler state sovereign power, disciplinary power, and the workings of biopolitics all help to analyze the attempted dismemberment of Indigenous societies and polities; at the same time, biopolitics as a mode of liberal governance can be a medium for Indigenous agency. In Foucault's formulation, biopower describes a distinct mode of modern state power while biopolitics describes the workings of that power. The advent of biopower as the increasingly dominant mode of state power in modern Europe from around the seventeenth century marked a transition from the older mode of sovereign power embodied by the monarch, once understood to receive their mandate to rule directly from God. Distinguishing these modes of power helps to convey the significance of biopower: sovereign power describes the absolute power of the monarch to kill— to take life, or to let live—whereas biopower describes "the power to *foster* life or *disallow* it to the point of death," and takes life itself as its object, beginning with the individual human body and aggregated into the body of a population (Foucault 1990, 261). Whereas sovereign power describes unilateral, centralized power (of state or sovereign) including the right to take life, biopower is decentralized, working through an array of state-authorized institutions and professionals, and particularly through discourse. Crucially, in Foucault's analysis, biopower does not displace sovereign power; rather, they coexist, which is an important feature of the settler-colonial context.

Foucault's concept of disciplinary power is also relevant to both historical and ongoing settler state efforts to dismember Indigenous societies.[22] Disciplinary power characterizes modern forms of social control aimed at rehabilitating individuals through containment in institutions and other forms of spatial sequestration, surveillance, and systems of normalization, all intended to make bodies more "docile." Lisa Stevenson's (2014) analysis of Inuit suicide prevention interventions in Nunavut shows how surveillance and care become entangled in contemporary settler state biopolitics. An "apparatus" of strategies and protocols characterizes virtually all Inuit youth as at risk of suicide, to be prevented with extensive education and information campaigns, anonymous hotlines, and close monitoring. But Stevenson discerns that the effect on Inuit youth of this "intense and often anonymous policing of the suicidal body" is alienation: they are inspired not to renew their commitment to life but to distance their desire for death from the auspices of the settler state (2014, 97).

Canadian legislation banning Indigenous ceremony and the persecution of leaders enacting Indigenous legal systems illustrate the historical significance of disciplinary power to settler colonialism, and its interface with state sovereign power. Although Indigenous health histories discussed above show that tactical engagements with settler-colonial biomedicine did not necessarily equate with abandonment of Indigenous medicine, ceremony and other traditional practices were often carried out amidst secrecy for fear of harassment and prosecution by missionaries and the Royal Canadian Mounted Police.[23] Amendments to the Indian Act banning the Sundance and Giveaway Dances in Western Canada, and the Potlatch and winter dances practiced by West Coast First Nations, were in place until 1951.[24] Missionary efforts to instill shame in Indigenous knowledge and practices continued through the twentieth century and are ongoing in some Northern communities. As theorized by Foucault (1995), those subjected to disciplinary control may internalize normalizing judgements and subsequently develop practices of self-surveillance. In the recent past, some evangelical Christian churches have incited Indigenous converts to publicly destroy traditional ceremonial items vilified as satanic, causing profound hurt and social divisions within their communities.[25] Another example of disciplinary power aligned with settler state sovereign power is the early twentieth-century prosecution by the Canadian legal system of respected community leaders who battled and killed Windigowag.[26] Among some Northern Peoples, including Cree and Anishinaabeg, the highly skilled practice of suppressing Windigo is essential to collective safety and protection of the vulnerable under conditions of extreme hardship. Indigenous legal systems are fundamental to collective and individual well-being, underscoring the breadth of Indigenous understandings of healing as interdependent with sovereignty, and the wide-ranging harm caused by imposition of a foreign justice system (Borrows 2010; Fiddler and Stevens 1985; Friedland 2018).

An unnamed nineteenth-century Indigenous leader observed that legislation passed by the nascent Canadian settler state intended to "break us to pieces" (Milloy 1983, 59)—in other words, fragment Indigenous societies and polities by individuation.[27] Central to this book's analysis is biopolitics as a mode of liberal governance that does this work for the settler state, particularly since the mid-twentieth century, while also, at certain historical junctures, allowing opportunities for Indigenous actors to channel resources for re-membering. In settler colonies including Canada, the territorial dispossession of Indigenous polities was driven by not only the insatiable quest for land for settlement, agriculture, and industry but also the threat their very existence poses to the rationality of individualism, foundational to liberal governance. Historian Ian McKay describes this dominant rationality as a "liberal order [that] encourages and seeks to extend across time and space a belief in the epistemological and ontological primacy of the category 'individual'" (2000, 623). In the liberal worldview, social relations are reduced to a market model and the naturalization of hierarchy, including human domination of the natural world. In contrast, as illustrated by healing histories, Indigenous social and political systems encompass epistemologies and ontologies permeated by relationality—not only among humans but among humans and the larger natural world, including other-than-human beings. As Dian Million writes, Indigenous ways of being and knowing may constitute "the only living models for different economic and social systems on the planet, ways of life that have the power to challenge capital cultures, even when they are not pure or untouched by capitalism" (2013, 161–62). Thus "eliminating" Indigenous Peoples as distinct societies and polities requires both undermining claims to territorial sovereignty and dismembering collectivities, substituting atomistic liberal identities and values for social and political systems predicated on interdependence.

The Canadian settler state's attempts at the social dismemberment of women and children from their nations since the late nineteenth century have caused profound disruptions to Indigenous societies, legitimated by liberal rhetoric and enacted through settler state sovereign power and disciplinary power. Initially, policy encouraging voluntary enfranchisement by Indigenous men was meant to dismantle collective ownership of reserves and enable individual property ownership, based on the white supremacist assumption that the men would readily abandon their own societies to adopt the ways of the colonizers (Lawrence 2004). When this state strategy was spectacularly unsuccessful, late nineteenth-century policymakers set about disrupting social reproduction and relations by assigning disproportionate social and political authority to men and removing children from their homes to residential schools.[28] Through the late twentieth century, settler state policies undermined women's often considerable political influence and attempted to radically reconfigure and sever their connections to family and nation by imposing patriarchal values derived from the British ruling classes.[29] As Bonita Lawrence (2004) notes, this imposition served the combined purpose of disrupting Clan-based systems of governance and enabling land theft by settlers. In residential schools, funded by the settler state from 1883, children were subjected to disciplinary power via violent proselytization by the Christian priests and nuns who administered the schools. The residential school system synthesized liberal ideals of individualistic development, punitive Christian morality, and the racialized paternalism that provided moral cover for liberal imperialism.[30] In the mid-twentieth century, members of the increasingly influential social work profession employed emerging liberal rhetoric of equality and modernization to criticize the role of the Indian agent in adoption practices and condemn the practice of placing children deemed neglected in residential schools (P. Johnston 1983). Their advocacy contributed to the inclusion of section 88 in the 1951 Indian Act amendment, enabling subsequent provincial-federal agreements for extending to reserves the provincial systems for surveillance of families, children's apprehension, and foster placement and adoption (Canadian Welfare Council and Canadian Association of Social Workers 1947). The ensuing mass removal of Indigenous children from their nations, among the most egregious attempts at Indigenous social dismemberment in the mid- to late twentieth century, exemplifies how mid-century white liberals championed the individual rights of members of marginalized groups yet continued to deny the collective rights of those same groups.

The history of the Indian hospital system illustrates how settler state sovereign power, disciplinary power, and biopower worked to constrain Indigenous lives through the mid-twentieth century and how Indigenous people attempted to navigate these coexisting regimes. The hospitals were sites for geopolitics as well as biopolitics. Historian Maureen Lux (2016) shows that through much of the twentieth century, Indigenous leaders asserted geopolitical claims to their peoples' entitlement to state-sponsored health care, integral to historic nation-to-nation relationships documented in treaties, with varying degrees of success. In the 1920s, two of the wealthiest and largest First Nations established their own hospitals on reserve lands: the Siksika's Blackfoot Hospital, and Six Nations' Lady Willingdon Hospital (Lux 2016). Both institutions developed pluralistic systems of care, including Indigenous healing and midwifery practice alongside biomedicine. Siksika council set hospital policies that suited their people's needs: visiting hours were flexible, patients were free to leave when they felt recovered, and the hospital offered care not only for the sick but also for healthy children and elders, thereby enabling caregivers to travel (Lux 2016, 139). Here we see Indigenous leaders' commitment to building and managing health care institutions in ways that align with their People's values and priorities, including continuation of long-standing healing knowledge and practice and caring for caregivers as integral to collective well-being, foreshadowing actions characterized as "health sovereignty" in the early twenty-first century (Morgensen 2011).

The threat posed by Indigenous-managed hospitals as sites for reinforcing distinct collective identities is underscored by the reassertion of the sovereign power of the settler state by Indian Health Service officials, who took control of both the Blackfoot and the Lady Willingdon hospitals by the 1950s (Lux, 2016). Like the reserve and residential school systems, the hospitals run by the federal government between the 1920s and 1980s were sites of disciplinary power for subjugating Indigenous Peoples: racially segregated institutions using techniques of containment, surveillance, and control of individual bodies in ways designed to reshape one's sense of self.[31] The Indian hospitals were part of the larger twentieth-century biopolitical project of moulding Indigenous people into junior citizens of the settler nation, with the disciplining of docile, compliant Indigenous patients seen by health professionals and policymakers as an interim measure towards eventual Canadian citizenship (Lux 2016). This strand of Indigenous health history reveals the coexistence of settler state sovereign power, disciplinary power, and biopower. The same period demonstrates the persistence of opposed Indigenous geopolitical claims, and what could be read as Indigenous appropriation of biopolitics through relational subjectification, elaborated below.[32]

Similarly, histories of Indigenous nursing show the settler-colonial entanglement of biopower and sovereign power and reveal how Indigenous women tactically navigated state systems to pursue their own social and political objectives, despite significant constraints. Historian Mary Jane Logan McCallum (2014) shows that many Indigenous women training as nurses in the mid-twentieth century were motivated by the desire to work in their home communities, only to be undermined by opposition from Indian Affairs bureaucrats. McCallum's archival research reveals officials fearful about the prospect of trained Indigenous nurses working with their own people, a fear that would be borne out as these women mobilized their professional "labour as activism" for advancing sovereignty over health and health care. For policymakers, Indigenous people's participation in higher education was another liberal mechanism expected to sever ties between the individual intent on self-improvement and their family and nation imagined as holding them back. As McCallum's analysis demonstrates, opposition to the idea of employing trained Indigenous nurses in their home communities was motivated by two conflicting fears: that nurses would reject their own communities based on their newly acquired sense of superiority, or, conversely, lose their hard-earned modern, assimilated identity through "cultural backsliding and undesirable social and familial influences" (2014, 195). Ultimately, McCallum shows, these women's claims to unique expertise predicated on Indigenous identity, professional training, and proximity to communities enabled them to gain influence in a range of political fora spanning federal policymaking, the National Indian Brotherhood,[33] and the Friendship Centre movement.

Indigenous nurses overcame myriad obstacles to gain employment in state health care, a system central to biopolitics as a mode of liberal governance that gained considerable traction through mid-century welfare policy. By the 1950s, residential schools were beginning to close, and the rapidly expanding welfare state became the main instrument for the intergenerational social dismemberment previously attempted through the schools, under the banner of a new policy discourse of Indigenous "modernization" and "equality" (Shewell 2004). Canadian policymakers created health and social programs intended to subjectify Indigenous adults as liberal subjects and future citizens reliant on professional expertise beyond their communities.[34] Day schools on reserves gradually replaced residential schools, meaning children were no longer apprehended and contained in institutions far from home.[35] Instead, parents were threatened with the withdrawal of the family allowance on which many had become dependent as traditional livelihoods were eroded unless their children attended school regularly. This less overt mode of coercion was still violently disruptive, particularly for those in Northern communities continuing to overwinter on traplines.

Beyond the education sector, health and welfare professionals intervened to devalue the knowledge, practices, and community authority of Elders and other knowledge keepers, straining relations with younger generations. The social disruption caused by biopolitical state actors is vividly demonstrated in Kim Anderson's (2011) book *Life Stages and Native Women*, in which she shares oral history accounts of how from the 1950s, medicalization of childbirth and child-rearing began to displace Indigenous midwives' roles in northern communities in Ontario and Saskatchewan. Embarrassed by high levels of infant and maternal mortality among Indigenous people that reflected destruction of livelihoods and state neglect, officials attempted to misattribute this evidence of settler state failures to Indigenous backwardness, to be corrected through education by health and social workers. The Indigenous practice of breastfeeding children until age two or three was specifically and falsely condemned by these state actors as contributing to infant mortality. Nursing stations and Hudson's Bay Company stores circulated rules for feeding babies that encouraged early replacement of breastfeeding with bottle feeding and processed foods (Burnett, Hay, and Chambers 2016). Ironically, such practices may be detrimental to child health, particularly in the absence of a reliable clean water supply. Maria Campbell described how a visiting nurse instructed women in her northern Saskatchewan Métis community that breastfeeding was unhealthy (K. Anderson 2011, 61). Anderson's contributors, including descendants of midwives, recalled Elders' emphasis on the importance of breastfeeding not only for health and maternal-child bonding but for mothers' authority over children (61–62). They observed that state interventions contributed to widespread abandonment of breastfeeding, causing children's deteriorating behaviour and the breakdown of intergenerational communication. In a complementary analysis based on oral histories from Anishinaabeg in northern Manitoba, Matthews et al. point to "ontological impairment" resulting from community nurses imposing biomedical paradigms and undermining Indigenous healing knowledge, alongside the decline of land-based activities and relations with Memegwesiwag, "semi-human spirit entities," fundamental to Anishinaabe epistemologies, or ways of knowing (2023, 158).

Settler nurses' efforts to transform Indigenous infant feeding practices were intended to subjectify young Indigenous women as "modern" mothers and devalue the expertise of their aunties and grandmothers. In Foucault's analysis of how biopolitics works as a mode of liberal governance, subjectification is central. Subjectification affords a focal point to investigate empirically how the work of state institutions and experts continue to shape Indigenous experience and social relations, even in the absence of overt coercion (sovereign or disciplinary power). As Judith Butler (1997) helpfully sums up,[36] subjectification is a dual process: an individual coming to identify as a particular sort of person (or subject), while also being subjected or subjugated to an external power. Subjectification involves the propagation, circulation, and individual internalization of ideas about how to live, ideas generated as part of the social production of biomedical and other scientific knowledge by state-authorized and -funded experts. Such knowledge encoded in language is described as discourse; biopolitical discourse can be powerfully persuasive at inciting individuals to change not only their behaviour but their sense of self, by conveying ideas about how best to live, often in terms of what is healthy, normal, and desirable, and what is unhealthy, abnormal, and problematic. Still, agency is pivotal to the working of biopolitics as a mode of liberal governance, since it involves tethering individual will, rather than relying on external coercion as does sovereign power. Indigenous people may sidestep biopolitical subjectification by refusing to cooperate with state interventions ostensibly addressing their well-being, for instance by disavowing the relevance of suicide prevention bureaucracy to their desire to die (Stevenson 2012, 2014).

Readers who believe that biomedical knowledge and health care is value-neutral and universally beneficial may not consider subjectification to be detrimental, and in many cases it may not be. Subjectification is not an inherently malevolent process.[37] But an extensive, long-standing literature demonstrates that biomedical and other scientific knowledge is socially produced and reflects the particular historical and political contexts of its production, and there are myriad examples of how medical knowledge and practice has aligned with colonialism, racism and white supremacy, misogyny, ableism, homophobia, and transphobia.[38] Working with the premise that subjectification is in itself neutral, in the remainder of this section I consider how tactical engagements with the expanding welfare state created opportunities for Indigenous social actors to subjectify other Indigenous people in relational ways, claiming them as kin worthy of care and co-inheritors of knowledge of enduring relevance. In this sense, re-membering involves subjectification. Academic literature on biopolitics and subjectification tends to focus on the work of state-authorized actors and institutions, but as I argue in this book, these dynamics are also at play in sites at the margins of and beyond the state, and discourses and practices for protecting life and promoting lifeways may align with a wide range of social and political projects (Rabinow and Rose 2006). Indigenous people employed in junior roles in the burgeoning mid-century health care system were often well positioned to counter the individuating subjectification inherent to these services.

Lux's (2016) history of the Indian hospitals, for example, reveals how Indigenous workers used the room afforded them for maneuvering to support patients, despite challenging, exploitative working conditions. Paraprofessionals such as nurse's aides, and manual workers such as janitors and drivers, were often called upon to translate and otherwise mediate between white professionals and Indigenous patients. This expectation and their close proximity to patients enabled them to extend care and comfort in an often-hostile environment, practices that we can read as relational subjectification, in contrast with many alienating and dehumanizing practices patients suffered (Lux 2016). The often ambiguous biopolitical roles performed by Indigenous workers in mid-century Canadian health care are captured by the concept of "colonial middle figures," crafted by Nancy Rose Hunt (1999) in her analysis of the colonial politics of birthing in a medical missionary institution in the Congo. The term *middle figure* characterizes how Congolese trained by the mission as teachers, pastors, nurses, and midwives performed "mediating" roles between British missionaries and Congolese colonial subjects (N. Hunt 1999). Similarly, mid-century Indigenous health care workers participated in the subjectification of those using services in ways both intended and unintended by policymakers. As Lux identifies, Indigenous middle figures' actions in the hospitals could exceed generic kindness to encompass support for explicit expressions of Indigeneity. Grace Anderson, Cree nurse's aide from Pinaymootang, worked at the Clearwater Lake Indian Hospital at The Pas, Manitoba. Lux documents how Anderson allowed Inuit women patients to play music and dance, activities prohibited by the white nurses. I characterize such expressions of reciprocal recognition and sometimes kinship as re-membering.[39] The social and political significance of mid-century Indigenous middle figures is heightened when we consider this was a period when a rapidly expanding, mostly white settler workforce of nurses, social workers, employment officers, teachers, and others attempted to reshape Indigenous subjectivities and social relations through intrusive and paternalistic interventions, such as the infant feeding prescriptions described above.

From the 1960s, the work of Indigenous community health representatives (CHRs) involved a dual process of subjectification, partially aligned with settler state goals of moulding willing patients for the dominant health care system, but simultaneously working beyond their remit by re-membering. Unlike the earlier hospital workers, the CHRs were explicitly conceived as middle figures by Indian Health Service officials, and expected to leverage their Indigeneity to encourage uptake of primary health care in the service of modernization and assimilation.[40] This instrumentalization of Indigenous culture marks a shift in policy rationality away from the earlier anticipation of Indigenous Peoples' inevitable disappearance, which I interpret as an early example of the politics of recognition in public services. CHR activities aligned with state efforts at subjectifying Indigenous people as self-regulating Canadian citizens: promoting childhood vaccination, discouraging smoking, inciting behaviour change to prevent and manage diabetes, and facilitating hospital admissions. State actors deliberately recruited those in existing healing roles, such as midwives and herbalists and their descendants, who then often came to be perceived by their people as junior agents of the settler state (McCallum 2014). As Matthews et al. observe, "They were invited to use their own prestige as known healers in the community to extend the reach of modern medicine which has historically trivialized their traditional knowledge" (2023, 159).

And yet many CHRs used their community-based, mediating role to actively pursue the renewal of traditional medicine and intergenerational relationships, and protect their people from paternalistic intrusions. These practices are evidenced by first-person accounts of CHRs' experiences from the 1970s to 2000s (National Indian & Inuit Community Health Representatives Organization [NIICHRO] 2010). Many CHRs self-identified as inheritors of enduring, if partially fragmented, intergenerational social networks of healing knowledge and reciprocal care. Alice Kimiksana of Ulukhaktok, Inuvialuit, described how a particularly rewarding aspect of her work was to "sit with an elder and a young adult and try to help them look after each other without the use of an interpreter" (NIICHRO 2010, 48). A poem written by Alice Carlick, CHR at Burwash Landing, Yukon Territory, also makes explicit reference to the restoration of intergenerational relations and Indigenous futures as part of her work (back cover). These accounts suggest CHRs' loyalty lay with their people, and their sense of responsibility and fulfillment in this role enabled them to persevere despite challenging conditions. Shirley McNab of Gordon First Nation explained how she advocated for community members, challenging white health professionals' paternalism: "Health professionals can be very cold and sometimes would not explain to the people why they were in the hospital...I would demand to the doctors to explain to me why the person is in the hospital and I wouldn't stand down when it came to the client" (61). Winnie Greenland of Fort McPherson also presents as a fierce advocate, stating bluntly, "I...see that my people's issues are addressed [by the health centre]" (37). And Yvonne Morin of Big River First Nation explains that CHRs have an enduring role in accompanying nurses on home visits because "our people still need us between them and the health staff" (62).

Women who participated in the Homemakers' Clubs established by Indian Affairs in 1937 were also mediating figures who employed settler state resources tactically to reassert caring roles and relationships in their communities. Loosely patterned on Women's Institutes and exemplifying the liberal ideal of self-development,[41] these clubs were intended by Indian Affairs officials to be sites to cultivate normative gender roles and attitudes towards citizenship.[42] But historians Aroha Harris and Mary Jane Logan McCallum (2012) argue that the clubs' members subverted this assimilationist agenda to develop their own analyses of health and social issues facing reserve communities and circulate these through translocal networks. Members articulated and addressed priorities aligned with protecting and promoting life within their reserve communities and were not readily swayed to wholesale adoption of state ideologies. These women promoted social cohesion through caring practices: they crafted and procured clothing and household items, obtained livestock, raised funds for material needs of families, cared for the sick and bereaved, and maintained traditional practices to produce a wide range of skilled crafts for sale. This work is tactical, harnessing labour within the individuated domains of home and family defined for women by the settler state to larger, collective Indigenous projects of perseverance and well-being. It also involves relational subjectification: members both affirmed their own roles and responsibilities within their communities, and subjectified other community members as worthy recipients of their caring labour at a time of few public services, when most organized care was delivered by Christian missionaries. The political significance of the Homemakers' Clubs is also supported by anthropologist Heather Howard's (2004) account of the life histories of women prominent in Indigenous politics in Toronto in the mid- to late twentieth century. Howard argues that participation in the Homemakers' Clubs shaped women's nascent political consciousness, enabling critical analyses of social suffering on reserves that contributed to urban community organizing later in the twentieth century.

Mid-twentieth-century federal "integration" discourse inadvertently bolstered urban Indigenous organizing by supporting the creation of Friendship Centres, which served as significant and long-standing institutional infrastructure, against the expectations of state actors. Integration became the mission of not only officials in Indian Affairs and Citizenship Branch, but a host of liberal white advocates affiliated with Christian churches, organizations such as the YMCA/YWCA, newly formed groups such as the Indian-Eskimo Association, and civil rights activists.[43] An illustrative series of meetings in the late 1950s organized by Winnipeg's Welfare Planning Council excluded Indigenous participation, but inspired the establishment of a new referral service, funded by all three levels of government, intended to assist Indigenous people with urban settlement (Langford 2016). Funding for Friendship Centres reflected a broader shift from the 1960s as policymakers and social scientists increasingly championed Indigenous "migration" to cities as desirable, while segregated reserve communities, once considered the ideal environment for gradual civilization, were reinterpreted as archaic obstacles to the ascendant liberal ideals of equality and integration. Settler state actors meant Friendship Centres to be sites for intensive subjectification of Indigenous city dwellers as junior members of settler society; they argued that short-term, culturally specific supports would enable adjustment to urban life, conceptualizing "culture" as a transitional stepping stone until Indigenous people, inevitably, abandoned their old ways to become fully fledged Canadians (Krouse and Howard 2009; Langford 2016; Peters 2001). The Winnipeg Indian and Métis Friendship Centre opened its doors in 1959. By 1966 there were nineteen Friendship Centres operating across Canada (Peters 2001). The following chapters show how Friendship Centres across Ontario were important sites for re-membering during the 1960s through the 1980s.

Thinking Indigenous Health and Politics Together: Re-Membering, Resurgence, Biopolitics

These health histories show how bringing health and politics into the same analytical frame affords insights into Indigenous navigations of a historically dynamic settler colonialism. Indigenous politics literature has tended to neglect the inter-related issues of collective health and well-being, healing, and interpersonal violence (Belcourt 2018; Hunt/Tłaliłila'ogwa and Simpson 2023; Ladner 2009; Million 2013). As Kiera Ladner (2009) argues, despite a pervasive assumption that self-determination enhances well-being, scholars have devoted little attention to how particular practices for enacting and enhancing self-determination might align with or undermine community well-being.[44] Meanwhile, Indigenous health is a burgeoning research field in Canada, Australia, and Aotearoa New Zealand, with growing participation by Indigenous researchers, but little cross-fertilization with the critical social and political analyses emanating from Indigenous studies, or Indigenous health historiography, summarized above. The Indigenous health literature often mentions settler colonialism (usually historical) and anti-Indigenous racism as determinants of contemporary health, but generally disregards Indigenous political agency, relations of power inherent to the social production of biomedical knowledge, and ongoing settler-colonial relations in the present. Further, literature on Indigenous health often reduces settler colonialism to an embodied "legacy," obscuring not only contemporary settler colonialism but biomedicine and health care as distinctly productive sites for observing and analyzing settler colonialism at work. In particular, Canadian Indigenous health literature often takes histories of residential school experiences as synecdoche for the full expanse of Indigenous colonial histories. The problematic effect has been to advance an understanding of residential schools as both an exceptional experience of colonialism and one universally shared by Indigenous people of a certain age, diverting attention from myriad other settler-colonial interventions aimed at Indigenous social dismemberment, many continuous with the present (Matthews et al. 2023; Maxwell 2017).

In this book I argue that theorizing Indigenous political agency around health and healing as an Indigenized biopolitics helps to bridge this limiting communication gap between the fields of Indigenous health and Indigenous politics, and also complicates the prevalent presumption that the politics of resurgence and reconciliation exist in binary opposition. My analysis builds on the work of a small number of scholars using a biopolitical framework to understand Indigenous health and healing as inherently political matters, often from feminist, queer, and Two-Spirit perspectives. Scott Morgensen (2011) interprets Indigenous and particularly Two-Spirit people's activism around HIV/AIDS as assertions of "health sovereignty" that engage and challenge settler-colonial biopolitics. Million problematizes the expansion of Indigenous healing programs under the rubric of the neoliberal settler state as, in part, the cynical instrumentalization of culture as a mode of self-management, but cautions, "that could never be the whole story" (2013, 166). This book builds on Million's critique of neoliberal settler colonialism and contributes another strand of the story by centring Indigenous accounts as a complementary narrative. By leaving room for Indigenous (bio)political agency, such analyses redress established limitations of settler-colonial theory as obscuring Indigenous social and political actors and knowledge and exaggerating the homogeneity of settler-colonial power (Kauanui 2016; Lambert 2022; Macoun and Strakosch 2013; Snelgrove, Dhamoon, and Corntassel 2014). These analyses also contribute to wider conversations about "biopolitics from below," showing that while critical and liberatory politics rarely operate entirely outside of dominant forms of governance, Indigenous Peoples, like other politically marginalized collectivities, challenge and appropriate the work of dominant institutions, professions, and discourses to construct their own politics of life.

Bringing biopolitical theory to bear on Indigenous experience requires critical awareness of Eurocentric blind spots inherent to Foucault's theory of state racism and the rise of modern state power in Europe, which, it has long been established, disregards the imperial contexts that enabled what is considered European modernity (Stoler 1995). For instance, biocitizenship is a prominent concept in the biopolitics literature, but is often used in ways that fail to interrogate how formulations of citizenship are entangled with long-standing colonial relations of power (Kolopenuk 2020b).[45] Earlier work on colonial biocitizenship in diverse imperial settings provides useful insights into how biomedical and welfare interventions effected Indigenous social dismemberment, legitimated by reference to anticipated social and political integration in a diminished form of citizenship, but tend to focus on processes of subjugation by imperial powers while devoting little attention to Indigenous agency or the social and political implications for Indigenous Peoples.[46] In contrast, Sarah Marie Wiebe's (2014) concept of "ecological citizenship" captures how Indigenous political organizing in support of life both overlaps with and exceeds conventional understandings of biopolitics. Wiebe considers organizing against industrial pollution among the Anishinaabeg of Aajiwnaang whose territory is close to "Chemical Valley," a source of toxic pollution threatening the health of humans and environment alike. Wiebe's analysis reveals how Anishinaabe understandings of citizenship are shaped by the interface of bodies with place, creating a politics of life that is biosocial, in the sense that their collective activism is in part inspired by their shared embodied experiences but equally concerned with health of the wider environment. These examples of Indigenous (bio)political agency reflect an understanding of citizenship as not only embodied but emplaced, encompassing a wider set of responsibilities to territory and other-than-human beings that constitute life, and challenging the individualism and disregard for place that characterizes much work on biocitizenship and biopolitics. While this book focuses on relations among humans rather than between humans and environment, my analysis similarly foregrounds biopolitics as a mode of liberal governance that can be a medium for agentive Indigenous tactics, resurrection of knowledge, and even resistance because it is a decentralized, productive mode of power that affords space for maneuvering.[47]

Re-membering provides a useful conceptual complement by making explicit how Indigenous biopolitical tactics connect to wider social and political relationships. This analysis aligns with the transformative potential of relationality for Indigenous societies (an important theme in the Indigenous resurgence literature), which stems not merely from (re)forming relations but "proliferation of relationships of care and nurturance, in which [Indigenous people] see [themselves] having concrete roles and responsibilities" (Starblanket and Stark 2018, 177). Re-membering focuses attention on the purposeful, practical reconstruction of social membership in the context of massive losses and social fragmentation. Marshall Jeffries (2015) uses re-membering to characterize health and healing work and the recovery of languages and historical knowledge, enabling the literal rebuilding of Occaneechi tribal membership.[48] Sandy Grande and Teresa McCarty (2018) analyze the experiences of Indigenous women in the academy, navigating caregiving as "life work" alongside intellectual production. Their use of re-membering inspires a renewed vision for academic work that "refuses" the artificial parsing of kin relations and scholarly production, insisting on the primacy of Indigenous scholars' roles and responsibilities as family and community members. In these accounts, and in the following chapters, re-membering is not only about sharing memories of stories and songs, or practicing Indigenous ways of knowing, being, and doing. It is also about how knowledge and practices work to reconstitute the collective membership of Indigenous families, societies, and polities: recovering neglected relationships with those who have died, other-than-human relatives, and living humans pushed to the margins by colonial violence, and supporting the latter to inhabit their own role and responsibilities in relation to the collective. It is a "non-colonial practice" that, as theorized by David Garneau (2016), values pre-contact knowledge while accepting the impossibility of simply reinstating pre-contact social organization. Re-membering therefore is not a straightforward resurrection of past institutions but a visionary, creative process informed by older Indigenous knowledge forms. Some academic work might itself be characterized as re-membering practice, since it aims to document and analyze Indigenous social histories and stories with the intention of supporting the healing and well-being of Indigenous nations in the present.[49] Finally, re-membering begs the question, "Membership of what?" or as articulated by Million, "What will our nations be?" (2013, 123). Acknowledging this as an open question offers a corrective to one limitation of the resurgence paradigm identified by Aaron Mills: the underdevelopment of what he describes as "Indigenous life ways," by which he means the core of collective identity defined by distinct ontologies and epistemologies that enable both social cohesion and adaptability through change, fostering a "thick sense of difference" (2018, 149).

    Re-membering, then, points to collective Indigenous health and well-being as not only inherently political but intertwined with the broader politics of resurgence. Activists and scholars use "resurgence" to describe the deliberate recovery, reworking, and sharing of Indigenous ways of knowing, being, and relating as inherent to the assertion of political autonomy, self-determination, and sovereignty, with a particular emphasis on territorial self-governance (Alfred 2009b; Corntassel 2012; Coulthard 2014; A. Simpson 2014; L. Simpson 2017). Re-membering as I explore it here centres on interpersonal practices intended to reconnect socially disconnected individuals to a larger social and spiritual whole. This dynamic is sometimes conveyed in references to the "everyday" in the Indigenous resurgence literature. For instance, in Ladner's discussion of the relationship between governance and well-being, she characterizes "honourable [Indigenous] governance" as "meaning that as a community we start picking up the pieces and looking after each other as all are our relations," and argues that "the re-integration of families and building consensus among families" constitutes "the basis of governance" (2009, 98).[50] Thus re-membering is part of what Sarah Hunt/Tłaliłila'ogwa describes as the "intimate decolonial work of transforming our everyday relationships into our resurgent practices and theories" (Hunt/Tłaliłila'ogwa and Simpson 2023, 131). Feminist, queer, and Two-Spirit commentators have called for more analytical attention to this intimate, everyday work as part of their critiques of how present-day modes of relating are often deprioritized and deferred by scholars and activists in the name of a future decolonization (D. Hunt 2023). Contemporary ethnographies of Indigenous social relations complement these analyses by providing empirical evidence for the endurance of strongly felt kinship-based responsibilities for providing collective care, enacted within and across urban and reserve settings (Downe 2021; Innes 2013).

The interconnectedness of re-membering and resurgence complicates the idea that Indigenous engagement with the settler state undermines the resurgence of Indigenous ethics, knowledge, and practices, rendering a "turn away" the most viable path towards the re-establishment of sovereignty. Perhaps the most influential iteration of this argument is made by political theorist Glen Sean Coulthard (2014) in his critique of the late twentieth-century liberal politics of recognition.[51] Coulthard argues that the politics of recognition, characterized by a superficial utilization of "culture" and enabled in part by the rise of liberal multicultural ideology from the late 1960s, contributes to deliberate misrecognition and undermining of Indigenous political claims grounded in inherent rights to territory. In this way, settler state recognition of Indigeneity works as another mode of political dismemberment: "a partial decoupling of Indigenous 'cultural' claims from the radical aspirations for social, political and economic change that once underpinned them" (Coulthard 2014, 19).

Some scholars of resurgence politics have recently argued that Coulthard doesn't intend to dismiss outright Indigenous engagements with the settler state, as his call to "turn away" has often been interpreted (Corntassel 2021; Stark 2023). Jeff Corntassel explains that while a politics of Indigenous resurgence necessarily entails "decentering the state," it may simultaneously be pursued "through state and other institutional engagements" (2021, 78). Corntassel illustrates such engagements, which I would characterize as tactics, with the example of Indigenous language learning, which he suggests may entail language instruction in and through the state education system and funding from state sources to enable large-scale resurrection of Indigenous language use, widely accepted as central to resurgence. By extension, although Coulthard contrasts the settler state's politics of recognition with practices of reciprocal recognition among Indigenous people inherent to resurgence politics, I argue that the Indigenous histories discussed above and in the following chapters show how tactical engagements with the settler state's liberal politics of recognition in the late twentieth century enabled access to resources for re-membering, supporting the everyday practices of reciprocal recognition foundational to resurgence politics.[52]

This evidence from Indigenous social histories suggests that the predominant representation in academic and activist circles of the politics of resurgence and the politics of recognition (or relatedly, reconciliation) as binary opposites may be an oversimplification.[53] Rigorous analysis of the risks and opportunities that coexist where Indigenous actors navigate engagements with state actors and institutions in the pursuit of re-membering requires attention to how such engagements play out in given, ever-shifting contexts, and an openness to the possibility of unexpected outcomes unfettered by ideological prejudice. Such nuanced, empirically grounded investigations are well illustrated by anthropologists centring Indigenous political actors in ethnographic research, who show how the latter navigate incommensurate worldviews and political and social structures to form tactical alliances with settler state agents and institutions—even becoming state agents themselves—to advance their peoples' sovereignty interests (de la Cadena 2015; Lambert 2022).

Working with concepts of re-membering and Indigenized biopolitics help us to see how, as Gina Starblanket and Heidi Kiiwetinepinesiik Stark (2018) argue, settler-colonial power is generative in ways that present opportunities for, as well as threats to, Indigenous resurgence. This simultaneity of opportunity and threat posed by Indigenous biopolitical tactics amidst ongoing social dismemberment demands that we consider the multiple meanings of biopolitics in the liberal settler colony, and its coexistence with necropolitics. Foucault argued that racist states oversee both biopolitical and necropolitical regimes in parallel.[54] Thus, biopolitics is also productive for examining how liberalism aligns with the workings of a racist settler state, a perspective often neglected by proponents of reconciliation politics, who tend to be uncritical of liberalism (Mills 2018).[55] Liberal rhetoric functions to enable and tacitly legitimate multiple modes of Indigenous social dismemberment: outright killing, deprivation of life essentials, and biopolitical individuation that jeopardizes Indigenous life by destroying its social substrate. Unlike "genocide," which, in current usage in Canadian public discourse, tends to obscure settler-colonial continuities, the concept of necropolitics pointedly calls our attention to "the relationship between politics and death" (Mbembe 2003, 16). While "making live" is the primary modus of biopolitics, necropolitics describes power over death—killing, or letting die—as the mobilization of sovereign authority, typically by state actors, to destroy human bodies and populations. Necropolitics is inextricably connected to biopolitics, because such deaths are legitimated by reference to political discourse around protecting the life and health of the social body from which those authorized for killing may be excluded (Foucault 2003). In the liberal settler colony, the social body is implicitly coterminous with white settler society, and Indigenous and other racialized people are readily construed as enemies, or surplus, whose death can be legitimated for the greater good (Moreton-Robinson 2009, 2015). As Tania Li notes in her helpful discussion of the politics of letting die, surplus populations are found where "places (or their resources) are useful, but the people are not" (2010, 69). In Canada, Indigenous people have frequently been treated as surplus, illustrated by the long history of settler state officials letting Indigenous people die through deprivation of the essentials of life (shelter, clean water, protection, food) and the systematic underfunding of public services (health care, family services, transportation).[56] The "over-policing but under-protecting" of Indigenous women and girls, including long-standing, systematic failure to investigate their deaths and disappearances, is a significant factor in their over-representation among the missing and murdered (Bourgeois 2018, 75–76).[57] The vulnerability of Indigenous defenders of their Peoples' territory to state-authorized killing is directly linked to the threat they pose to liberal values of property and the unfettered pursuit of profit: "efforts at reclaiming land expose the necropolitics of settler geopolitics" (Dietrich 2023, 32).[58] Wet'suwet'en land defenders in Unist'ot'en territory protesting pipeline construction have been targeted for killing by state agents (Dhillon and Parish 2019). Anne Spice (2018) explicates how this authorization is underpinned by liberal rationality: settler state sovereign power is extended through legislation expanding the definition of security, affording aggressive protection to oil and gas pipelines as "critical infrastructure." This move renders pipelines coterminous with national interest, with the effects of undermining Indigenous territorial claims, and criminalizing Indigenous opposition to fossil fuel extraction. Similarly, necropolitical discourse implicitly legitimates murder of Indigenous people by settlers by invoking threat to the sacrosanct liberal value of property and equating Indigeneity with criminality.[59]

Amidst necropolitics, Indigenous values, knowledge, and practices continue to support Indigenous life via (bio)political agency and tactics. Sandy Grande (2023) shows that while settler-colonial biopolitics of aging attempt to displace Indigenous knowledge with biomedical understandings, subjectifying elders and caregivers in ways that segregate elders from communities, alternate Indigenous understandings of aging persist, carrying the potential to shape relations with elders differently. Indigenous knowledge of aging offers an alternate model for how to live, one that could be translated into policy and programming as a transformative Indigenized politics of life. In Aotearoa New Zealand, Brendan Hokowhitu and colleagues (2022) argue explicitly for an Indigenous biopolitics to shape health research strategies. For Hokowhitu et al., biopolitical theory offers a tool for critique of settler state biopolitics as enacted through Indigenous health research, complementary to Māori principles and models, such as the concept of mana motuhake (autonomy, sovereignty, political self-governance). Claiming an Indigenous biopolitics is important, they argue, because Māori concepts in themselves are insufficient to critically analyze the political relations underpinning Indigenous health in the settler-colonial context; thus, they aspire to "Māori biopolitical self-governance" (Hokowhitu et al. 2022, 105).

These analyses suggest that Indigenous approaches to the politics of life can and do exceed engagement with and opposition to state institutions, constituting an "alter-politics," or the enactment of an alternative way of being pointing the way to transformative change. Ghassan Hage argues for the importance of alter-politics to transformative social and political movements, observing "the structure of the radical political imaginary at any given time is characterised by a certain balance between 'anti' politics and 'alter' politics" (2015, 28). In this formulation, visionary ideas and affect representing social and political transformation (what Hage describes as "the radical political imaginary") incorporate both critical analysis of existing structures and relations, and commitments to and enactments of alternative social and political forms, such as Indigenous resurgence. Hage argues that older Marxist politics prioritized anti-politics (critical analyses of and opposition to capitalism) over the active envisioning of alternative social and political systems, but globally, more recent movements show a heightened interest in alter-politics. Late twentieth-century Indigenous political movements in North America complicate Hage's timeline, encompassing anti-politics and alter-politics decades prior to the recent examples of the latter observed by Hage. Red Power of the 1970s was connected to international anti-colonial struggle, but diverged from movements in the Global South by emphasizing the importance of resurgent Indigenous knowledge for revitalizing Indigenous societies (Coulthard 2019; Rutherford 2010). Coulthard's (2014) contemporary analysis continues this tradition and wields it to critique central elements of dominant leftist thought, for instance by pointing to how Marx's theory of primitive accumulation disregards Indigenous land theft under settler colonialism.[60] Coulthard asserts the scope of anti-colonial struggle as beyond material reclamation of territory and inclusive of social systems characterized by place-based epistemologies and relational ontologies.[61] Indigenous alter-politics are constantly in flux, subject to reworking in line with divergent visions of Indigenous futures and the transformations needed to enact them. Indigenous feminist, queer, and Two-Spirit critiques have addressed masculinist and heteronormative biases and misogynistic practice inherent to the Red Power movement and still prevalent in contemporary Indigenous politics, including resurgence movements (Barker 2018; D. Hunt 2023; S. Hunt 2015; Hunt/Tłaliłila'ogwa and Simpson 2023; Innes and Anderson 2018), alongside the problem of limited attention to health and social domains as foundational to resurgence politics and sovereignty struggles, discussed above. These critiques implicitly suggest the significance of biopolitics as a substrate for Indigenous political agency. In this book, I argue that an Indigenized biopolitics may afford scope for an alter-politics enabling expansive movement from biopolitical tactics to biopolitical strategy as inherent to sovereignty, while sharpening anti-political critique of how liberal systems and discourses of Indigenous health and healing can continue settler-colonial relations of power.

Methodology, Scope, and Overview

My research methodology was shaped by interdisciplinary training in anthropology and history, relevant scholarship, particularly from Indigenous studies and settler-colonial studies, and professional experience as a medical anthropologist in public health and health care settings across three continents. As the preceding discussion conveys, my research centres Indigenous actors against the backdrop of shifting social and political contexts, including the experiences and effects of policies, programs, practices, and discourses around Indigenous health and healing. The following chapters trace Indigenous social and political action addressing collective well-being from the 1960s to the early twenty-first century, spanning demands for equality and civil rights in public service delivery, Native Alcoholics Anonymous, the revival of powwows and the Drum, Red Power activism including armed occupation, the early Friendship Centre movement, a street patrol to prevent and respond to violence and deaths from exposure, prison visiting, women's organizing against gendered violence and social and political dismemberment under the Indian Act, and the psychosocial effects of residential school abuse and trauma. I show how Indigenous social and political actors have navigated shifting public policy ranging from the 1969 White Paper and its aftermath to C-31, the Royal Commission on Aboriginal Peoples to *Gathering Strength*, and by turns collaborated with, co-opted, and critiqued the workings of dominant institutions spanning hospitals, hostels, research institutions, prisons, government ministries, and universities.

The critical social approach to health and well-being used in this book needs to be distinguished from applied research conducted by health professionals working within a biomedical or public health paradigm and intended to evaluate the effectiveness of policies and programs according to externally defined criteria. To enhance research reliability, evaluative health research is rightly concerned with systematic sampling to produce the most representative data describing whatever is being investigated. This book does not claim to provide a systematic historical survey of Indigenous healing across Canada, Ontario, or Treaty 3 territory. Instead, I offer a critical analysis of specific healing histories located in time and place, across shifting scales. My analysis has involved synthesizing the accounts and interpretations of interlocutors with my own interpretations, in dialogue with social and political theory and other academic work.[62] As elaborated in the preface, I've chosen to focus on these histories because I believe they convey perspectives and experiences insufficiently represented in ongoing academic, activist, public, and policy conversations, and because of the relationships I've formed with these interlocutors. The book draws on conversations with and oral histories shared by a wide range of mostly Indigenous interlocutors between 2008 and 2020, almost all of whom asked to be identified by name in published work. Contributors to this research have each played a significant role in Indigenous healing: as community organizers and advocates, providers and managers of services, and/or policymakers. More detailed information about my research methods, including how I approached these conversations and relationships with contributors, appears in the appendix.

Subsequent chapters document Indigenous social histories at a range of scales, spanning small urban centres and adjacent reserves in Northern Ontario, larger cities in the south of the province, and organizing at provincial and national levels. The first three chapters are set in the province of Ontario in central-eastern Canada, the boundaries of which overlap with the traditional territories of the Algonquin, Anishinaabe (Ojibwe), Cree, Delaware, Haudenosaunee Confederacy (Mohawk, Onondaga, Oneida, Cayuga, Tuscarora, Seneca), Mississauga, Odawa, and Potawatomi peoples. Virtually all waters and lands within the borders claimed by Ontario are subject to treaties that document agreements between these First Nations and Britain or Canada dating back to the late 1700s.[63] The province is also home to many Métis, and in the federal capital, Ottawa, the largest number of Inuit outside of their traditional territory. Ontario includes the largest Indigenous and settler populations in the country and the fourth-largest landmass of any province or territory.

Chapter 1 provides a social history of Anishinaabe re-membering in the small city of Kenora in the northern part of Treaty 3 territory beginning in the 1960s. This chapter centres on the caring work of Giizhiiganang (Don Morrison), including his innovative synthesis of Alcoholics Anonymous principles, Anishinaabe philosophy and ceremony, and historical-political analysis. Oral histories show how re-membering as healing was predicated on intertwined ceremonial, spiritual, and social resurgence, particularly relations with Grandfather Drum. It was also enabled by tactical engagements with liberal civil rights discourse and white health professionals who supported the establishment of urban Indigenous infrastructure, in the form of the short-lived but historically significant Kenora Waystation hostel.

Chapter 2 documents the expansion of Indigenous biopolitical tactics in Ontario during the 1970s and 1980s, through social histories of engagements with dominant institutions aimed at re-membering some of the most vulnerable and marginalized individuals. Shifting Indigenous and settler state politics after the 1969 White Paper, including the rise of Red Power politics and opportunities arising from liberal multiculturalism, provide the contexts for these tactics. Oral histories and archival source show how Indigenous community organizers in a range of sites spanning Northern and Southern Ontario challenged ongoing social dismemberment in prisons, hospitals, and on urban streets, asserting the value of Indigenous knowledge and subjectifying other Indigenous people as extended family members worthy of care.

Chapter 3 is an account of Indigenous women's organizing against family violence across Ontario between the early 1970s and 1990, including social histories set in Thunder Bay and Robinson-Superior Treaty territory, and province-wide organizing and research undertaken by the Ontario Native Women's Association. Drawing on their extensive experience of providing grassroots care for families, these women developed critiques of both liberal, white-dominated feminism and Indigenous politics dominated by men and their interests. The association's vision for "family healing" articulated a new, multivalent discourse linking Indigenous nationhood to individual and collective well-being, one which emphasized Indigenous legal systems' capacity to respond to interpersonal violence more appropriately and effectively than the settler state.

Chapter 4 considers the trajectory of re-membering as Indigenous healing migrated into public and policy discourse, in Ontario and nationally, under neoliberal settler colonialism from the 1990s. As tactical engagements with biopolitics expanded exponentially, the idea that colonialism is etiological of Indigenous social suffering that demands healing gained traction and was mobilized in divergent ways, creating both new opportunities for re-membering and new modes of biopolitical individuation and social dismemberment.

The following chapters encourage readers to think critically and carefully about the politics of Indigenous healing amidst settler colonialism, show how Indigenous social histories and social and political theory can work in complementary ways to support this aim, and suggest questions and directions for further inquiry. This work is not meant as a comprehensive or definitive account of Indigenous healing histories in Treaty 3 territory, Ontario, or Canada. On the contrary, I'm conscious of significant gaps and limitations in my analysis. Perhaps the most obvious is that by focusing on Indigenous social relations among humans, the book largely reproduces an anthropocentric understanding of health and well-being inconsistent with Indigenous understandings of human well-being as interdependent with that of nonhuman life. This limited perspective is the result of my early research orientation towards critical analysis of the dominant health care system, and that most of my early interlocutors worked primarily within the constraints of settler state policy and urban institutions, although land-based healing practices were sometimes part of this work, and Leanne Betasamosake Simpson argues that "all Indigenous practices are land-based practices" (Hunt/Tłaliłila'ogwa and Simpson 2023, 139). It is not my intention to detract from the fundamental importance of relations with territory, land, water, and other-than-human beings to Indigenous people's collective health and well-being, and I appreciate scholarship (McGregor 2018; Spice 2024; Watts 2020) and activist writing (Women's Earth Alliance and Native Youth Sexual Health Network 2016) addressing this interrelationship.

A second omission that some readers will note is a lack of detailed ethnographic vignettes depicting ceremony and other healing practices, or extended discussion of Indigenous philosophy. Some of my interlocutors were generous in sharing Anishinaabe teachings, and I was invited and encouraged to participate in ceremony on multiple occasions. But I have decided against writing about these learnings and experiences in any detail, for two linked reasons. First,

I'm conscious of anthropology's history of misrepresenting Indigenous Peoples in ways that caused significant harm—an important focus of my undergraduate teaching work—and second, I'm aware of the limitations of my own very basic knowledge, particularly given that I don't speak Anishinaabemowin, and of the risk of causing further harm as a white settler scholar writing about important and sometimes sensitive matters. I hope that those who wish to learn more will seek out appropriately qualified teachers and, meanwhile, that readers will find my basic knowledge of Indigenous worldviews sufficient to support the analytical account offered here. This account begins with the re-membering work of Giizhiiganang in Treaty 3 territory in the late 1960s.

Giizhiiganang and Anishinaabe Re-Membering, 1965–1980

GIIZHIIGANANG (MORNING STAR) is remembered by many older Anishinaabeg in Treaty 3 territory and beyond for his role in re-membering Anishinaabe society between 1967, when he himself became sober, until his death in 1990. But in the mid-1960s, Giizhiiganang, also widely known by his English name, Don Morrison, was "known as a town drunk" in Kenora.[1] He was a veteran of the Second World War, one of many enlisted Indigenous soldiers who drank legally alongside other Canadians.[2] Returning home, they endured the humiliation of being refused service in bars, as nineteenth-century colonial prohibitions against Indigenous people's consumption of alcohol remained intact. Racialized prohibition was gradually reversed through the 1950s, part of the post-war "integration" of Indigenous people into white settler society, and Don was one of those Anishinaabeg who sought comfort from alcohol as it became available for legal purchase. But he and others continued to be refused service in the bars of Kenora. There, white residents were reportedly both "ashamed...and embarrassed" by Indigenous public drunkenness, and perceived it as a vague threat to the sensibilities and safety of white women in particular, who were a significant presence in local drinking establishments.[3] Beyond concerns with decorum, inebriated Anishinaabeg in the streets of the town may have reminded white residents of an uncomfortable truth: their own prosperity from the pulp and paper industry was predicated on dispossessing Indigenous people of their territory, livelihoods, and once well-functioning societies.

One night early on in his sobriety, Don dreamt of a ceremonial Drum. Anishinaabeg know this Drum as Grandfather Drum, a living being and relative.[4] This Drum was originally received by the Anishinaabeg as a peace-making gift from the Sioux in the late nineteenth century.[5] In one of several conversations I had with an "old guy from Naicatchewenin,"[6] a member of Don's Drum group from the early 1980s, he explained to me, "When we choose to walk that way of life, there's always something we receive. Don received a message from the Creator, a vision, to make the Drum. When you're meant to make a sacred item, you *know* how." He shared an illustration from his own life: "My oldest granddaughter asked me to make a tikinaagan (traditional cradle board). At first, I said 'I don't know how.' Then...I remembered watching my father make it as a boy. I did make one for her...she still has it."[7] Don's dream, and his subsequent acts of building the Drum, Waakebiness, and supporting many men and women in achieving and maintaining sobriety, involved recovering and enacting multiple layers of traditional knowledge, or rememberings: Anishinaabe technology; the spiritual, therapeutic, social, and political significance of the Grandfather Drum; how relations to other-than-human beings enable relations among humans. Both remembering and forgetting are profoundly social practices with the capacity to shape individual social actors (Lambek 1996). I understand Don's process as not simply recovery of himself, as an Anishinaabe man, but a recovery of his sense of self *in relation to others*, meaning as a person shaped through a social web of relatedness and mutual responsibility spanning generations. This understanding can be conveyed through the concept of relational subjectivity. The Old Guy's automatic response to his granddaughter's request, *I don't know how to make a tikinaagan*, signalled a forgetting deliberately instilled in him by the workings of disciplinary power through the residential school system, where he'd been taught that Indigenous knowledge was backwards, worthless in the modern world, and relational selfhood was discouraged as children were encouraged to consider themselves as apart from their relatives. In remembering, he overcame the stultifying effect of deliberately instilled shame, in the process recovering himself—not only as the son of an Anishinaabe father who transmitted this knowledge but as a father and grandfather himself, who recovered his own capacity to perform this act of caring, crafting technology that would protect his great-grandchild. This assertion of the endurance and contemporary relevance of Anishinaabe knowledge has clear material implications for social and political relationships. In this sense, we can understand remembering as not only a powerful antidote to shame but also a moral practice (Lambek 1996). In the context of the extraordinary violence, multiple losses, and intergenerational ruptures of settler colonialism, those who can remember may experience this capacity as a shared moral responsibility to future generations (Myerhoff 1982).

In this chapter, I discuss how Giizhiiganang and others in Treaty 3 territory in the 1970s practiced re-membering by recovering previously suppressed Anishinaabe knowledge as part of their response to social dismemberment resulting from Canadian settler colonialism. "Re-membering," as discussed in the introduction, signifies the double meaning of recovering knowledge and enacting social repair. In my use of re-membering as a central concept, I intend to both build on earlier anti-colonial scholarship and redress shortcomings that limit its applicability to Indigenous experiences under settler colonialism. Most famously, Frantz Fanon's (2004) analysis of the psychosocial effects of colonization considers the celebration of pre-contact indigenous society as a route to recovery.[8] Fanon's work is structured around the colonizer/colonized dualism, an overly simplistic formulation for analyzing Indigenous experience in the context of an ongoing colonial project spanning centuries, and cannot do justice to the many tactical engagements with the settler state enabling Indigenous survival through the twentieth century (discussed in the introduction) or the diversity of experience obscured by the "colonized" category.[9] Ngũgĩ wa Thiong'o's (2009) concept of re-membering builds on Fanon, but is more attentive to divergent social locations, for instance, how postcolonial and post-slavery social divisions of class and geography shape engagements with social memory. Thus, he posits the recovery and revitalization of indigenous knowledge, such as the use of indigenous languages, as a dynamic social and political process inflected by divergent contemporary social locations and political commitments across the African diaspora. But like Fanon, Ngũgĩ's analysis neglects how the profoundly gendered effects of colonialism have important implications for contemporary (post)colonial subjects. As elaborated in the introduction, I mean "subjects" in a dual sense: social actors and people who have been subjugated (Butler 1997). As Indigenous feminist scholars argue, not only do women and men and Two-Spirit people experience colonization differently, contemporary Indigenous political and social responses to colonization also need to be analyzed through a gender lens (Barker 2008; Million 2013; A. Wilson 2018). As a practice explicitly focused on resocializing, re-membering is broadly aligned with such feminist approaches. But like the larger resurgence movement, re-membering is pursued amidst ongoing effects of gendered dismemberment and the larger structure of settler colonialism. We therefore can expect that practices of re-membering and resurgence may by turns challenge and reproduce colonial gender norms.

This chapter centres oral histories shared by and about Anishinaabe men to elucidate their roles and experiences of re-membering in Treaty 3 territory during the 1960s and 1970s. Analyzing men's experiences of and contributions to re-membering can generate insights into how their gendered identities are reshaped or reaffirmed in this complex matrix, where Indigenous efforts at resocialization are shaped by both external and internalized constraints. Analyses of masculinities can complement the growing body of work on Indigenous women and Two-Spirit experience (Innes and Anderson 2015; McKegney 2014b). And as Robert Alexander Innes and Kim Anderson (2015) note, there is a pressing need to understand Indigenous masculinities beyond the dichotomous roles of victimizer/protector, which can obscure men's experiences of violence and vulnerability and work as caregivers. Oral histories in this chapter show how Anishinaabe re-membering was not only about recovering, adapting, and putting into practice Indigenous ways of knowing, being, and doing, such as constructing and using a tikinaagan or powwow Drum. It was also about how that knowledge supports reconstituting collective membership of Indigenous families and societies, by recovering neglected relationships with those who have died and with other-than-human relatives, reconnecting with living humans pushed to the margins by colonial violence, and reflecting on one's own violent behaviour. In the 1970s re-membering by Don and others focused on reconnecting with those struggling with alcohol abuse—predominantly men, but also some women—by affording protection from violence and death in the hostile public spaces of Kenora and rebuilding social and spiritual relations centred around the Grandfather Drum. The latter practice included difficult conversations about men's participation in lateral violence, including gendered and interpersonal violence and betrayal.

Anishinaabe re-membering needs to be understood in the context of mid-twentieth-century Canadian settler colonialism, compelling attention to how Indigenous social actions are embedded in but can also challenge and exceed *ongoing* colonial relations. In this period, these relations entailed both the continued social dismemberment of families and societies and the rise of liberal civil rights discourse. As discussed in the introduction, settler state approaches to attempted elimination of Indigenous Peoples shifted during the period after the Second World War when the rapid expansion of the liberal welfare state marked the intensification of biopolitics as a mode of liberal settler-colonial governance. Welfare state institutions and actors attempted to subjectify Indigenous people as liberal subjects whose habits and desires would increasingly resemble those of white Canadians.[10] Paradoxically, mid-century state racism relied on a discourse on "equality" and the professed intention to treat "Indians" the same as other Canadians. This liberal ideology then enabled policymakers to dismiss Indigenous entitlements derived from Treaty Rights as "segregation," constituting obstacles to citizenship and full participation in Canadian society (Shewell 2004, 282). But the liberal ideology dominant in Ottawa and among white professionals in southern cities did little to challenge white supremacist values embedded in many settler communities and state institutions alike. Anishinaabe experiences in Kenora show that state actors and white citizens continued to engage in everyday practices of violence and exclusion.

Forgetting Re-Membering: Civil rights and Biopolitical Tactics

In November 1965, two years before Don became sober, hundreds of Anishinaabeg marched "in quiet dignity" (Anglin 1965, 8) through the streets of Kenora, convening to present a set of demands to the town council. Their demands asserted their civil rights to employment and fair working conditions, life-saving modern infrastructure, public health care services, and full participation in Kenora's consumer society without racist discrimination. Spokesmen Fred Kelly and Peter Seymour drew heavily on universalist ideas of human rights and equality, with multiple implicit references to the Black civil rights movement in the United States. Simply put, the protestors sought "opportunities the same as the white man" (*Globe and Mail* 1965).[11] This tactical engagement with liberal rhetoric proved effective at galvanizing support from white advocates, including human rights activists and liberal professionals, but also obscured how Indigenous rights, both inherent and Treaty, are prior to and distinct from the civil rights claims of Black and other racialized groups. For instance, the speeches hardly mentioned Treaty 3, signed by these Anishinaabeg's ancestors and the Crown nearly a century before.

Reflecting on the significance of the 1965 Kenora march in 2015, Kelly characterized it as "the turning point for our people" marked by "the beginning of a new assertiveness" (Assembly of First Nations 2015).

Anishinaabe opposition to colonial domination was long-standing; what was unprecedented was a new reliance on the "equality and dignity" language and methods of the Black civil rights movement originating in the United States. Earlier in the decade, media commentators had begun to characterize anti-Indigenous racism in Canada as analogous with anti-Black racism in the southern United States, but the 1965 Kenora march was the first instance in which Indigenous protestors in Canada publicly took up this discourse, fuelling wider comparisons with the Black civil rights movement south of the border (Rutherford 2017).[12] In this sense, the march marked a significant historical shift, not only for Anishinaabeg but for Indigenous political protest more broadly.

From a longer historical perspective, Kelly's characterization of Anishinaabe assertiveness as "new" is misleading. When the traditional leaders of this dispersed, egalitarian society signed Treaty 3 with representatives of the Crown in 1873, Anishinaabeg agreed to share the soil with incoming white settlers, but insisted that their traditional livelihoods of fishing, hunting, trapping, and wild rice harvesting, with which their social, political, and spiritual systems were co-constituted, not be interfered with. Almost immediately, it became clear that the Crown would not honour this commitment. In the following decades, Anishinaabeg acted in multiple ways to challenge Treaty violations by the federal and provincial governments and white settlers. These actions spanned a range of channels: diplomatic (such as the 1892 petition to the king of England expressing concerns about flooding and overfishing in the Lake of Woods), direct action (deliberate destruction of commercial fisheries' trawler nets in 1898, led by Treaty signatory Chief Powassin), and legal (in 1923, retention of a lawyer by Naotkamegwanning [Whitefish Bay], Wabaseemoong [Whitedog], and other communities to ascertain the status of Anishinaabe funds from sale of timber) (Kinew 1995). From the 1920s through the 1940s, new provincial laws authorized Ontario game wardens to increase policing of Anishinaabe wild harvesting—denying hunting and fishing licences, confiscating boats and equipment, laying charges that led to fines and/or jail time. Some Anishinaabeg repeatedly defied these unjust laws (Kinew 1995, 142).[13] Clearly, assertiveness was a long-standing feature of Treaty 3 Anishinaabeg's relations with the Canadian settler state.

But a significant shift in relations between Indigenous Peoples and the settler state did occur mid-century: post-WWII modernization and integration policy, and its psychosocial effects. Kelly, who grew up during the 1940s and 1950s, might have read the assertiveness of the 1965 march as "new" because the post-war period was one of particularly intense subjugation. Historian Hugh Shewell suggests that these effects are discernible in archival sources from the 1950s: written communication from First Nations leaders across Canada conveys what he argues are historically emergent "feelings of inferiority to whites and a negative, collective self-image," a growing resignation to the inevitability of labour market participation and welfare dependence, with some Band Councils taking up the language of "integration"—all in contrast to the distinctly more assertive tone of submissions from the previous decade (Shewell 2004, 287). While integration began to displace long-standing segregation under the banner of "equality," state policy and discourse continued to frame Indigenous people as premodern and reinforce doubt as to their capacity to manage their own affairs. For example, administrators of the new relief payments to Status Indians were advised to issue cheques and vouchers only to those "who can be relied upon to purchase essential items of food with a minimum of supervision" (265). These interventions aimed to reshape Indigenous people's sense of themselves, to subjectify them as junior citizens who embraced dominant gender roles, organization of domestic life, and kinship relations consistent with the normative expectations of white, urban, middle-class Canadian society. By the 1960s, the Old Guy from Naicatchewenin wryly observed, "No one wanted to be an Indian. Everybody wanted to be a white man."[14]

Against this backdrop, we can see that in fact the 1965 Anishinaabe protestors' demands for equal opportunities to employment and health care were quite well aligned with the liberal thinking increasingly influential within settler state institutions. But one comment stands out as of a slightly different character: "Even our traditional occupations meet pressing government restrictions…

Is there any wonder that so many of our people turn to alcohol?" (quoted in Rutherford 2017, 166). Linking the systemic undermining of Anishinaabe livelihoods to the indignity of chronic drunkenness powerfully conveys the particularity of Indigenous experience of settler colonialism as corroding social worlds and selfhood. Unspoken, but no doubt understood by the older Anishinaabeg present, was the extent to which "traditional occupations," far from a narrowly economic activity, are bound up with kinship, Clan, and broader social, political, and spiritual relations and responsibilities, among humans, past, present, and future, and including other-than-human beings in Anishinaabe territory.[15] This social and political specificity contrasts with the other, universal civil rights demands, which would have been recognizable to colonized, racialized, and marginalized peoples in almost any mid-twentieth-century socio-political context. Also striking is spokesmen Kelly and Seymour's sympathetic presentation of Anishinaabe alcohol abuse, not as inherent weakness or pathology, as dictated by popular and biomedical discourses of the time, but as an understandable response to the degradation of unemployment, welfare dependence, exploitative service labour, and suppression of traditional livelihoods.

This link drawn by the spokesmen between Indigenous dispossession and social suffering departed from the universalized, liberal politics that otherwise shaped their address. Their subsequent demand for assistance from a state institution, the Toronto-based Addiction Research Foundation (ARF), could be read as consistent with the dominant modernization paradigm, but also as an invocation of settler state responsibilities in the context of enduring Treaty Rights. Did this implicit confidence in the ability of these white, credentialled experts to intervene effectively in Anishinaabe alcohol abuse reflect a loss of faith in Anishinaabeg's own approaches to supporting and reintegrating suffering individuals through ceremony? Or had these approaches simply been suppressed or forgotten?

In the 1960s most younger Anishinaabeg's inexperience of ceremony was the result not only of the residential school system's partial success at inciting shame in their people's traditional knowledge, as described by the Old Guy, but also of targeted attacks by the settler state and Christian missionaries in the first half of the twentieth century.[16] As discussed in the introduction, Canadian legislation banned all forms of Indigenous ceremonial dance between 1906 and 1951. This was not simply Christian intolerance for other religions: state actors understood very well that ceremony had a central role in the Indigenous social, political, and economic systems they were attempting to destroy (Pettipas 1994). In Treaty 3 territory, Kathi Avery Kinew (1995, 136–37) notes two occasions in the early twentieth century when white observers contacted the Canadian military after becoming aware of practices of Anishinaabe ceremony: in 1902 a "religious ceremony" held at Windy Point, and in 1912 a Midewiwin ceremony at Blueberry Point, outside of Kenora. Oral histories indicate that although Drum and Midewiwin ceremonies continued through the prohibition period, they were practiced by small groups, often deep in the bush, to avoid hostility from settlers and officials. Even after the repeal of the ban, some state agents continued to perceive Indigenous ceremony as a threat, intrusively monitoring Anishinaabe gatherings. The Old Guy recalled, "In the early 1950s, the RCMP would come in when there was a ceremony going on, watching. I don't know if they were ready to take people away. I heard the ceremonies were outlawed. The Shaking Tent, the Midewiwin had to hide to do that."[17] Many Anishinaabeg experienced lingering anxiety, uncertainty, even shame towards ceremonial practice; family members became secretive with one another about ceremony and spirituality.[18] For example, Don's son, Joseph Morrison, only learned that his maternal grandfather was an active participant in the Midewiwin Society throughout his life after the man's death.[19]

The 1965 Anishinaabe protestors' demand that a welfare state institution direct its expertise and resources towards alleviating Indigenous suffering was consistent with a civil rights framework and settler-colonial biopolitics; it was also a tactic that enabled Anishinaabeg in and around Kenora to cultivate re-membering on an unprecedented scale. By characterizing their people's suffering not as evidence of backwardness or inherent dysfunction but the outcome of colonial suppression and racism, they diverged from the paternalistic assimilationist discourse of the day. Their alternate framing presented a public challenge to dominant ways of "knowing" Indigenous people, signalling the emergence of tactical Indigenous engagement with biopolitics in urban settings, characterized by a historicized and politicized understanding of social suffering. Although these Anishinaabe political actors did not publicly attest to the value of their people's own knowledge for supporting recovery from alcohol abuse, they helped to create the conditions under which such a healing renaissance could occur and relational subjectification could flourish.

The Kenora Waystation: Biopolitics and Re-Membering, 1967–1970

In February 1967, with temperatures averaging minus twelve degrees Celsius, the Kenora Waystation first opened its doors to inebriated men and women and anyone else seeking shelter. Intended, quite literally, to save lives, its short-lived existence was both testament to the effectiveness of Anishinaabe tactical engagement with civil rights discourse and state biopolitics and, I argue, an instantiation of an Indigenized politics of life. Housed in a centrally located two-storey building, the Waystation was conceptualized by the ARF and the Mayor's Committee as a pilot project consisting of "a combined hostel and detox facility which could serve as an alternative to jail."[20] The then emergent "addictions" approach favoured rehabilitation of the "acute common drunk" as a modern alternative to criminalization.[21] Most white Kenora residents had little interest in the project of rehabilitating Anishinaabe drinkers: their priority was to conceal inebriation from public view, not necessarily to prevent or treat it.[22] This widely held imperative partially explains why criminalization continued to disproportionately affect Anishinaabeg in Kenora: in 1970 every day the court sentenced more than twenty people on alcohol-related charges, following procedures that one visiting ARF researcher described as "only vaguely legal…casual and off-handed, or perhaps mechanical."[23] Of course, alcohol consumption was at least as prevalent among whites, but they drank in bars, the Legion, and private homes, meaning they were far less vulnerable to arrest. And if police happened to spot a drunk white man wandering along the street, chances are they would give him a ride home rather than throw him in jail.[24]

The Waystation's first director was Dr. Allan Torrie, a local physician widely known for his respectful relationships with Anishinaabeg; employed to assist Dr. Torrie were Len Hakenson and Peter Kelly (brother of Fred Kelly, organizer and spokesperson of the 1965 march).[25] The upper floor housed offices, a large kitchen, washroom, and comfortable lounge. Downstairs was the hostel-cum-detox space. An ARF researcher visiting from Toronto in 1970 described it thus: "an entrance with a rather battered desk, then a partition behind which was the main room—large, empty of all but a few chairs and mattresses piled in a corner. It was not overly clean...Men and women were sitting against the walls. Behind the main room, there is a man's and woman's washroom...a storage room and women's sleeping quarters having poor ventilation and no noticeable fire exit."[26]

Anishinaabe counsellors staffed the hostel space; according to the visiting researcher, "the white staff and a small portion of the elite Indian staff never seemed to venture downstairs."[27] Don was among the first of many Anishinaabe counsellors hired at the Waystation. Don had attended Cecilia Jeffrey Indian Residential School outside of Kenora for ten years before serving in the Second World War. Don's son, Joseph, told me that his father returned from the war "with a different outlook... more rough, violent."[28] Don began drinking heavily during these years and beating his young wife, Ada (née Crow). Alcohol and spousal abuse went together for many Anishinaabe men (Ontario Native Women's Association 1989); this issue was apparently not publicly addressed by Indigenous community organisers and their allies in the 1960s and 1970s. In the 1980s Indigenous women's groups in Ontario and elsewhere began to publicly raise the issue of spousal abuse as a social and political priority for their nations (discussed in chapter 3). When his father was drunk and became violent, Joseph would run outside to hide. Eventually, Ada asked Don to leave, and he survived for some years on the streets of Kenora.

The vulnerability of Anishinaabe life in late twentieth-century Kenora shows how equality rhetoric circulates alongside discrimination, coercion, and overt forms of violence. These conditions help to define liberal settler colonialism: the foundational ethos of profit-making shapes the workings of biopolitics, while older modes of disciplinary power persist where dictated by dominant economic interests, such as keeping drunken Natives out of public view. Although federal and provincial legislation began to dismantle the Indian Act's long-standing racialized prohibition during the 1950s, the ethos that Indigenous people, with their "genetic weakness to alcohol and civilization" (Vizenor 1994, 29), needed to be controlled by whites endured in the liquor regulations, criminal justice system, and everyday prejudices of white Canadians.[29] Among many possible illustrations, section 94(b) of the Indian Act, which made it an offence for a Status Indian to be intoxicated outside of a reserve, was not removed until 1970.[30]

The book's introduction discusses how the politics of life (biopolitics) is intertwined and interdependent with the politics of death (necropolitics) in the settler state's sovereignty project (Mbembe 2003). Settler-colonial interventions aimed at "making live," such as providing a twenty-four-hour hostel and counselling services for chronic drinkers, coexist with practices of "letting die" those who cannot be assimilated into liberal settler society. Groups implicitly marked as surplus or disposable can be neglected to the point of death, or targeted for killing by state or non-state actors (Li 2010). In the northern part of Treaty 3 territory during this period, some Anishinaabeg were useful to the tourist and recreational fishing industry, which employed them as guides and maids until 1970 when it was devastated by mercury poisoning caused by the pulp mill in Dryden. Beyond this, it was Anishinaabe territory, not labour, that was valuable to the pulp and paper industry, the dominant source of wealth and employment in the region, which continues to wreak environmental devastation to this day.[31] In Kenora, exclusion from public spaces, combined with a lack of basic shelter and public transportation, rendered those Anishinaabeg weakened by alcohol consumption ready targets for interpersonal violence, at times lethal, by both racist white Kenorans and other inebriated Anishinaabeg.[32] They were also at risk of death by exposure or drowning, and experienced a relentless cycle of arrest, court appearances, and fines that they often couldn't afford to pay.[33]

Not only was the biopolitical intervention of the Waystation the result of Anishinaabe community organizing, its services were shaped by Anishinaabe knowledge and experience, delivered in ways quite different to what government policymakers and ARF directors must have envisioned. Counsellors were recruited from among those using the Waystation, consistent with the Alcoholics Anonymous (AA) principle that recovering alcoholics can most effectively support one another. Anishinaabe counsellors channelled the resources flowing through this biopolitical project to support practices of re-membering. In his role as counsellor, Don drew on his intimate knowledge of life on the streets of Kenora and his understanding of Anishinaabe ethics and ceremony. Don and other Anishinaabe counsellors hosted bi-weekly AA meetings upstairs, supervised the downstairs hostel space, translated in court for accused Anishinaabeg not fluent in English, provided informal counselling in the Waystation and on the street, and drove people freshly discharged from prison home to their reserve. They also travelled to surrounding reserves in a rented station wagon, where they visited with residents and encouraged informal discussions about alcohol abuse, sometimes screening films and hosting AA meetings. These visits would become central to Don's job description in the 1970s, when he was hired permanently by the ARF.[34]

In 1967, with sobriety and employment affording a new stability to Don's life, he began to repair relationships with his immediate family members, initiating communication with his estranged wife, Ada Crow, and his and Ada's only son, Joseph Morrison, with whom relations were also strained in the wake of his extended time living on the streets.[35] In early March, shortly after being hired at the Waystation, Don wrote a letter to Joseph, by then age twenty-six and living with his wife, Gloria, and two young children in Winnipeg, where he was studying accounting.[36] Don wrote of his recent employment and ongoing efforts to stay sober and reconcile with Ada. He portrayed the Waystation as a site of lively, sometimes rowdy social life, affording shelter to a wide range of Anishinaabeg from the surrounding communities: "Saw lots fellows from Sioux Narrows yesterday, guess they got paid. We got about 30 guys here some of them drunk some of them they hard to handle. Had one girl here and she only about 17 or 18 years of age. And some want to play cards and other games." As if reflecting on the vulnerability of young, inebriated Anishinaabeg, Don opens his next paragraph by expressing his fervent wish for his son and daughter-in-law to stay sober: "And I hope you could keep away from drinking too Joseph, and Glo too." Don's use of the conditional tense "could" conveys his hesitancy in prescribing action to Joseph and Gloria. Interpersonal communication in Anishinaabemowin is replete with such tentative expression, consistent with the high value Anishinaabeg place on individual autonomy.[37] In this, AA philosophy is in alignment, advising that people should not be told to quit drinking.

In the same paragraph, perhaps as a non-directive reminder of this path to sobriety, Don shares reflections on his participation in the AA group at the Waystation: "And I been in A.A. meets once a week, and it nice to listen them talking about drinking and how they stop. And I know it's hard." In affirming the difficulty of quitting drinking, Don seems to both emphasize his own struggle and validate efforts that he hopes his son and daughter-in-law are making. His next paragraph shares news of his recent visit with Ada, perhaps an implicit reflection on both the consequences of long-term alcohol abuse and the possibility of subsequent relationship repair. Reflecting further on the challenges of staying sober at a time when so many of his people were drinking, Don added, "And I don't go out much out in street and lots boys ask me to go with them to pub and I tell them I don't like to drink and trying to keep away from it." In the last substantive paragraph, Don urges his son to focus on his studies: "Well Joseph, I hope you keep with school every day and don't miss any school days eh."

In closing, Don conveys his strong desire to maintain regular correspondence with his son, by repeating requests for a return letter

("I hope you drop a line"; "Write soon eh"). Underlining "take care," and double underlining "Dad" in his sign-off, he gives special emphasis to these expressions of caring and relatedness.[38] In the early 1970s Joseph and his family moved to Wauzhushk Onigum (Rat Portage reserve) just outside of Kenora, and Don and Ada, who reconciled around the same time, became actively involved in caring for their grandchildren. By repairing relations with his closest kin, Don established the conditions for the reinstatement of intergenerational caring and sharing of knowledge, thus revitalizing Anishinaabe social reproduction and starting to scale up re-membering.

During a visit to the Waystation in 1970, Toronto-based ARF researcher G.W. Mercer surveyed the selection of films screened by the Anishinaabe counsellors and was mystified. In his report, he observed that "The films seem irrelevant...How [they] will affect the Kenora area Indian's drinking problem is a bit obscure."[39] Mercer's comment suggests a lack of political and historical analysis in dominant professional approaches to understanding addiction. In contrast, taken together, the films suggest that, like the spokespersons at the 1965 march, Anishinaabe counsellors were developing a contextualized analysis of Indigenous experiences of alcohol, which attended to social, political, and historical relations. *Circle of the Sun* (Low 1960), filmed in 1956 and 1957, documents the (erroneously) anticipated demise of the Kainai (Blood) Sundance ceremony in Western Canada, through the eyes of a young Kainai man. *Bitter Wind* (1963) is a Mormon-produced, proselytizing drama about how a Dine father's alcohol abuse nearly destroys his family (Hard-to-find Mormon Videos 2015). *Indian Memento* (Régnier 1967) documents the powerful, Indigenous-created "Indian Pavilion" exhibit at Canada's Expo 67. All three films convey the persistence of Indigenous relations with kin and territory, in contexts of countervailing settler colonialism: pressures to "modernize" by leaving home for formal education and wage labour; the presumed inevitable fading away of Indigenous ceremony and spirituality; ongoing efforts at Christian conversion. Notwithstanding overt missionary bias, *Bitter Wind* (the only film addressing alcohol) portrays alcohol abuse as an inherently social phenomenon, with profound implications for kin relations. Don screened this film dozens of times during visits to Treaty 3 reserves in the mid-1970s.[40] This socialized perspective contrasts with dominant professional and public discourse at the time, which tended to focus on the isolated figure of the implicitly male "alcoholic," who was presumed to have moved permanently beyond the reach of caring relations. Anishinaabe re-membering, in contrast, practiced a relational subjectification that continued to claim the most marginalized as kin and worthy of care, denying estrangement as inevitable and permanent. I've witnessed and heard accounts about this ethical practice many times during the years I've been visiting Treaty 3 territory.

A fourth film in the Waystation collection, *The Queen in Canada, 1964* (Sparling 1965), suggests that the Anishinaabe counsellors connected their people's contemporary social challenges to the longer history of colonization and betrayal of Treaty relations, a powerful reframing of the dominant model of addiction. The film documents Queen Elizabeth's 1964 visit to Canada, in commemoration of the hundredth anniversary of two 1864 conferences leading to Confederation: part of the political pre-history to these Anishinaabeg's own Treaty 3, signed with representatives of Queen Elizabeth's great-great-grandmother, Queen Victoria, in 1873. The Waystation workers' inclusion of this film in their repertoire is evidence of their historical-political analysis of Anishinaabe alcohol abuse, including an enduring understanding of Anishinaabeg's nation-to-nation relationships with the Crown structured by Treaty, illustrating another way in which these Anishinaabeg Indigenized state-dominated biopolitics.[41]

Concluding his 1970 report on the Waystation, the ARF researcher wrote, "It is the Indian in transition from one culture to the other that has a drinking 'problem.'"[42] In contrast to the sophisticated, historically and politically grounded perspective reflected by the Waystation counsellors' film repertoire, and the explicit connection between alcohol consumption and loss of livelihoods noted by spokespersons at the 1965 march, ARF research about Anishinaabe drinking and the Waystation showed a marked absence of nuanced, contextualized analysis. Dominant discourse about Indigenous alcohol consumption obscured past and ongoing dispossession, instead identifying the root problem as challenges inherent to the necessary but treacherous path towards assimilation. In a circular logic, assimilation is then held up as the best solution to Anishinaabe alcohol abuse. In an illustrative ARF report researched prior to the opening of the Waystation, anthropologist Carol Yawney identified a perceived excess of leisure time as driving Indigenous alcohol abuse, and urged, "The ARF must convince [the Indian] that steady employment and other improvements in his circumstances are necessary before he will be likely to moderate his drinking," and advised that ARF workers counter this alleged instinct towards slothfulness by inciting "a measure of enterprise and capitalist 'frenzy.'"[43] But ARF commentators were well aware that other white Canadians might be skeptical of their liberal assessment of alcohol abuse as linked to the challenges of assimilation, to be redressed by "habilitation."[44] The pervasive view among white Kenorans was that a tendency to alcohol abuse was innate to Native people—a view that was arguably reinforced, albeit from a liberal assimilationist perspective, by the ARF researchers' disregard for social, historical, and political contexts in their analyses. As change was deemed unlikely, many white Kenorans supported expanding local jail capacity as a more appropriate response than rehabilitation.[45] Yawney (and other researchers) expressed concerns that this "antiquarian attitude" of white residents and officials in Kenora would inhibit the success of the ARF rehabilitation intervention.[46]

Sure enough, as a concession to pressure from white residents, the ARF closed the Waystation's hostel service in June 1970. From the perspective of the white social scientists, it had been a resounding failure, in part because white management staff, whose role was to train the Anishinaabe counsellors as social workers, themselves lacked "any training to speak of in psychology, sociology, counselling or data collection," and the project as a whole lacked "efficiency and productivity."[47] During the Waystation's operation, there was no measurable reduction in arrests for public drunkenness, white hostility towards Anishinaabeg had not relented, and only about 10 per cent of approximately 150 Anishinaabeg hired as workers reportedly maintained "extended sobriety."[48] Despite this perceived failure, the ARF presence in Kenora was solidified in October 1969, reportedly because this work was seen by the federal government as well aligned with the community development approach articulated in the 1969 White Paper.[49] Several Anishinaabeg, including Don Morrison and his friend Sam Copenace, remained employed in counselling roles.[50]

I suggest that this lack of white professional management may have been precisely what allowed the conveniently located Waystation hostel to flourish as hub for Anishinaabe re-membering. Beyond affording safety and shelter for about seventy people per day, including sleeping-off space for the inebriated, the Waystation provided a space where families from the reserves, visiting town to pick up cheques and purchase food and supplies, could socialize without fear of racist harassment.[51] Don's granddaughter, Beverly (Bev) Williamson, told me about her memories of being taken to the Waystation with her younger brother to bathe, since their shack at Wauzhushk Onigum (Rat Portage reserve) had no running water. Among Waystation workers who maintained long-term sobriety, many went on to "become leaders among their people," in the words of one ARF commentator: detox worker and Wauzhushk Onigum Chief Madeline Skead, court worker Charlie Fisher, reserve constable Clifford Skead, and many others.[52] An Anishinaabeg-dominated urban social space and refuge that not only saved many lives but cultivated an ethos of reciprocal recognition and care, the Waystation launched future trajectories not of professional social workers but of men and women known as committed helpers of their people. I suggest this history can be interpreted as the emergence of an urban, Indigenized politics of life at the margins of but also exceeding settler state biopolitics. Through the 1970s and 1980s (and beyond), some members of this cohort continued to extend re-membering practice and launch new projects supporting Indigenous life in Kenora, discussed in chapter 2.

Anishinaabe Re-Membering: Native Alcoholics Anonymous and the Lake of the Woods Drum Resurgence

"For me, Alcoholics Anonymous was the answer. For you? This is something you must decide for yourself."[53] Thus Don concluded his often-repeated short lecture to his Anishinaabe audience, during AA meetings held upstairs at the Waystation, or at Doug and Madeline Skead's home at Wauzhushk Onigum, or in fledgling AA group meetings in towns and reserves across Treaty 3 territory.

Abstinence from alcohol as spiritual practice has been central to historical Indigenous spiritual renaissance movements, in diverse territories across North America, since at least the early 1800s—well before AA was established in 1935 (Million 2013, 154). The fact that AA is "spiritually open-ended" renders its ideology and practice sufficiently flexible to incorporate—or be incorporated by—Indigenous spiritualities (153). The non-directiveness inherent to AA philosophy is one of several elements that overlap with Indigenous subjectivity, ontology, epistemology, and ethics; others include individual responsibility, interdependence within the collective, and storytelling as an important medium for sharing knowledge.[54] These common elements enabled AA to serve as a useful framework or medium for resurrecting Anishinaabe philosophy and, most importantly, transmitting it widely. In his talk, Don described his own route from social drinker, through his "descent" to the "degrading...depths," and finally to sobriety. He was unequivocal on two points: that the AA philosophy and practice enabled his own recovery, and that he did not intend to impose this approach on any other person.[55]

In the years after the Waystation hostel's closure in 1970, Don's continued employment as an outreach counsellor at the ARF centre enabled him and his colleagues to expand the reach of re-membering in support of sobriety across Treaty 3 territory. His practice of re-membering was shaped particularly by his close relationships with Madeline and Doug Skead of Wauzhushk Onigum and their extended family, with whom he developed a distinct approach to maintaining sobriety and supporting others in doing so, synthesizing AA philosophy with the resurgence of Anishinaabe ceremony. Madeline and Doug became sober in 1969, a couple of years after Don; Madeline worked at the Waystation before being employed at the detox centre and in the early 1970s was elected Chief of Wauzhushk Onigum (Rat Portage reserve).[56] The Skeads hosted weekly AA meetings at their home, where attendance ranged from Don plus one or two others (his son Joseph and wife Ada sometimes attended), to larger groups of up to eighteen people. It was around this time that Don and Ada reconciled, and they remained together until his death in 1990.

Don travelled regularly, visiting at least ten different reserves across Treaty 3 territory, often in response to invitations from Band Councils, and towns with significant Anishinaabe communities. The Old Guy described to me the significance of Don's visits to his community of Naicatchewenin (Northwest Bay) in the early 1970s, part of a much longer narrative about his own trajectory from "Indian politics" to a healing path. At that time, in his words, "maybe 90 per cent of our people were drinking." He recalled, "I knew who he was, knew he was sober, but at that time, I didn't care. But he kept coming back. I thought, what is he doing anyway? I used to wonder: Was he just being nosy, that old man?" Don's friendly, open approach and refusal to lecture made a lasting impression on the Old Guy, who recalled, "He just visited, didn't preach or anything, just talking. He never told anyone, 'You gotta quit drinking!'"[57]

In Kenora, Don regularly visited Anishinaabeg interred at the jail, in hospital, and at the detox centre, and received visitors, including travellers from surrounding reserves, at the ARF centre. Don's nephew Albert Morrison, raised in Onigaming (Sabaskong Bay), sometimes accompanied him on visits to reserves; Albert later became a respected Healer and ceremonialist.[58] In September 1978, leaving Fort Frances at the end of a four-day trip to communities in the area, Don met an Anishinaabe woman who told him that "her son was in Emo Hospital from drinking too much." He promised to visit the man on his way home. Don's ledger records that he stayed about an hour visiting with the man. On other occasions, Don might attend a funeral service or participate in a meeting to plan a hockey tournament. In short, his work of re-membering was embedded in the Anishinaabe social fabric that stretched between reserves and small rural and urban centres of Treaty 3 territory.

In the early 1970s, Don and Ada joined with the Skeads "to celebrate sobriety" by establishing the Lake of the Woods Powwow Club.[59] The increasing significance of the powwow group, Grandfather Drum, and Anishinaabe songs in Don's life and work is discernible in his ledger from 1974, when he begins to record Waakebiness and "Indian songs" as part of his community visits and AA meetings. A powwow renaissance was just beginning in Treaty 3 territory at this time.[60] As elsewhere in North America, alcohol use was common among powwow participants (Weibel-Orlando 2009).[61] But for Don and the Skeads, powwows became a means to honour and sustain sobriety and well-being and encourage and support other Anishinaabeg to do so, demonstrating spiritual resurgence and collective well-being as mutually constitutive.

The Grandfather Drum and the powwow served as powerful focal points for embodied re-membering, on multiple levels: spiritual, social, physical, and psychological. For Anishinaabeg, relationships with the Drum, singing, and dancing enable reconnection to the Creator. For older Anishinaabeg who had participated in ceremonies in their younger lives, decades earlier, the working of sensory and embodied memory may also support the healing effects of these activities: memories suppressed by the conscious mind (through the workings of internalized shame, for example) may be recollected via an experience of moving to the drumbeat or hearing a long-forgotten song. Reflecting on her work with Jewish elders who'd suffered multiple losses through migration and the Holocaust, Barbara Myerhoff (1982) suggests that such embodied re-membering powerfully reintegrates fragmented parts of the self in the wake of such multiple, cumulative losses. As I've been taught by many Anishinaabeg, the Grandfather Drum and Anishinaabe songs and dances also have inherent physical and psychological healing properties. The Drum that Don built, Waakebiness, became widely known as a healing

Drum. The Old Guy told me a story that illustrates the Drum's healing effects:

> I've seen that Drum help a lot of people that were sick. One time in the mid-1980s, there was an old man from Red Lake, Minnesota who was diagnosed with cancer, told he would live a couple of months or less. So he came to the Drum. I was there with Don, who accepted tobacco from the man. He had no hair or eyebrows, his fingernails were falling off, he was very weak...Don asked us to sing a song for the old man, and told him he didn't have to dance, "Let other people dance for you." Don told him to hold the staff.

Later, they learned that the man fully recovered from the cancer. Further, participation in a powwow entails receiving the care of those whose labour facilitates the ceremony (Berbaum 2000). Women contribute substantial efforts in producing food and regalia for powwows; this process of creating is itself considered by Anishinaabeg to be a healing practice.[62] Finally, powwows are a significant space for socializing, within and between generations, and among Anishinaabeg from communities near and far, presenting an opportunity for re-membering kinship and other important relations.[63]

Perhaps both practical and symbolic considerations motivated the Lake of the Woods Powwow Club members to choose Cecelia Jeffrey residential school as the site for the first powwows they hosted in the mid-1970s.[64] It was (and remains) a beautiful site: grassy and open, overlooking Round Lake, with ample space for camping. The school was equipped with infrastructure to a standard lacking on many Northern reserves for much of the twentieth century: road access, an indoor water supply, washrooms, and laundry facilities.[65] But given the significance of the school in their personal and family histories, this cannot have been a neutral choice, emotionally, spiritually, or politically.[66] It seems probable that Don, the Skeads, and other participants experienced gathering with the Drum, singing, dancing, and socializing on the former school grounds as a way of actively asserting the enduring value of Anishinaabe knowledge and relationships, a celebration of the ultimate failure of that institution. In August 1974, segments of the powwow were captured on film. Within weeks, Don was screening this footage for Anishinaabeg during his outreach work at the ARF, including one meeting at the Kenora Jail for sixteen women interned there.[67]

But after two consecutive years of hosting powwows at the former Cecelia Jeffrey residential school site, the legacy of the school forced the club to relocate its powwows. As explained to me by Andy White, an early participant in the Drum revival at Whitefish Bay who attended the Lake of the Woods powwows, on both occasions a traditional dancer collapsed during the powwow and later died.[68] A Shaking Tent was held at Wauzhushk Onigum to determine the cause of the deaths, and it was learned that a child buried in the school grounds was being disturbed by the powwows. After that, different sites were used. This concern foreshadowed by several decades widespread and publicly expressed Indigenous consternation about undocumented deaths and unmarked graves of children who attended the schools.

The celebration of Anishinaabe tradition, identity, spiritual and social relations inherent to the powwow profoundly shaped the childhoods of the youngest Skeads and Morrisons. Don's granddaughter, Beverly Williamson, and Cindy Piche, one of Madeline and Doug Skead's daughters, were both under ten years old when their families founded the Lake of the Woods Powwow Club. In conversation with me and Bev, Cindy explained how their parents and grandparents made explicit decisions to create an alternate social space for them: "I remember them telling us they wanted something better for us than a life with all the drinking: they gave us the powwow life instead."[69] Much of the heavy drinking and linked violence on reserves happened on weekends, following Friday payments of wages and welfare cheques. But as Cindy recalled, "We didn't even know what went on on the rez on the weekends. On Thursday nights we'd do laundry and pack. Right after school and work on Friday, we'd be gone, and get back late Sunday evening." The children enjoyed social spaces where they could play freely and safely outdoors and visit with extended family members. Bev recollected the feeling of closeness to her father, Joseph Morrison, and grandparents, Don and Ada.[70] And from as young as age five, at what would have been one of the earliest public powwows in the area, Bev was dressed by her older sister Ava in beautiful regalia sewed by Ada and invited to dance in the circle. She recalled, "I remember standing in line, just waiting to go in for the Grand Entry. It was just natural to be in regalia." Cindy's and Bev's recollections attest to how re-membering worked intergenerationally to shape the selfhood of young Anishinaabeg, cultivating a relational subjectivity. The Lake of the Woods powwows provided meaningful supports for the founding members to maintain sobriety, but more than this, these were intergenerational social spaces in which members of their extended families and fellow citizens were warmly invited to join them on this path.

Intergenerational re-membering fostered during the powwows also included young adults. In his early thirties, after over a decade of heavy drinking, Don's son Joseph started "going to sit with the old fellas at the Drum."[71] Joseph described to me how his conversations with older men around the Drum inspired him to reflect on his relationships. The men spoke about the importance of respecting himself and other people: "When you're drinking, you're not doing that. I didn't know if I'd hurt anyone [while drinking]. That got me thinking maybe I need to change." Joseph went on to play a leading role in developing community services for Anishinaabeg in Kenora and Fort Frances, including the Ne-Chee Friendship Centre and Street Patrol (discussed in chapter 2), and later was appointed a justice of the peace.

The Old Guy remembered the first time he heard the Lake of the Woods singers in the mid-1970s, at a powwow at Pithers Point Park on the Rainy River, outside of Fort Frances. It was common knowledge that members of this group were all sober, while the Old Guy, like many singers and even some dancers, regularly drank at powwows.[72] When he eventually sobered up, in 1982, Don approached the Old Guy at a powwow: "The first one who came to me was that old man,

Don Morrison. He told me, 'Come [*beckoning with his hand*], we need you [at the Drum]. You're a good singer.' Don congratulated me that I took that step into recovery. He welcomed me. So I stuck with him. Whenever I felt down, I went to them, Don and his son Joseph. They supported me to build up my strength, supported me in my recovery."[73] The Old Guy had been through residential treatment at the Smith Clinic in Thunder Bay but struggled to grasp some of the AA principles. Don explained these in Anishinaabemowin and, the Old Guy emphasized, "He *knew* when to use that language, he used to say, 'One day at a time, my friend.'"[74] Over time, the Old Guy developed a special relationship with the Drum Don had built: "One day he talked to me about his Drum, Waakebiness. I knew there was something powerful in that Drum, I felt it. He said, 'I'm going to support you to sit on the South side.' He gave me tobacco, and he gave me a song. I still have it to this day, still remember. If someone asks me 'Sing your song', I'll sing it."[75]

Don shared a lot of stories around the Drum, many that served as reminders of how alcohol abuse can damage important relationships, advancing the settler-colonial project of dismemberment through lateral violence. During a long phone conversation in 2020, the Old Guy explained to me how Don drew on his own challenging experiences and spoke openly about his own weaknesses and history of violence in his stories. In one story the Old Guy remembered, Don and a friend were returning from Winnipeg by train, sharing a case of wine purchased by the friend.[76] As the train approached the station where Don's friend would disembark, he went to the washroom. Don took the opportunity to steal his friend's wine, transferring it to his own pack. "That's how powerful alcohol is, it makes us do things that we don't normally do when we're sober," Don said at the time when he told that story. Some of Don's stories were suitable for mixed gender audiences. Others the Old Guy categorized as "relationship stories [that] he used to talk to us about, *as men*." These stories included Don's experience of becoming violent towards his wife, Ada, when he was drinking, their separation, and eventual reconciliation. Don's generous sharing of stories with other Anishinaabeg underscores the extent to which he equated his own suffering and well-being with theirs.

These Anishinaabe men were engaged in conversations about how to align masculine roles and responsibilities with the well-being of the larger community and develop "living models of non-dominative and empowered Indigenous manhood" (McKegney 2014a, 5). These were groundbreaking conversations, several decades prior to scholars' calls for more attention to Indigenous masculinities as part of gendered analyses in Indigenous studies (Innes and Anderson 2015; McKegney 2014a, 2014b). But as the following chapters discuss, it would be decades more before the gendered social and political dismemberment experienced by women and Two-Spirit people began to be taken seriously in larger Indigenous political arenas.

Adolphus Cameron from Wabaseemoong Independent Nations (Whitedog) told me about his first conversation with Don, around 1978, which he clearly recalled more than forty years later.[77] At the time Adolphus was twenty-one years old, five years out of residential school, and had worked a series of jobs in logging, construction, and Band Council administration. He approached Dr. Torrie at the Lake of the Woods hospital in Kenora and asked for his help to quit drinking. Adolphus recalled, "[Dr. Torrie] said he would get someone to come and talk to me, so I stayed in the hospital for the night. Don came... and we recognized each other. He asked me, 'So are you serious about quitting drinking, or do you want to learn to control your drinking?' I thought about it. It was the first time I'd heard that question, I didn't know I had options. So, I said, 'I want to learn to control my drinking.' Without saying another word, Don turned and walked away from me!" Returning to Kenora from the AA-based residential treatment program at the Smith Clinic in Thunder Bay, Adolphus met Don again. Mindful of their previous interaction, he made no further mention of "controlling" drinking: "We met over coffee. I told him that I was serious, and that, I just...I needed help. I asked if he would be my AA sponsor. He said he wanted three things from me. He wanted my commitment, he wanted me to read, and he wanted me to talk with him before speaking in a meeting."[78] Eventually, Adolphus asked Don why he'd walked away from him during their first conversation: "He told me that he works with people who are serious about staying sober.

If someone wants to learn to manage their drinking, he told me, 'I don't know how to do that, so I don't waste my time.'"[79]

Don used the AA framework as a teaching tool to facilitate Adolphus's re-membering, reconnecting him with Anishinaabe knowledge as a means to re-awaken his sense of belonging and responsibility to his people. Speaking most often in Anishinaabemowin, sometimes in English, Don taught Adolphus that "culture and AA were basically the same thing."[80] The AA language describes a relationship with "God *as we understood him*," which Don and the Skeads reconceptualized as a relationship with our Creator and the spirits, enabled by ceremony. They grouped the Twelve Steps into four stages of three steps, each corresponding to one of the four directions, East, West, South, and North. The first three steps represent the East. Adolphus explained, "In our culture, that was getting to know our Creator, relying on our Creator, trusting our Creator, building a relationship with our Creator." As part of that process, Don directed Adolphus to make a fire offering of tobacco, "and say that I'm leaving the control of drinking over to my Creator, or to the spirits." This ceremonial practice is an enactment of the first of the Twelve Steps, which centres on an admission of powerlessness over alcohol. Steps four through six were linked to the southern direction. "That represented getting to know yourself, being honest and truthful about yourself. Identifying all of your strengths, and also your weaknesses." The third stage corresponds to the West and relationships with other humans, including "really honestly talking with somebody, and letting them know who you are," which is Step Five in the AA model. And in his teachings for this stage, Don emphasized forgiveness of self and others. Adolphus reflected, "Because I blamed a lot of people, things, institutions. But it was just something that was out of my control, and I had to find forgiveness. And I had to start demonstrating that, through the way I live, on a daily basis. To stop doing certain things, and to relearn how to do other things. And that would help me with the relationship part. That's how I remember him explaining it to me." The final stage, corresponding to the North, Adolphus characterizes as being about wisdom, integrating all the earlier teachings into everyday life as lived.

This integration involves a conscious, daily practice of reflection: "Take a daily review of everything and try to find a way to forgive and release all those things that are building up." These teachings left Adolphus trusting that "eventually the spirits would take my desire for drinking away."[81]

Adolphus and Don's relationship shows how Anishinaabeg adapted AA teachings as a vehicle for re-membering, resurrecting their own spiritual-philosophical knowledge and sharing it with others as a means of strengthening Indigenous society, both between and within generational cohorts. Don told Adolphus the story of his own route to sobriety and stressed the importance of working with other Anishinaabeg of his own generation through the Drum, and Adolphus carved out a similar path for himself. While continuing to attend AA meetings, he was welcomed to join a recently established Drum in his home community of Wabaseemoong, where, he recalled, "They passed on a lot of teachings to us, around the Drum." In later years, Adolphus participated in the Treaty 3 Drum, with Clifford Skead, Tommy White, and Gilbert Smith. The older men told him to listen and observe, and he would learn. Eventually, when he was in his late forties or early fifties, Adolphus attended a Treaty 3 gathering where Clifford was offered tobacco to pray for some offerings. He accepted the tobacco, then passed it to Adolphus, saying, "'You've been here, you've been listening, you've been observing, you know how we do things. You're going to be taking over as an Elder.'"[82] That was the first time Adolphus was invited into that ceremonial role.[83] All of the older men in the Treaty 3 Drum were supportive of younger Elders taking on such responsibilities. Thus, intergenerational transmission of knowledge and ways of relating—Anishinaabe social reproduction—was reinstated, thwarting the permanent disruption of that process intended by the architects of the residential school system.[84]

Don's notes for his talk are titled "To a people in trouble comes this message of love."[85] His conceptualization of his audience as "a people" affirms the collective understanding of Anishinaabe nationhood, suggesting that Don's work was informed by this political consciousness. He told his audience, "[I] truly understand your problems, because I have had similar troubles in my own life...I have walked the streets you have walked, been through the hells you have been through." We can't know which of the many troubles of Don's early life would have come into the minds of others in the meeting as they listened to his words: The systematic destruction of their family's livelihood, and associated dignity? The loss of a parent to infectious disease as a young child? Years interned in a violent, foreign institution? The trauma of the First World War battlefields? Struggles with one's own violent behaviour and resulting estrangement from spouse and children? The humiliation of everyday racism in the businesses and streets of Kenora? But we can be confident that Don's words, despite their appearance of universality, were particularly familiar to Anishinaabe listeners. Don wanted to help alleviate others' suffering, not as an outsider but as one of them who understands the nature of that suffering rooted in experiences of colonial social dismemberment. In his words, this practice was "a sharing of experience to remind and comfort us all."[86] In this, he was "absorbing his own needs and desires in the needs of the broader community," enacting Anishinaabe masculinity in ways consistent with traditional values of relationship "through proactive gestures of kinship responsibility" (McKegney 2012, 263).[87] The next chapter considers how, through the 1970s and 1980s, a diverse range of Indigenous social actors in Northern and Southern Ontario employed an expanding set of biopolitical tactics in their efforts to re-member at a larger scale.

2

Re-Membering and Biopolitics in Urban Ontario, 1973-1980s

WHEN THE ADDICTION RESEARCH FOUNDATION closed the Waystation hostel in Kenora in 1970, Anishinaabeg lost an important place of refuge, and nearly two hundred died preventable deaths on those streets over the subsequent three years. The ongoing dismemberment of the Anishinaabe nation included deaths by drowning and exposure due to the state's denial of basic public services to a population deemed surplus, and planned attacks on vulnerable individuals by white supremacists that local police failed to curb. In this chapter, I analyze Indigenous tactics for re-membering during the 1970s and 1980s as challenges to social dismemberment in the urban spaces and public institutions of Ontario. I argue that these tactics represent an Indigenized biopolitics: efforts to promote and protect Indigenous life, understood not only in biological but in social and political terms, in ways that enact well-being as collective and relational. Cultivating inter-Indigenous relationality and wellness in these contexts, especially at a larger scale, required Indigenous biopolitical actors to cultivate relationships with settler state institutions and professionals and tactically engage with biopolitical discourses, enabling them to create infrastructure and claim resources in support of re-membering.

These social histories of an emergent Indigenized biopolitics point to often unacknowledged intersections between Indigenous struggles for civil rights and the liberationist Red Power movement of this period. In Kenora, Anishinaabeg employed divergent political tactics to address the shocking number of preventable deaths in public spaces. A 1973 report *While People Sleep: Sudden Deaths in Kenora Area*, published by Grand Council Treaty #3 and based on a collaboration with white Kenorans and University of Manitoba researchers, drew on data from the coroner's office and other sources to document an average of five deaths per month since the Waystation's closure (Kenora and District Social Planning Council and Concerned Citizens Committee 1973). The analysis in this report links the deaths to unequal public services, using civil rights discourse very similar to that of the 1965 march described in chapter 1.[1] The same year, the newly formed Ojibway Warriors Society occupied the Kenora office of the Department of Indian Affairs for thirty-six hours. Their demands used more critical language, including a call for "an end to the overtly racist actions and physical brutality against First Nations in Kenora" (Rutherford 2010, 79). Such occupations were a characteristic tactic of the American Indian Movement (AIM) and the wider youth-led Red Power movement spanning the Canada–United States border.[2] Months prior to the Ojibway Warriors Society's occupation in Kenora, the Oglala Sioux and AIM members occupied the town of Wounded Knee on the Pine Ridge reservation, site of the late nineteenth-century massacre by US troops, and attracted widespread support, including a convoy from Winnipeg, just west of Treaty 3 territory (Smith and Warrior 1996). But as the Indigenous histories below reveal, many political actors who participated in the direct action associated with liberationist politics were also willing to employ more conciliatory tactics, including working closely with settler state institutions. These histories suggest that techniques of "resistance" of liberation movements as conventionally understood, such as armed occupations, may coexist with a diverse range of tactics, without implying inconsistent ideological commitments.

The Indigenous biopolitics emergent in Ontario was further shaped by the politics of gender and settler colonialism, including Indigenous women's critiques of both male-dominated Indigenous politics and white liberal feminism. Indigenous women began establishing their own organizations, often as offshoots of Friendship Centres, extending protection and sharing knowledge and skills to ensure women were among those re-membered in life-threatening urban and institutional settings. As the demands made during the 1965 civil rights march in Kenora illustrated, men's experiences of ongoing colonial relations were most prominent in Indigenous political discourse of this period. Initially, the earliest urban biopolitical interventions, such as the Waystation and, later, the Ne-Chee Street Patrol (discussed below) were staffed mainly by men. This pattern was consistent with men's domination of leadership roles across public political domains, including civil rights organizing, the Indian Act politics of Band Council governance, and the emerging Red Power movement.[3] Although more women participated in Red Power activism of the 1970s than in Band Council politics at that time, their experiences are less well-documented than those of the men who were the public face of the movement (Barker 2018; Hightower-Langston 2003). Indigenous women's relative invisibility has been exacerbated by the tendency of the historiography of Red Power to focus on struggles over territory, typically led by men despite women's participation, and neglect activism focused on social issues in which women played leading roles (Krouse and Howard 2009). Anishinaabe re-membering by Don Morrison and others focused on supporting those struggling with alcohol abuse, more often men, and centred on the Grandfather Drum with whom women were relegated to a more distant relationship. As we saw in chapter 1, Don and other men privately discussed the ongoing issue of gendered abuse, but experiences of colonial violence and lateral violence suffered disproportionately by women and children were given little public attention by Indigenous political actors and their white allies during this period. Across Canada, Indigenous women's organizing through the 1970s and 1980s helped create the space for increasingly public discussions of interpersonal violence, including histories of abuse in the residential schools (Million 2013). By the 1990s most Indigenous-managed health and social services in urban Ontario would be led and staffed by women.

Indigenizing Biopolitics: The Ne-Chee Street Patrol

The idea of a "native foot patrol" to protect Indigenous life in Kenora was initially proposed in the *While People Sleep* report.[4] A careful reading of this report generates insights into some of the tensions inherent to biopolitical tactics. The authors' analysis of structural factors contributing to Indigenous deaths in Kenora echoes the liberal civil rights framework presented during the 1965 march. Indeed, the recommendations articulated in *While People Sleep* overlap considerably with the demands made during that march, underscoring government inaction in addressing Indigenous people's civil rights in the eight intervening years. In essence, the report argues that the disturbing number of preventable deaths could be explained by the continuing denial of full citizenship rights to Indigenous people, including access to services and opportunities of a similar standard provided to white Canadians. Ultimately, the report settles on individual Indigenous people, rather than dominant structures and relations of power, as the target for recommended interventions, including a "native foot patrol to work in close cooperation with police," conceived as a "crisis service" (Kenora and District Social Planning Council and Concerned Citizens Committee 1973, 23). As we'll see, the street patrol as eventually established did significant work to protect Indigenous lives and well-being. But the framing of the report, which analyzes the deaths as part of "a complex syndrome of social problems" (vii) experienced by Anishinaabeg, aligns with the paternalistic settler humanitarianism resurgent in state policy since the mid-twentieth century in assuming that Indigenous people themselves, rather than ongoing settler colonialism perpetuated by white citizens and their governments, are the locus of problems (Shewell 2004; A. Simpson 2008). This framing illustrates how biopolitical tactics are tricky: services may be urgently needed to protect and promote lives, but advocacy framed mainly in terms of service delivery often entails individuating complex social and political issues, and thus obscuring how ongoing structures of settler colonialism effect Indigenous social and political dismemberment.

Illustrating the coexistence of divergent political framings during this period, the same report includes an argument about how urban homelessness and state failure to provide services are interconnected with Indigenous people's dispossession of their land. This more critical perspective, however, is buried in an appendix and unreferenced in the body of the report, in a brief presented to the Kenora Town Council on August 9, 1973, by Peter Kelly on behalf of Grand Council Treaty #3. Kelly's brief links Indigenous homelessness in Kenora to the social disruption, including disruption of Clan systems, resulting from the relocations of several reserve communities surrounding Kenora during the prior two decades, and the 1959 closure of Indian House in Anicinabe Park. A fourteen-acre space on the shore of the Lake of the Woods and long-standing Anishinaabe gathering place, Anicinabe Park was purchased by the Department of Indian Affairs in 1929 and designated as a camping area for families visiting their children at nearby Cecilia Jeffrey Indian Residential School. In 1959 the Department of Indian Affairs sold the park to the city of Kenora, whose administrators then closed Indian House so that the park could be opened to tourism (an increasingly significant industry in Kenora with the decline of logging and pulp and paper over the course of the twentieth century). Prior to these changes, according to Kelly, Indian House was a space where visitors from reserves could stay overnight while conducting business in Kenora. This closure was part of a larger pattern of white opposition to Anishinaabe space in the town, which continued through the early 1960s, when efforts by the Presbyterian Fellowship Centre to establish a hostel for Anishinaabeg were undermined by both federal and municipal governments.[5]

In the summer of 1974, the creation of an Anishinaabe street patrol gained renewed impetus from the Ojibway Warriors Society's occupation of Anicinabe Park, which included expressed demands for improved public services alongside the return of stolen land.[6] Approximately five hundred people, including activists from elsewhere in Canada and members of AIM from the United States alongside Treaty 3 Anishinaabeg, attended the Ojibwe Unity Conference and powwow, organized by the Ojibway Warriors Society during the weekend of July 20–21 (Burke 1976). Immediately following the conference, between one hundred and two hundred people, some armed, occupied the park for thirty-nine days (Burke 1976). The occupiers, who included members of the Warriors and other local Anishinaabeg as well as visiting activists, received extensive support from local Anishinaabeg, including many women. Beyond the return of Anicinabe Park, the occupiers' demands reiterated the call for action to prevent the deaths of Anishinaabeg in Kenora expressed in the *While People Sleep* report, and asserted the need for a radical overhaul of the racist criminal justice system, improvements in housing and health care, public transportation between Kenora and surrounding reserves, and the creation of a local human rights committee.[7] Young Anishinaabeg who took part in the occupation, including Joseph Morrison, and those who supported it, such as Charles Copenace, came away with a vision of changes they wanted to implement in Kenora, which included establishing a Friendship Centre and a street patrol.[8] Their vision for the latter was likely informed by conversations with AIM activists from Minneapolis during the occupation: the AIM Patrol was one of the first programs initiated by the newly formed organization in Minneapolis–Saint Paul in the summer of 1968 (Smith and Warrior 1996). Early AIM members in Minneapolis–Saint Paul were mostly Chippewas from reservations north and west of the cities, and while this urban centre is much larger than Kenora, both were settler-dominated spaces in which Natives "had a presence" (Smith and Warrior 1996, 128). According to Paul Chaat Smith and Robert Allen Warrior (1996), the AIM Patrol was inspired by the work of the early Black Panther party in Oakland. It had a similar mission "to decrease police brutality against Native people" (B. Wilson 2023), and its workers wore distinctive red jackets, provided legal support for those arrested, and used cameras and tape recorders to document arrests (Smith and Warrior 1996).[9]

Many years later, I met with Charles Copenace at the East End Café, where the Trans-Canada Highway leads east out of Kenora. Over soup and bannock, Charles told me, "Keeping people safe, helping people out, is the first step towards healing. Helping people get home. Feeling safe is a big part of healing."[10] According to Charles, the founders of Ne-Chee Friendship Centre intended it to be a safe, welcoming social space in town, where Anishinaabeg could come together, sit indoors, and visit with each other between appointments, instead of sitting at the taxi station, as had become the practice after the Waystation closed. Charles's oral history of Ne-Chee and the street patrol, detailed below, emphasizes how helping and being helped, providing safety and feeling safe, are all intertwined in this social practice of re-membering and healing, in which Anishinaabe men are both protectors and themselves in need of protection. Charles's relational understanding of safety, which incorporates men's vulnerability, contrasts with the most prominent and enduring public representations from the Anicinabe Park occupation of Indigenous men as warriors.

In the conference keynote address by AIM director Dennis Banks, protection was a central theme; a subsequent demonstration of taekwondo continued the focus on masculine interpersonal violence (Rutherford 2010). In the Red Power discourse, "protection" evokes the warrior as a rugged individual, implicitly male, ready to assert himself and ensure the safety of his People through violence, while patriarchy and sexism were marginal issues in AIM (in common with other liberationist movements of the time), and some male activists, including leaders, were themselves perpetrators of violence against women (Barker 2018; Mihesuah 2001). In dominant media outlets, the most widely circulated images from the Anicinabe Park occupation depicted a lone young man holding a gun: the Red Power activist as reincarnation of "the romantic warrior figure that had simultaneously fascinated and scared white people for centuries" (Rutherford 2010, 86). As critical scholars have noted, these images reflect both white stereotypes and some Red Power activists' preoccupation with revitalizing a narrowly conceived Indigenous masculinity (McKegney 2012; Rutherford 2010). The harm caused by this constraining subject position was demonstrated in grassroots organizing for healing in subsequent decades: by women's efforts to respond to gendered violence within families and communities (the focus of chapter 3), and many men's difficulties in discussing their own experiences as victims of physical and sexual abuse, notably as suffered at the residential schools.

The Ne-Chee Street Patrol was intended to extend the protection previously afforded by the Waystation beyond the confines of an immobile shelter. It was piloted in 1976, one of the two original programs delivered by the newly established Friendship Centre. The Copenace family were among a small number of Anishinaabeg (including the Morrisons) able to secure housing in Kenora at that time. Charles recalled his family's concern about growing numbers of Anishinaabeg from the surrounding reserves drinking in town, having nowhere to go, encountering "trouble," and being beaten up. Each member of the Copenace family became centrally involved in the early days of the Friendship Centre and its programs: Charles was the Street Patrol's first coordinator, while his father, Sam, an early member of the Lake of the Woods Drum and former Waystation counsellor, sat on the Friendship Centre's Board of Directors; his sister worked as secretary; and his brother worked with the youth program.[11] Joseph Morrison was both a founding member of the Ne-Chee Board of Directors and one of the original foot patrol workers.[12] Between 6:00 p.m. and 2:00 a.m., Joseph and his co-worker walked the streets, looking out for vulnerable people at risk of incurring harm through violence, exposure, or drowning, including unsupervised children and intoxicated youth and adults, or people threatening violence against others.[13] The patrol worked Thursday to Sunday, when public drinking and its collateral damage were most prevalent. Boathouses along the docks were popular places for Anishinaabeg to seek shelter and sleep, while some sought refuge underneath a local hotel.[14] The pilot was funded by a nine-thousand-dollar grant from the Ontario Ministry of Community and Social Services, enabling organizers to establish a small office above the bus depot and purchase equipment, including four winter jackets with "Street Patrol" emblazoned on the back.[15]

The Ne-Chee Street Patrol demonstrated both classic elements of biopolitics, as defined by Michel Foucault (1990), and a distinctly Indigenous approach to service development and delivery centred on relational subjectification, showing continuity with the work of Don Morrison and others at the Waystation. The Street Patrol's basic goal of keeping people alive might be characterized as a "minimalist biopolitics" typical of international humanitarian interventions, widely critiqued for failing to address the wider political contexts of suffering (Redfield 2005). Funded by the settler state, the Street Patrol's mission to protect Indigenous life was operationalized through interventions designed and managed by experts. Its workers produced knowledge about those using its services through monitoring reports that relied heavily on quantification and statistics.[16] All of these characteristics are hallmarks of biopolitics. But I argue that the early Ne-Chee Street Patrol modelled an Indigenized biopolitics in several important ways. Street Patrol workers were recruited based on personal experience of alcohol abuse, knowledge of the dangers faced by Indigenous people on the streets of Kenora, and ability to speak Anishinaabemowin.[17] This understanding of expertise contrasts markedly with the elite, credentialled professional knowledge central to state-dominated biopolitics as theorized by Foucault, and aligns with Alcoholics Anonymous and the earlier Waystation practice of hiring formerly alcoholic Anishinaabeg as counsellors, underscoring that Anishinaabe political actors adapted and appropriated biopolitics in ways aligned with their own socio-political goal of re-membering. The relationship that a credentialled professional (such as a physician or social worker) forms with a patient or client within a biopolitical regime is characterized by the authority of their role and discourse, regulated through formal systems maintained by institutions that are part of the settler state apparatus. In contrast, the Street Patrol and Waystation workers were less likely to perceive themselves as socially distinct or removed from or in any way superior to those they were helping. This relational approach to providing care also contrasts with the "othering" inherent to humanitarian practice, in which those being helped in the name of a universal humanity remain in some sense alien to the helpers, by virtue of nationality, impoverishment, race, or Indigeneity (Barnett 2011). Like Don's approach to supporting others in staying sober, shaped by his own experience of suffering and healing as an Anishinaabe man, the early Friendship Centre and Street Patrol were premised on workers serving and supporting not patients and clients, or pitiable racialized others, but their own extended families and communities—even their past and future selves, as Charles's case vividly illustrates.

For Charles, the job at Ne-Chee was an opportunity to do meaningful work and an incentive to quit drinking; he couldn't have known at that time that the Street Patrol would one day help to save his own life.[18] A couple of years earlier, he had angrily quit his previous job as a forest technician with the Ontario Ministry of Natural Resources after two years, having been passed over for a permanent job given instead to a less qualified white man. Charles was driven to numb his pain through excessive alcohol consumption. Despite his enthusiasm for the work at Ne-Chee, Charles was not able to stay sober indefinitely: he struggled with ongoing personal and family problems and resumed drinking, finally leaving his position around 1976. He wouldn't sober up permanently until 1993. During his years of drinking in Kenora, Charles benefitted more than once from the care and protection of the Street Patrol. He recalled, "One time I passed out among the garbage bins behind the Northlands Hotel. The Street Patrol let me sleep but kept checking up on me until I got up and made my own way safely." On another occasion, in the late 1980s, Charles was attacked in the streets while drunk, suffering severe damage to his eye. Street Patrol workers administered first aid, kept him safe and facilitated emergency medical transportation to a hospital in Winnipeg, where he received surgery that saved his vision.[19]

The relational, collectivist ethos of the Street Patrol extended to the conditions of its workers, again suggesting a distinctly Anishinaabe approach to biopolitics: one that subjectifies workers as simultaneously members of Indigenous families, communities, and nations. Biopolitical analyses often focus on how users of services are subjectified, but the subjectivities of those providing services are also shaped by the material and discursive conditions of their work (Crowley-Matoka and True 2012). Eschewing the rigid bureaucracy typical of welfare state institutions, the early Street Patrol was organized to provide its workers with an unusually flexible schedule. Although the ministry's memorandum of agreement stipulated employment of four staff, in practice the program employed a total of sixteen people: seven people who worked most shifts, and another nine who worked far fewer.[20] This structure allowed regular workers more time for family responsibilities, participation in ceremonies, and wild harvesting activities, while generating income for four times as many people as envisaged by ministry officials. In this sense, the program could be considered to have maximized redistribution of wealth to Anishinaabeg via the settler welfare state, while limiting the extent to which the subjectification of Street Patrol workers as social service employees undermined their ongoing participation in Indigenous social life and traditional livelihoods.[21] This creative restructuring of caring labour provides a powerful illustration of how Indigenous re-membering practice challenges capitalist culture (Million 2013). The larger workforce with flexible scheduling also made the organization responsive to fluctuating levels of need; for instance, a higher level of staffing could be provided in response to a local hockey tournament or powwow. By 1978 each pair of foot patrol workers included one woman and one man, a change that may reflect participation in the program's management committee by the Kenora Native Women's Association, established in the mid-1970s.[22]

The Street Patrol's efforts to care for and protect other Anishinaabeg are both an assertion of relatedness, and an attempt to compensate for the Canadian welfare state's failure to ensure Indigenous people's access to basic public services: safety, shelter, and transportation. This failure can be at least partially explained by the incompatibility of reserve-urban interconnectivity in the settler-colonial imagination, in which reserves are considered places for containing unassimilated Indigenous people, and those residing in towns and cities are presumed to already be assimilated and so disconnected from reserve life. In contrast, Charles's historical account emphasizes a web of Anishinaabe relatedness, interdependence, and reciprocity extending between reserves and urban centres as foundational to the Street Patrol project, similar to the enduring connections underpinning the work of Don Morrison and the other Waystation counsellors described in chapter 1. Charles's family history also underscores the profound challenges and constraints of re-membering in the face of ongoing social dismemberment. The Street Patrol was unable to ensure the safety of Charles's father, Sam Copenace, one of the Ne-Chee founders and a board member, who drowned while crossing the frozen Lake of the Woods while drunk. His decision to take that route may have been motivated by the ongoing threat of physical attack by white Kenorans along the golf course road leading to Wauzhushk Onigum (Rat Portage). The divergent roles played by members of the Copenace family in this history of re-membering—by turns leader and victim, provider and user of services—illustrates the extent to which this early Indigenized biopolitics was both inspired by and intertwined with ongoing experiences of colonial social dismemberment.

Re-Membering in Settler-Colonial Institutions

Two thousand kilometres southeast of Kenora, in the much larger and wealthier city of Toronto, members of the Native Canadian Centre's Ladies' Auxiliary initiated a practice of visiting prison inmates. Considered alongside Don Morrison's practice of re-membering Anishinaabeg in the Kenora jail and hospitals, this parallel points to an enduring felt social responsibility among Indigenous social actors, and the value and malleability of re-membering as practical response to ongoing social dismemberment. A more detailed comparison of these social histories generates further insights into the range of mid-century Indigenous social trajectories leading divergent actors to the adoption of biopolitical tactics. Anthropologist Heather Howard (2004, 2009) suggests that the women in Toronto constituted an emerging Indigenous middle class. They had moved from First Nations reserves in Southern Ontario in the 1920s and 1930s to pursue higher education in nursing, teaching, and secretarial work, and to take up domestic employment with elite white families. Making effective use of their relations with white employers to access fundraising, some of these women were central in establishing the North American Indian Club in Toronto in 1950 and the Native Canadian Centre in 1962.[23] A year later, the Native Canadian Centre's Ladies' Auxiliary was established by Ella Rush, from Six Nations of the Grand River, and Millie Redmond (née White) its first president, from the Potawatomi Nation on Bkejwanong (Walpole Island). Both had previously participated in women's social and political organizing on reserves through the federally sponsored assimilationist Homemakers' Clubs established in 1937, discussed in the introduction.

    Howard describes a shift over time in how the Ladies' Auxiliary members understood their practice of visiting other Indigenous women incarcerated at the Kingston Penitentiary, 250 kilometres east of Toronto, from what she characterizes as "middle-class activism" to solidarity work. She argues that prison visiting was initially conceived of as charity work by women who may have felt some paternalistic sense of distance from those they were visiting, as typically characterizes humanitarian work to alleviate the suffering of "others," and perhaps subscribed to the moral judgement of those incarcerated embedded in the dominant morality in Canada.[24] But developing a heightened awareness of the social and political contexts of Indigenous women's disproportionate incarceration, in part through the influence of Red Power activism on those working at the Native Canadian Centre, they came to conceive of these prison visits as solidarity work that dovetailed with the Auxiliary's mission to promote traditional craft skills (Howard 2004). This vision is powerfully expressed by Josephine Beaucage (née Commanda) of Nipissing First Nation, who described teaching craftwork to women in the penitentiary as contributing to a "mission to bring traditional practices and elements of Native culture to spaces where they might re-affirm Native identity and forge links of cultural solidarity" (Toronto Native Oral History Project 1983c, quoted in Howard 2004, 158). As I discussed in chapter 1 with reference to crafting powwow regalia, the creativity inherent to Indigenous crafts production is characterized by Elders as healing. It is also potentially of economic significance: the Auxiliary played a central role in developing a market for Indigenous arts and crafts in Toronto, an important source of revenue for the Friendship Centre and some members of the community (Howard 2004, 161).

The Ladies' Auxiliary practice of re-membering incarcerated women can be understood as (bio)political interventions to enhance Indigenous life—both individual and collective—and oppose the ongoing settler-colonial dismemberment of Indigenous nations through criminalization and incarceration. While the visiting teachers incited a shift in the incarcerated woman's sense of herself through their practice of teaching crafts, (re)affirming these women as members of a larger whole, members of the Auxiliary were apparently themselves subjectified. Howard's account suggests that their own subjectivities shifted from a sense of belonging to a paternalistic middle class, towards a paramount identification of solidarity with Indigenous Peoples, regardless of ethnonational identification or socioeconomic status. In comparison, Anishinaabe re-membering in Treaty 3 territory was about reconstituting relationships within a dispersed Indigenous society whose members, however marginalized and alienated, shared geopolitical origins and the language of Anishinaabemowin (at that time still widely understood), the descendants of signatories of Treaty 3 and those with long-standing family and social ties to that people, regardless of whether individuals had status or resided on a reserve. As becomes clear below, in culturally and economically diverse urban Indigenous communities such as Toronto, consciousness of shared experiences of colonization became increasingly significant for constituting a shared sense of membership through biopolitical tactics. Through the 1970s and 1980s, Indigenous community organizers brought practices of re-membering into colonial institutions in Ontario (and elsewhere in North America) wherever opportunities emerged, sometimes through the presence of sympathetic white biopolitical actors, typically professionals including physicians, psychiatrists, and social workers, such as Dr. Torrie, who supported the Waystation and facilitated Adolphus's fateful meeting with Don described in chapter 1. During the late 1980s and early 1990s, two men who worked closely with members of the Ladies' Auxiliary at the Native Canadian Centre, Vern Harper (Asin; Cree) and Jim Mason (Ojibwe and Mohawk), extended the practice of prison visiting to the Don Jail in Toronto's east end by collaborating with white social worker Leslie Saunders. Notably, both were also active in the Red Power movement. Vern spent time in California during the early days of AIM, participated in the Anicinawbe Park occupation and the Native People's cross-country Caravan to Ottawa in 1974, and was an early commentator on gender dynamics in Indigenous political movements.[25]

As we have seen, Indigenous biopolitical tactics for navigating state institutions often came up against the challenges of re-membering under conditions of profound and ongoing social dismemberment of families and nations. Such conditions are embodied by those who have endured the child welfare system and incarceration in succession. At the Don Jail, a significant number of those incarcerated in the 1980s were Anishinaabe, Cree, and Oji-Cree men from Northern Ontario (Treaty 3 and Nishnawbe Aski Nation territories). Their early lives followed a common pattern: removed from family and community at a young age; placed in private or institutional foster homes; abused drugs and alcohol to cope; committed a minor theft or assault while incapacitated; charged, convicted, and imprisoned.[26] Jim and Vern were invited to visit the Don Jail by Leslie Saunders, as part of her efforts to reinvigorate the flagging Native Sons support group.[27] Sharing oral history about this work, Leslie explained to me how, having been taken from their homes in early childhood and undergone a great deal of trauma, these men often had little or no memory of early experiences with other Indigenous people and practices. Like many of those who attended residential schools, they were ashamed of being Indigenous, but their shame was instilled not by priests, nuns, and teachers but by white foster families and institutions. As Leslie explained, this trajectory often led to reluctance to participate in the Native Sons activities. She recalled, "I'd have to discuss with them for a long time to get them to come to the program. Because if I'd go up to them and say, 'Do you want to go to the Native Sons Program tonight?' they'd say 'Oh, I wasn't raised with Native people. I don't know anything about it.' And this shame, this veil of shame would come over, because they felt they weren't worthy of being in that room. They wouldn't know how to behave. They wouldn't know what to say." Once Leslie persuaded the men to participate, their initial reluctance quickly dissipated: "Once they got up there, just even the first time, there was no more fear. They were very comfortable, because they quickly realized that they did not have to be an expert in Aboriginal culture."[28] This comfort was skillfully fostered by Vern and Jim. Leslie described how the expertise that Vern and Jim mobilized to develop meaningful relationships with the men included not only knowledge of ceremony but shared knowledge of Indigenous life under colonial conditions: experience of criminalization, institutionalization, racism, and, in Vern's case, adoption by a white family who shamed him for being Indigenous, and reconnection with his Cree family and culture later in life.[29] For the men working with Vern and Jim, experiencing their personal trajectory as readily understood and contextualized within a shared history of loss and disruption was especially transformative: "their [personal] history seemed to *already be known* by the person facilitating the program, and they thought this was miraculous."[30]

Like the earlier prison visiting by members of the Ladies' Auxiliary, this urban institutional re-membering shows an openness to embracing other Indigenous people as kin regardless of ethnonational identity and territory of origin, based on an understanding of how individual experience is patterned by larger historical, political, and social forces, and a shared personal history of social dismemberment as part of the basis for membership. In this context, unlike earlier re-membering in Treaty 3 territory, those participating in mutual recognition often didn't share an Indigenous language, biological relatedness, or origins in the same nation and territory. Leslie's account conveys how, for these incarcerated men, being recognized by older, caring, and knowledgeable Indigenous men based on a common history was a healing experience, because this recognition enabled them to reframe personal suffering as the expected outcome of colonial policies and institutions, rather than individual failure. As an Indigenized biopolitics gained ground in public services from the 1990s, enabled in part by the ascent of reconciliation politics in Canada, this distinct mode of reciprocal recognition came to the fore, characterized by new Indigenous subjectivities and groupings coalesced around personal histories of surviving the residential school and child welfare systems, respectively. These developments are discussed in chapter 4.

Like prisons and residential schools, hospitals were significant sites of social dismemberment and individuation, so establishing the Native Healers Program at the Lake of the Woods Hospital in Kenora was a logical extension of the Powwow Club's project of challenging colonial domination of Indigenous lives.[31] This hospital was created in 1968 through the merger of two previous, racially segregated institutions, Kenora General and St. Joseph's. The latter was established as a missionary hospital in 1903, a site where settler-colonial biomedical knowledge and authority legitimated the social dismemberment of Anishinaabe families. Here, Indigenous patients were diagnosed with tuberculosis and sent to Thunder Bay for treatment; some would never return. New mothers were (and still are) coerced into giving up their babies, while hospitalized children were at risk of apprehension by Children's Aid Society workers.[32] Members of the Lake of the Woods Powwow Club collaborated with white physician Dr. Allan Torrie to access funding from the province's community mental health budget, which supported employment of an Anishinaabe coordinator to administer the program, and the costs of compensating traditional Healers from Treaty 3 territory and beyond. These Healers visited the hospital, treated patients, supported family members staying in the adjacent hostel, conducted ceremony in the hospital grounds, and even visited people in need at their homes on reserves surrounding Kenora. Through this project, the Lake of the Woods Powwow Club members asserted the continuing importance of Anishinaabe knowledge and practices to their people's well-being, mounting a powerful challenge to the dominance of biomedical knowledge, with its claims to privileged insight and the authority to devalue Indigenous lives. Like the employment practices of the Ne-Chee Street Patrol, the Native Healers Program demonstrates the importance of Indigenous knowledge to an Indigenized politics of life.

Such Indigenous biopolitical projects aimed at re-membering within settler-colonial institutions are at once potentially transformative and, like other tactical engagements with settler state actors, vulnerable to myriad constraints and reversals. Indigenous re-membering in hospitals and prisons has the effect of reconfiguring dominant power-knowledge, reversing the effects of the "anonymous care" of inmates and patients whose identities are defined by their position as subjects of state control (Stevenson 2014).[33] The relational, reciprocal recognition inherent to re-membering challenges the racialized hierarchy of worth that permeates Canadian society by defiantly enacting forms of care that demonstrate that Indigenous lives are valued, not as "bare life" to be saved at any cost without regard for context or meaning, but as inherently social, spiritual, and political lives, whose meaning is created through relations with others as members of a larger collective. Given this analysis, it is unsurprising that settler state actors might experience these interventions as threatening and attempt to suppress them through bureaucratic control. At the Don Jail in Toronto, prison guards' deliberately obstructive actions eventually made it impossible for Vern and Jim to continue visiting. In Kenora, although the Native Healers Program endures at the time of writing, its operation was undermined by opposition at multiple levels: petty bureaucrats within the institution and skeptical funders in the provincial civil service. Although Indigenous efforts at re-membering within dominant institutions continue, the cumulative effects of everyday racism and obstruction fuelled the determination of many organizers to establish their own service infrastructure.

Tactical Engagement with the Politics of Recognition: Pedahbun Lodge

As an addictions counsellor at the Native Canadian Centre in Toronto in the 1970s, Joe Sylvester (Ojibwe, Beausoleil First Nation on G'chimnissing) routinely referred those struggling with alcohol abuse to white-dominated treatment settings. But as he observed, "They did not respond to that treatment" (Sylvester 1980). Sylvester's frustration inspired his vision of a Native-run rehabilitation treatment centre in Toronto for those struggling with alcohol and drug abuse, as he recalled in an oral history interview: "I thought to myself, then we must have our own rehabilitation unit."

As early as the 1960s, there were signs that service provision for Indigenous people in urban centres is an issue that reflects and magnifies divergent perspectives on Indigenous political identities and relations with the settler state. Indigenous political leaders and community organizers in the early Friendship Centre movement asserted the need for Indigenous-provided services; to them, urban residence was not incompatible with Treaty Rights and First Nations citizenship. In contrast, federal policymakers explicitly disallowed the development of "parallel services" for Indigenous people under the terms of funding for the earliest Friendship Centres. They envisioned the centres as short-term measures to facilitate "integration" of "migrating Native people" who would quickly come to identify primarily as citizens of the provinces, hastening the demise of Indigenous political identities (Peters 2001, 76). In other words, settler state policymakers saw Indigenous people's use of existing, provincially funded services as a useful mechanism towards their political dismemberment. Distinct services provided by and for Indigenous people undermined this strategy, so state actors used the liberal discourse of "equality" to condemn such innovations as akin to segregation, the hallmark of racial discrimination targeted by influential Black civil rights protests in the United States.[34]

The 1969 White Paper legislation, introduced by Pierre Trudeau's Liberal government, blamed the historic "special treatment" of Indigenous Peoples for their current suffering, and advocated for the pursuit of "equality" and "integration" by abolishing the Indian Act and eliminating Indigenous Peoples' special status and rights. As Dale Turner has argued, by misrepresenting Indigenous rights as "merely a class of minority rights" (2006, 15) rather than distinct and innate political rights, the White Paper bolstered the equation of Indigenous Peoples' *sui generis* relations with the Canadian state as a form of discrimination, and the liberal understanding of individual rather than collective rights as sacrosanct. Although the government backed down in the face of intense First Nations opposition to this proposal, the tenor of Indigenous–state relations shifted permanently in its wake. Multicultural ideology was intimately intertwined with White Paper racism and the renewed push for the assimilation of Indigenous Peoples, and actively depoliticized Indigenous struggles for self-determination, as critiques of the politics of recognition in settler-colonial settings have elaborated (Coulthard 2014; Povinelli 1998, 2002).

But the ascent of multiculturalism in Canadian policy discourse simultaneously created new opportunities for Indigenous political actors to challenge the late twentieth-century liberal orthodoxy of equality as assimilation. Multicultural ideology was not only a superficial celebration of cultural diversity, it also enabled meaningful, material change by expanding access to control of public services essential to survival and social reproduction. In the domains of health care and social services, not only bureaucrats but health professionals and community organizations from racialized and immigrant communities employed multicultural discourse to advocate for change. This period saw growing acknowledgement among policymakers and service providers that "cultural" models of care, including "ethnic matching" in service delivery, might improve service access and effectiveness for those from marginalized groups.

For proponents of Indigenous re-membering in urban settings, this shift created opportunities to employ biopolitical tactics to claim public resources to establish their own services.

Glen Coulthard (2014) derides the Indigenous pursuit of state recognition that such tactics represent, on the grounds that this approach "decouples" Indigenous assertions of cultural autonomy from potentially more transformative social and political change, arguing instead for a "turning away" from the state towards a more transformational politics of resurgence. Considering Indigenous biopolitical tactics to develop relevant and accessible health and social services, I argue that such critiques need to be tempered by two stark realities of urban Indigenous life under late twentieth-century settler colonialism: first, recognition enables access to scarce resources (Andersen 2014), and second, meaningful and effective care is impossible in the absence of recognition (Taylor 2008). The politics of recognition, in the form of liberal multiculturalism, drove shifts in public policy that made it somewhat easier for Indigenous organizers in cities to (re)claim public resources to develop infrastructure and services tailored to the needs of Indigenous people during the 1970s and 1980s, including the provision of care and interventions intended to facilitate reciprocal recognition and re-membering. While this model is far removed from Indigenous understandings of inherent rights to sovereignty over service delivery and Treaty entitlements to quality services, the social and political significance of service infrastructure should not be underestimated (Anand, Gupta, and Appel 2018). In urban Ontario, the late twentieth-century politics of recognition enabled the growth of Indigenous biopolitical projects often connected to and supportive of the larger resurgence movement.

Like Sylvester, other frontline service workers and volunteers in the early Friendship Centres found that their referrals to generic public services led to racist encounters, or simply a misfit of dominant practices with Indigenous needs.[35] Frustrations mounted as they observed increasing experiences of alcohol abuse, homelessness, incarceration, and other forms of suffering and social dismemberment in rapidly growing urban Indigenous communities. At the same time, as illustrated by the projects described above, community organizers increasingly appreciated the value and effectiveness of their own traditional knowledge and practices for supporting those in need.[36] Meanwhile, as illustrated by the experiences of the Ladies' Auxiliary members, Indigenous people with higher levels of formal education and professional employment might have formed a distinct middle class but they too continued to experience racism from white Canadians, and the rise of Red Power and ideas of solidarity encouraged them to identify more strongly with Indigenous people using services than with white, middle-class society.

Sylvester went on to share his inspiration for a Native-run rehabilitation unit with other community organizers linked with the Native Canadian Centre, and together they submitted the first Ontario application to the newly established federal Native Alcohol Abuse Program.[37] Pedahbun Lodge was housed in a former nursing home on King Street in downtown Toronto, and the first urban residential alcohol abuse treatment centre for Indigenous people in Canada.[38] Their archived application shows how activists made instrumental use of dominant knowledge to bridge Indigenous need and settler state funding sources. Like Don Morrison and others active in supporting their people's recovery from alcohol, they drew on the dominant Alcoholics Anonymous model, which understands alcoholism as a disease: "We support research into the problems of the Native alcoholic and the seeking of better solutions to the disease alcoholism."[39] This paradigm subjectifies those struggling with alcohol abuse as a knowable figure, "the Native alcoholic" (encountered in the discourse of the Addiction Research Foundation in chapter 1) while reinforcing a stigmatized subject position loaded with historical and political baggage.

But accounts from other sources of how these community organizers approached treatment at Pedahbun Lodge reveal a program designed for re-membering, a very different form of subjectification entailing a mutual recognition of relatedness between Indigenous people. The relationship may be as close kin, members of a shared nation, or simply one of shared history and social location. "Patients" at Pedahbun Lodge participated in ceremonies (including a Sweat

Lodge constructed in the grounds), attended a weekly drumming group at the Native Canadian Centre, and travelled to powwows and land-based ceremonies outside of Toronto.[40] In 1977 a group of residents, staff, and volunteers embarked on a therapeutic road trip, intended to "further the spiritual awareness of the Pedahbun group" (Simard 1977); travelling through western Canada and the northern United States, they visited the Chicago Indian Friendship Centre, Cree reserves, and a conference hosted by the Stoney community at Mînî Thnî (then Morley), Alberta (Simard 1977). Harper was one of the volunteers on this trip: a photograph published as part of coverage in the *Toronto Native Times* shows a young Vern in braids tending to the barbecue, alongside a woman identified as "Linda." These 1970s organizers clearly understood recovery as a simultaneously spiritual, social, and political process, one that hinged on facilitating opportunities to form relationships with other Indigenous people, locally and across the continent, in urban and reserve settings. This social history underscores the imbrication of re-membering and resurgence politics, suggesting that tactical engagement with the politics of recognition can sometimes support social and political transformations. Further Indigenous initiatives aimed at supporting their people's well-being were established in Toronto through the 1980s, including the primary health centre Anishinaabe Health Toronto, with Joe Sylvester playing a central role.

Gendered Political Dismemberment

In 1984 Wally McKay, executive director of Tikinagan Child and Family Services, brought up the topic of family violence at a meeting of Nishnawbe Aski Nation Chiefs in Sioux Lookout, Northern Ontario and met a wall of dead silence: the male political leaders of Northern First Nations were unwilling to discuss the issue (Ontario Native Women's Association 1989, 25). At that time, First Nations leaders tended to prioritize land and Treaty Rights over social issues; spousal abuse and other forms of interpersonal violence in Indigenous families barely featured in their public discourse.[41] The leaders of urban Indigenous organizations did focus on social issues, but seem to have been similarly reluctant to act against spousal violence in this period (Janovicek 2009). Notably, Friendship Centres across Ontario employed court workers who helped men charged with family violence offences, but not the women who were their victims (Ontario Native Women's Association 1989, 50).

The implications of the 1969 White Paper for Indigenous politics went beyond the threat it posed to existing protections for collective rights, however limited. In its wake, the Indian Act became "a lever" for political gains by the male leadership of the National Indian Brotherhood (K. Jamieson 1978, 83). Indigenous feminist scholars challenge the narrative that heralds unprecedented Indigenous political unity after the White Paper, pointing out that both Indigenous and white male politicians' support for the continuation of women's systematic political dismemberment under the Indian Act became entrenched in this period (Suzack 2005). The White Paper created a political climate that enabled male leaders to undermine the claims of Indigenous women and their supporters as based on "individual" rights, a stance they alleged to be foreign to collective Indigenous social and political systems (Cannon 2019). Thus, an unprecedented alliance of First Nations and Canadian political leaders mobilized to oppose Indigenous women's long-standing demands to be re-enfranchised subsequent to their excision from nations and families under the Indian Act.[42]

Through the 1970s and 1980s, Indigenous women challenged male political leaders' disregard for how patriarchy and colonialism are mutually constitutive. A new genre of literary and autobiographical writing, built on the anti-colonial analyses of the Red Power movement with vivid accounts of Indigenous women's experiences, exposed the long-standing neglect of gender relations by male Indigenous politicians.[43] Women's lived experiences of everyday interpersonal struggles in the crevices of settler colonialism were initially propelled into the public domain with the 1972 publication of Maria Campbell's autobiographical *Halfbreed*, triangulating with organized challenges to gendered dismemberment by Jeannette

Corbiere Lavell (Anishinaabe, Wikwemikong) and Yvonne Bédard (Haudenosaunee, Six Nations of the Grand River) to expose the profoundly gendered nature of Canadian settler colonialism. During Lavell's and Bédard's unsuccessful legal challenges to their disenfranchisements as Status Indians and Band members, the subsequent joint committee consultative process involving the National Indian Brotherhood and the federal cabinet, and the constitutional debates of the 1980s and 1990s, many First Nations governments worked to actively exclude Indigenous women from political discourse, refusing to examine the extent to which their own politics were shaped by settler-colonial patriarchy (Cannon 2019). Cultural production became a site where Indigenous women illuminated the inadequacies of dominant, masculinist representations of colonialism and Indigenous dispossession focused narrowly on the geopolitical (Huhndorf and Suzack 2010; Million 2013).[44] Far from a separate, apolitical domain, Cheryl Suzack (2005) argues that Indigenous women's early literary treatments of colonial violence spoke back to First Nations political leaders, challenging their narrow and exclusionary definitions of membership. For instance, reading *Halfbreed* alongside Lavell's and Bédard's unsuccessful legal challenges to the Indian Act's discriminatory membership provisions, Suzack compares Campbell's historical account of the "loss of cultural cohesion and personal dignity" that ensued from Métis dispossession from their Red River territory with the experiences of Lavell and Bédard, "dispossess[ed]...of their status as Native women" by the National Indian Brotherhood in concert with settler state actors (Suzack 2005, 79). An understanding of how colonial dismemberment is gendered is important for making sense of gendered approaches to re-membering and healing, discussed in the next chapter.

In the mid-1980s, *A Gathering of Spirit*, a collection of Indigenous women's creative works edited by Degonwadonti (Beth Brant), a Mohawk lesbian feminist from Tyendinaga, Southern Ontario, powerfully conveyed the complex positioning of Indigenous women struggling against a social and political system designed by and for white men, and further undermined by the disregard of Indigenous men and white feminists.[45] Asserting, "We are not victims. We are organizers, we are freedom fighters, we are feminists, we are healers," Brant claims these overlapping subject positions as agents of social and political transformation for Indigenous women (1983, 7–8).[46] By challenging stereotypes of passivity, linking these identities to the imperative to value Indigenous women's lives, and explicitly critiquing the geopolitical model advanced by male Indigenous leaders with "their limited vision of what constitutes a strong Nation" (7), Brant's essay and the collection as a whole work to create space for a more fulsome Indigenous politics centring relationships. The contents of *A Gathering of Spirit* demonstrate how Indigenous women express "felt experience as community knowledge" (Million 2013, 57). The next chapter focuses on the social history of Indigenous women's organizing in Ontario and documents their political agency in launching a movement for what they described as "family healing," and illustrates how biopolitical analysis grounded in Indigenous knowledge can have profoundly geopolitical implications.

3

"Family Violence Is Weakening Our Nations"

Indigenous Women, Political Dismemberment, and Family Healing, 1972–1990

IN THEIR 1989 REPORT *Breaking Free: A Proposal for Change to Aboriginal Family Violence*, the Ontario Native Women's Association (ONWA) link urgent concerns for individual and collective well-being to an assertion of Indigenous Peoples' legal sovereignty. In so doing, I suggest, they offer an unprecedented synthesis of an Indigenized biopolitics and resurgence politics.[1] Their analysis reflects their members' extensive experience of providing frontline services as part of the expansion of Indigenous biopolitical tactics in urban Ontario during the 1970s and 1980s, described in chapter 2. Over decades, Indigenous women's caring work brought them up against the limitations of re-membering amidst ongoing, settler-colonial dismemberment, including not only settler state interventions, but also male Indigenous leaders' purposeful exclusion of women from political decision-making. Through this period, conversations among women living on and off reserves, Status, non-status, and Métis, crystallized a collective consciousness of how their lives were dominated by the combined workings of settler colonialism and patriarchy. This perspective inspired their redefinition of colonial violence to include both abuses suffered by women and children in their own homes, and the destruction of the socio-legal systems that once enabled Indigenous societies to respond effectively to interpersonal conflict.

In this chapter, I argue that the *Breaking Free* report represents a milestone in the emergence of an Indigenized biopolitics in Ontario. Paul Rabinow and Nikolas Rose identify three elements—"truth discourses," "strategies for intervention upon collective existence in the name of life and health," and "modes of subjectification" (2006, 197)—as essential criteria defining biopower and biopolitics as conceptualized by Foucault. ONWA's analysis of colonialism as etiological of interpersonal violence in Indigenous communities advanced a new "truth discourse" about Indigenous life, several years before mental health professionals Maria Yellow Horse Brave Heart and Eduardo Duran developed Indigenized applications of the related concept of historical trauma.[2] Their report also generated impetus towards "strategies for intervention upon collective existence," justified by invoking Indigenous well-being, involving new "modes of subjectification" under the rubric of healing that invite individuals "to work on themselves...in the name of their own life or health, that of their family" and nation (Rabinow and Rose 2006, 197). With the *Breaking Free* report, Indigenous healing histories reached a crucial juncture where insights gained from decades of re-membering enabled a vision of transformative change for Indigenous and settler societies. While this vision remains unrealized, ONWA's analysis undoubtedly fuelled the rise of Indigenous healing in public and political discourse in Ontario and Canada from the 1990s.

To fully appreciate the subversive force, courage, and analytical insight conveyed by this report, we must consider the political context of ONWA's work in the 1980s. *Breaking Free* used the rubric of "family healing" to challenge multiple orthodoxies at once: the misleading distinction between individual and collective rights then prevailing in both Indigenous and settler state political discourses led by men; conspiracies of silence around family violence in Indigenous communities; Canada's illegitimate claim to jurisdiction over Indigenous families and nations; and trivialization of spousal abuse by most members of the Canadian government, alongside white liberal feminists' increasingly influential campaign to criminalize perpetrators. ONWA's members refused to accept the incarceration of male perpetrators of violence who are also their relatives as a solution. Instead, they championed the capacity of Indigenous legal systems to respond to interpersonal violence more appropriately than the settler state. This assertion of legal jurisdiction aligns ONWA's arguments with Indigenous Peoples' broader struggle for sovereignty and self-determination. It is in this sense that I characterize their analysis as geopolitical: an assertion of the inherent, territory-based rights of Indigenous Peoples to govern themselves (Rifkin 2017). Their argument for the resurgence of Indigenous law predates the emergence of Indigenous legal studies as an academic field, and while Indigenous and other political and legal actors had called for Indigenous justice systems on reserves during the decade prior to *Breaking Free*, it appears ONWA were the first to explicitly link this demand to family violence.[3] ONWA's family healing paradigm expanded the scope of what could and should be discussed under the rubric of sovereignty, linking Indigenous nationhood to healing, and rendering individual safety, recovery, and well-being political matters. But beyond advising Band Councils to develop legal frameworks to protect the rights of abused women and children to remain in their family home, the report presents little concrete guidance on how Indigenous law is to be resurrected.

    ONWA's commitment to Indigenous sovereignty notwithstanding, the imperatives of redressing systemic state neglect and mobilizing resources for safety and healing, alongside the reluctance of male leaders to discuss family violence, prevent these women from "turning away" from the state. Instead, they offer extensive biopolitical analysis that adds empirical weight to their principled argument about the illegitimacy of the settler state's claims to jurisdiction over Indigenous lives. The report provides a strong critique of how settler colonialism, past and present, not only contributes to interpersonal violence in Indigenous families but actively prevents victims from accessing support, for instance through lack of basic infrastructure for Northern and reserve communities.

Indigenous Women Re-Membering in Ontario

After years of studying ONWA's work, in autumn of 2019 I was grateful to have the opportunity to meet and learn from Marlene Pierre, a founding member of ONWA and its executive director when *Breaking Free* was published, in Thunder Bay.[4] During a subsequent conversation, Marlene situated the origins of the family healing concept developed by ONWA in the volunteer labour of women, who organized locally to shelter and care for other women and their children fleeing violent homes:

> That word, *healing*, came from the years of work, of seeing all of the hardship and violence and impact on the family. And coming to realize all of the laws and regulations established by all levels of government designed to dismantle the family, our governance, everything that was our life before they came. So after many years of dealing with all of the problems, we knew that our People were hurting, and we needed to do something to help them get over that. That's where the word *healing* came from: the strongest way to identify what needed to be done, in order to make a difference for our families and our children in the future...We could no longer just...keep doing the work, the first stage of comforting people and getting them settled so that they would have a secure home, all that kind of stuff, then look at the impact that the violence had on their family...that's where healing really was the key, to all of the violence. We were focusing on the women, but

it became very evident that the men were in need of the healing as much as we did...It was complex, and none of us were educated in any of those fields. But we knew what had to be done.[5]

Marlene's long-standing leadership role in re-membering and family healing, in Thunder Bay and beyond, can be traced to how her early life experiences instilled a deep appreciation for Anishinaabe kin and a strong sense of responsibility to work hard and care for others.[6] Born in 1944, Marlene was the oldest daughter of Margaret Keebuck and Cyril Pierre, one of nine children. Most of the year, Marlene's family lived in a little two-bedroom house on Rosslyn Road, on the western outskirts of what is now the city of Thunder Bay. Marlene's parents "set good examples of how to care for your family and yourself," regularly hosted visitors in their already crowded house, and helped other Anishinaabeg in the area. Like many Indigenous families in mid-century Northern Ontario, hers sustained themselves through a combination of her father's waged labour, and hunting by her brothers (who snared rabbits and shot partridge close to their home) and uncles (who hunted moose and deer in their traditional territory in the Dog Lake area, nearly one hundred kilometres northwest of Thunder Bay). Decades earlier, the Keebucks had lived largely beyond the control of the Indian Act: not registered as a Band, but organized and largely self-governing through their own system of kinship-based governance. Marlene's maternal grandfather, Jack Keebuck, was a respected leader of his community, a strong traditionalist who maintained Ojibwe spiritual practices, for instance ensuring that all his grandchildren received Spirit Names through ceremony. Until age sixteen, Marlene spent every summer with Jack and her grandmother, Elisabeth Keebuck, aunts, uncles, and cousins at Dog Lake. There she picked blueberries, watched animals, enjoyed living in the bush, and learned what it means to be Anishinaabekwe, which Marlene sums up as "a freedom that you're with your own."[7]

Marlene's expression, "freedom that you're with your own," foreshadows an important theme of ONWA's family healing paradigm and its divergence from dominant liberal feminist ethics. Whereas the liberal ideal of freedom hinges on a minimally constrained individual liberty, Marlene conveys the sense of emancipation she experienced as part of a larger social whole, in a time and place where Anishinaabe society was relatively unconstrained by everyday enactments of illegitimate settler state authority, since her mother's family lived outside of the Indian Act. Simultaneously, she expresses how her sense of herself as a person within her particular social setting—her subjectivity—is, in part, defined by her connections and responsibilities to kin and collective. Philosopher and Anishinaabemowin instructor Maya Ode'amik Chacaby explains an Anishinaabe understanding of freedom, expressed by the concept dibenindizowin: "to have all the means necessary to fulfill one's responsibilities, as your Clan, as whatever you are in the world" (K. Anderson et al. 2018, 315). This definition of freedom conveys the relational subjectivity or selfhood that is central to re-membering. Freedom to take the actions necessary to fulfill one's responsibilities was part of the conditions and the effects of the urban Indigenous biopolitical tactics of the 1970s discussed in the previous chapter: the Ne-Chee Street Patrol's flexible employment conditions allowing workers to maintain kinship and ceremonial responsibilities, and the Native Canadian Centres' Ladies' Auxiliary members' efforts to forge bonds of solidarity with incarcerated women by teaching traditional craft skills. This model of relational subjectivity would be equally foundational to ONWA's concept of family healing as a response to spousal violence, contrasting with the decontextualized, autonomous model of personhood and limited notion of freedom underlying the liberal feminist preoccupation with criminalizing perpetrators.

    A profound resentment of the Indian Act's control over Anishinaabe lives is also part of the legacy of Marlene's childhood. Marlene's father's family lived on the Fort William reserve,[8] where her parents settled after their marriage in 1938. Before Marlene's birth in 1944, her parents and two older brothers were pressured into moving off the reserve. Marlene explained, "There were a number of families who were asked to leave the reserve. I know all those people today, and I feel a kinship with them, because something outside, a negative force outside of our own life had caused a division [between] those of us who could live on the reserve, and those of us who couldn't. Those of us who could be called 'Indian' by the government. That was very influential to me as I grew older. I didn't like the injustice" (Pierre 1994). Marlene's family history of political dismemberment and the ensuing crystallization of her values also foreshadow ONWA's family healing analysis and the approach of the larger Indigenous feminist movement, specifically, a commitment to an inclusive definition of membership spanning off-reserve, non-status, and Métis alongside those with Status living on reserves.

In 1969 Marlene began work as a volunteer with a youth group operating out of the Friendship Centre in what was then the city of Port Arthur. Established five years earlier and incorporated in 1968 as the "Thunder Bay Indian Youth Friendship Society," it was one of the first Native Friendship Centres in Canada, housed in a small red Insulbrick-covered building on the corner of Cumberland and Clavet Streets in the city's north end (Thunder Bay Indigenous Friendship Centre, n.d.).[9] Marlene was twenty-five years old and, like many Indigenous women in Ontario at that time, a single mother. Through her work at the Friendship Centre, she learned how to organize volunteers, fundraise, work with white people, and create social change. These experiences, and supportive mentoring by founding Executive Director Xavier Michon, equipped her to take on subsequent leadership roles. This work also deepened painful awareness of how continuing colonial relations shaped Indigenous lives in the present: "we saw firsthand our People's poverty, and their experiences of discrimination on the streets, in stores and in the courts."[10] And she gained a new appreciation for her own harmonious upbringing, as she learned that many other Anishinaabe women and their children suffered violence from family members, usually male relatives, in their own homes.

Like others established across Canada, the Thunder Bay Friendship Centre created new urban Indigenous social spaces where women could build trusting, mutually supportive relationships with one another. Thunder Bay had long been a destination for a diverse group of Indigenous people seeking employment, education, and services, including women pushed from their home reserves by disenfranchisement under the Indian Act, and those fleeing violence at the hands of men often protected by other family members and community leaders.[11] Marlene and other women working as volunteers gradually got to know the women using their services. They listened to them recount experiences of violence at the hands of domestic partners, abuse that went unreported to authorities because of the women's well-founded fear of further social dismemberment: a domestic violence report would lead the Ontario Children's Aid Society to apprehend their children.[12] Indigenous women's profound mistrust of state institutions is powerful testament to the illegitimacy of liberal state actors' claims to be carers or protectors of Indigenous people while routinely dismembering their families. Marlene noted that women suffering from abuse often struggled with feelings of shame, making it difficult for them to confide in others about their situation. Alcohol consumption was almost always involved in the abuse, a pattern that ONWA's subsequent research would confirm was consistent across Ontario. Many of the women were non-status, not entitled to Band membership or any federal services; most survived on a very low social services income that couldn't cover even basic expenses. Pervasive racism among private landlords coupled with a lack of public housing meant that shelter was difficult to find, adding another obstacle to the already challenging process of leaving an abusive partner.

These conversations among women generated momentum for change. In 1972 Marlene and other volunteers formed an Indigenous women's organization, Anishinabequek, and quickly identified their priority as providing shelter for women and children fleeing violence. As Friendship Centre volunteers, they had already acquired skills in social and political organizing.[13] Marlene had developed advanced proposal-writing skills, honed through her many years performing the gendered labour of secretary in meetings of the Ontario Federation of Indigenous Friendship Centres, then a male-dominated organization. Taking advantage of a Friendship Centre business trip to Toronto, Marlene and her colleagues met with the women who had recently established Anduhyaun, the first publicly funded Indigenous women's centre in Canada, and learned from them about possible funding sources, policy development, and operations.[14] Marlene's trajectory is consistent with existing historiography of Indigenous women's organizing in urban centres, which documents a pattern whereby women acquired skills and experiences in the early Friendship Centre movement that they then utilized in mobilizing around the particular experiences and needs of women (Krouse and Howard 2009). As Sylvia Maracle (2003) notes, this historical sequencing of Friendship Centres preceding women's centres also reflects women's inherent commitment to universal community well-being, almost always prioritized above their own, gendered needs.

When Marlene and the other members of Anishinabequek established Beendigen in Thunder Bay in 1978, it was the only shelter with a mission to serve Indigenous women in all northwestern Ontario, a region of hundreds of thousands of square kilometres including more than seventy First Nations reserves and many off-reserve Indigenous communities. As both inaugural president of Anishinabequek and housing manager at the Friendship Centre, Marlene was well positioned to advocate for resources to establish a women's shelter: "I just walked across the hall to Xavier's office and asked him if we could have the next available house."[15] The first property was "an ordinary four-bedroom house on Syndicate Avenue,"[16] with a mission to "provide culturally sensitive emergency shelter for Native women and their children" (Janovicek 2009, 63). The founders were aware that when attempting to access shelter services run by white women, Indigenous women often felt misunderstood, unwelcome, and fearful that shelter workers would contact Children's Aid, which would then apprehend their children. The validity of these fears is supported by research in the 1980s that found evidence of overt racism among white women using shelter services in Western Canada (W. Jamieson 1987; MacLeod 1987). Beendigen, which translates into English as "Come on in," would be a space where "women did not have to explain their circumstances" (Janovicek 2009, 65–66).[17] By 1982 Beendigen was providing emergency accommodation for 187 families. Across Ontario, Indigenous women were similarly preoccupied with attempting to provide shelter and other supports for women fleeing spousal violence.[18] But according to Marlene, they rarely paused to consider why these services were so acutely required: "Many of us, including the leadership, didn't know our history."[19] Their purposeful efforts to re-member these histories became central to envisioning the Indigenous societies they wanted to recreate.

In regional and annual provincial meetings, ONWA's collective re-membering of women's social and political roles prior to colonial social dismemberment strengthened their analysis of how current systems needed to change. Hundreds gathered to compare experiences, deepen their understanding of the historical and political roots of their Peoples' social suffering, and learn about the "impact of the patriarchal system."[20] Elders described past Indigenous societies in which women had been respected, indicating that the pervasive violence they witnessed was a recent phenomenon. They circulated copies of the Indian Act, which most of them had never had the opportunity to read, and discussed the origins of the reserve system, and the role and social effects of Christian missionaries and residential schools.[21] Ultimately, they came to understand contemporary male violence against themselves and their children as a function of patriarchal values, enshrined in the Indian Act and Christian theology that had governed most Indigenous communities for over a century.

With this heightened historical and political consciousness, ONWA members came to recognize the persistence of patriarchal values and practices in contemporary First Nations political culture. Marlene vividly described to me the dismay she felt when, in 1980, she realized that the gendered social and political exclusion that they'd analyzed in the Indian Act was now actively perpetuated by male First Nations leaders.[22] That year, Ontario Premier Bill Davis invited representatives of ONWA and the Ontario Federation of Indian Friendship Centres to participate in discussions with the provincial government, alongside the First Nations political organizations in the province: the Association of Iroquois and Allied Indians, Union of Ontario Indians, Grand Council of Treaty #3, and Grand Council of Treaty 9.[23] The meeting was to plan for the upcoming First Ministers' conference focused on patriation of the constitution and the Charter of Rights and Freedoms. Premier Davis informed the group that he would provide funds for selected representatives of all the organizations to participate in the Ottawa conference, scheduled for September 1980. Marlene recalled, "When Davis asked, 'And what about the women?' the response from the Treaty 9 leadership was an outright 'No, we don't want the women there.' I was stunned. He'd been part of the youth group at the Thunder Bay Friendship Centre, and I thought of him as a friend. It was unbelievable." Each of the organizations in turn was asked if they would include Indigenous women's representatives in their delegation. Each representative refused. To Marlene's amazement, Davis then said, "'Well, if you don't want them, the province will take them." These political maneuverings around the inclusion or exclusion of Indigenous women point to how liberal settler state actors can exploit entrenched patriarchy in First Nations leadership. Women might be able to take short-term tactical advantage of such opportunities, as did Marlene and her colleagues, but state-driven gendered inclusion doesn't address the fundamental challenge of dismantling colonial misogyny in Indigenous politics.

The only Indigenous women who participated in this historic conference, Marlene and three ONWA colleagues took a particular interest in advocating for the passage of section 15 of the Charter of Rights and Freedoms, and they met with every single provincial minister for Aboriginal affairs to solicit support.[24] Male First Nations leaders were concerned that section 15, which amended the Canadian constitution to guarantee individual rights,[25] could undermine the collective rights enshrined, however imperfectly, in the Indian Act. Indeed, once the charter was enacted in 1982, the presence of section 15 generated significant momentum towards the passage of Bill C-31, amending the Indian Act in June 1985.[26] After decades of advocacy by Indigenous women, the Canadian government finally accepted the imperative to reverse over a century of legislated gender discrimination.

But the resulting legislation satisfied no one and fostered conflict in many communities and families.[27] The Canadian government's mismanagement of the legislative process echoed that of the 1969 White Paper, in that Indigenous input was invited and then ignored—except that in the case of C-31, the bill went on to become law (Innes 2013). Most First Nations leaders resented the imposition of state control over membership that undermined what they perceived to be a basic tenet of self-determination afforded them under the Indian Act: control over who belongs to the Band, and is therefore eligible for the entitlements of this constrained mode of citizenship. Many members of reserve communities were understandably wary of what they anticipated would be a large influx of new residents who would overburden already inadequate resources and infrastructure, particularly housing. Even those supporting in principle the reversal of the Indian Act's gender discrimination were dissatisfied with the new forms of exclusion created by the bill, dubbed "discriminatory leftovers" by Martin Cannon (2019, 67). The implicit introduction of blood quantum as a basis for reckoning identity meant that children of reinstated women, or of any new mixed (Status and non-status) marriages, would gain status themselves, but would not be able to pass status on to their children. As Cannon observes, the ostensibly anti-patriarchal reforms didn't consider or redress how the sexism and racism inherent to the Indian Act were mutually implicated. In other words, the political dismemberment of women was not separate from but integral to the racialization of Indigenous people as Indians, so any changes to the first element of the act necessarily has implications for the second. It was in this politically fraught climate of the late 1980s that ONWA launched their research into family violence.

ONWA's "Family Healing": Indigenous Sovereignty and Biopolitics

By redefining family violence as the result of settler colonialism, ONWA problematized analyses of power relations in both male-led Indigenous resurgence and white liberal feminist politics of the period. In the male-led Red Power and broader resurgence movements depicted in chapters 1 and 2, public discussions of colonial violence did not extend to violence perpetrated by Indigenous men against their own women and children.[28] And ONWA had an ambivalent relationship with white liberal feminists, like many Indigenous women's organizations (Barker 2018). Liberal feminists' organizing and advocacy effectively drew attention to spousal violence as a matter of public policy, creating conditions in which a wider range of women's organizations, including ONWA, might access public funds.[29] But while liberal feminists forced public acknowledgement of men's abuse of female partners, their work was informed mainly by white women's experiences, and they were often blind to how Indigenous and other racialized women's lives and options were further constrained by spectrums of colonial and racialized violence, including disproportionate incarceration (Monture-Okanee 1992).[30]

ONWA's *Breaking Free* report broke new ground by navigating lateral violence as both a biopolitical and a geopolitical matter, pertaining at once to individual behaviour and suffering, collective well-being, and sovereignty over law governing interpersonal and family relations. *Breaking Free* not only presents an unprecedented public acknowledgement of lateral violence, but frames this violence as symptomatic of a geopolitical issue: the illegitimacy of settler-colonial rule and the imperative to resurrect Indigenous self-governance, including legal systems. The report supports this argument with biopolitical analysis that advances a new "truth discourse" linking Indigenous family violence to colonial histories and settler state neglect. It also compellingly demonstrates the need for new interventions in the name of Indigenous well-being, drawing on original survey data quantifying the scale of the problem and the impact on Indigenous lives. And it advocates Indigenous-led biopolitical interventions in the form of services aimed at changing individual behaviour in the name of healing. At the same time, ONWA demonstrates their commitment to Indigenous ontologies and sovereignty, analyzing kinship networks as fundamental political and legal units and targets of ongoing colonial dismemberment. This is a geopolitical assertion that shows the irrelevance of dominant liberal feminist analyses to Indigenous Peoples, and the importance of transforming colonial relations—namely, dismantling settler state domination and resurrecting Indigenous self-governance—as a central strategy to redress family violence. At the same time, they make clear the inevitability of tactical engagement with the settler state, demanding adequate infrastructure and services and resources to develop Indigenous alternatives to criminalization of male perpetrators.

ONWA's approach to research synthesized their (bio)political savvy, including an understanding of the value state actors attach to population data, with their embeddedness in their communities and deep knowledge of Indigenous women's lives. This expertise informed a research methodology designed to reach women usually excluded from social research (ONWA 1989, 5–6). Members of ONWA locals across the province distributed questionnaires to women through their personal networks, enhancing the validity of the results by increasing women's confidence in the research process and encouraging frank, detailed responses. By comparison, research conducted by outsiders in Northern Ontario reserves commonly elicits suspicion and withdrawal, as illustrated by the conversation between Mary Equay Letander and her sister with which this book began. During the period of ONWA's research, a separate project found that Indigenous women working as community health representatives refused to even respond to questions about abuse in their communities (Timpson et al. 1987). Most of the 104 women who responded to ONWA's survey lived outside of urban areas: on reserves (45%), and in rural (17%) and isolated (8%) communities; two-thirds lived in communities where Indigenous people make up at least half of the population (ONWA 1989, 6–7). The survey results were triangulated with interviews, conducted with an additional 167 people: victims of abuse, Elders, Band Chiefs and Councillors, and a wide range of frontline professionals and paraprofessionals in relevant fields, who validated survey findings about the scale of spousal abuse in Indigenous families.[31]

Given their extensive experience of frontline service delivery, ONWA members no doubt understood the potential risks associated with public discussion of social problems within Indigenous nations, such as inadvertently validating colonial stereotypes of dysfunction, and legitimating yet more violent state interventions into family life.[32] Their interpretation of family violence as "a reaction against systems of domination, disrespect and bureaucratic control" (ONWA 1989, 3), an explicit critique of the long history of settler state interventions, may mitigate this risk. Their previous experience did not fully prepare ONWA leaders for the scale of abuse revealed by their research: 80 per cent of responding women had personally experienced family violence, a figure eight times higher than the reported incidence of domestic violence against all women in Canada at that time.[33] Nearly a quarter of respondents knew of cases where family violence had led to death, usually of a woman. In their analysis, ONWA are very purposeful in locating these troubling data in their social, political, and historical contexts. Their framing of family healing as an expression of sovereignty is grounded in an analysis of the foundational role of kinship in pre-contact Indigenous political and legal systems, pointing out that the "family" in family healing signifies not just a kinship unit but also the "customary and fundamental socio-political unit" (21). Individual and collective well-being and social harmony are integral to nationhood, as they elaborate: "Family violence is not a personal or even a family issue; it affects the whole community on a spiritual, social, mental and physical level. It drains the energies and strength of a community when they are needed for more productive uses. Community leaders have a responsibility to promote the well-being and welfare of their People, and family violence is something they must help stop" (29). This argument simultaneously conveys an Indigenous relational subjectivity at odds with the individualism underlying liberal feminist understandings, and a subtle critique of First Nations leaders' failure to redress family violence. They discuss policies, institutions, and agents of the Canadian settler state aimed at social and political dismemberment: the residential school system led to loss of role models and undermined the development of parenting skills; women's disenfranchisement under the Indian Act for marrying non-status men disrupted the extended family's important role in raising children; children fostered and adopted by non-Indigenous families were denied the opportunity to learn about the importance of families to their cultures. They were among the first Indigenous commentators to publicly argue that these experiences of colonization are etiological of contemporary Indigenous family violence; in so doing, ONWA both crafted a powerful biopolitical framework that would be widely taken up in the larger healing movement, and attempted to align their analysis with First Nations' struggles for sovereignty and against continuing domination by the Canadian settler state.

ONWA support their argument for understanding family violence as a matter of sovereignty with critical analysis of how an imposed foreign legal system not only disproportionately criminalizes and incarcerates Indigenous people, but fails to consider Indigenous women's needs for safety under dominant property law. In 1986, three years before publication of the ONWA report, the Supreme Court of Canada ruled in *Derrickson v. Derrickson* and *Paul v. Paul* that provincial laws regarding ownership and possession of real property do not apply on reserves.[34] Mary Ellen Turpel, co-researcher and co-author of *Breaking Free*, argued that these rulings were further evidence of the ongoing domination of Indigenous Peoples by Canadian legal institutions and actors, wrongly preoccupied with "which branch of the state should control which aspect of aboriginal life, not the very matter of state control itself" (1991, 30). Responding to commentaries on the rulings, Turpel challenged both liberal feminists[35] and those sympathetic to First Nations' leadership.[36] She noted that neither Supreme Court decision considered the experiences of women and children in their deliberations, and thereby enabled the continuation of their vulnerability to violence. Indigenous women were condemned to dire options: remain in a violent home, seek shelter elsewhere on the reserve in an already overcrowded home, or leave their home community and risk not being welcomed back. ONWA's research demonstrated that the third of these possibilities, a form of gendered social dismemberment, was the most probable outcome. A woman seeking safety from spousal violence would usually have to leave her reserve or rural home to seek shelter, often a great distance away: "she will then look like the one who abandoned her home, and her community, simply because she has nowhere else to go, and no protection to remain" (ONWA 1989, 38). As noted by research contributor Loren Mitchell, the value attached to collectivity in reserve communities means that those who flee for their own safety may be shunned as "outcasts" upon their return (26). These challenges overlap with the experiences of white women in small rural communities, particularly in Northern Canada, which Linda MacLeod describes as "double isolation": the social isolation of secret abuse, where women are less likely to report assault due to the "value the community places on maintaining relationships" (1987, 22), and the isolation of being unable to access support services due to geographic distance.

But compared with the white woman who is the implicit subject of liberal feminist discourse, much more was (and is) at stake for an Indigenous woman contemplating leaving home to escape abuse. As the ONWA report makes clear, loss of a home on reserve represents the loss of *homeland*: potentially the only access a woman and her children have to their culture, language, territory, and family. For these reasons, ONWA insists that "an abused woman...gain interim possession of the matrimonial home, until such time as the batterer can be treated and the family can be restored to a healthy and safe environment for the women and children" (1989, 38). Their proposal is consistent with the principle of self-determination: rather than amend the Indian Act as recommended by some white feminist commentators, they urge Indigenous Peoples to develop and enforce their own legal frameworks. Most urgently, Band Councils should "develop a by-law providing Aboriginal women with protection so that she can remain in their community" (38); ONWA offered to develop a model for such by-laws. To better understand the experiences of Indigenous women living off-reserve, they noted the need to assess how the Ontario Family Law Reform Act relates to Métis and First Nations women and how it is working in practice.[37]

ONWA's central argument that family violence must be taken seriously as a political issue inherently linked to sovereignty and the necessary resurrection of legal orders anticipated the work of Indigenous legal studies scholars by several decades. The report explains the failure of effective collective action to redress violence by invoking the colonial destruction of Indigenous legal systems. Prior to colonial regulation of Indigenous societies, interpersonal relations were organized by "behavioral codes and social mechanisms," "predicated on the respect and dignity of the individual" (ONWA 1989, 8). These once-effective values and practices of kinship and broader social relations have been "lost or distorted by oppressive policies and legislation," creating the present situation "in which abuses, such as family violence and alcoholism, have been allowed to flourish" (8).[38] Three decades later, Indigenous legal studies scholar Hadley Friedland (2018) made a similar argument that historical suppression of Indigenous legal systems enabled increasing levels of abuse by constraining communities' capacity to act against that abuse.[39] Friedland asserts that by deliberately undermining Indigenous socio-legal orders, settler state and Christian missionary actors fostered uncertainty and chaos, to the point that it became increasingly difficult for community members to discuss certain subjects, such as violence against women and children, which "become unspeakable because they are forced to remain unspoken for so long" (xv). This breakdown of socially embedded legal systems led to collective silence and a culture of impunity for perpetrators, which, as Friedland points out, "are ideal conditions for abuse and abusers to flourish" (xvii).

ONWA's assertion of Indigenous legal sovereignty grounded in kinship relations is a direct challenge to liberal feminist arguments that consider the family to be an inherently patriarchal institution from which women must be liberated. Dominant feminist discourse on spousal violence in the 1980s centred on a dyad of "victim" and "perpetrator" and presumed that justice necessitated a radical rupture in family relations to liberate victimized women and punish violent men. Tellingly, for liberal feminists advocating criminalization of spousal violence, "it became unpopular to even talk of relationships": their assumption was that women who received appropriate support would "forge a new life without violence and probably without the batterer" (MacLeod 1987, 4). Further, they presumed "woman" to be a universal category of autonomous individuals bearing the fundamental rights and freedoms foundational to liberal thought, and failed to consider how cultural and political contexts shape divergent subjectivities with implications for understandings of justice, and thus their analyses disregarded collective rights. To many Indigenous women, this analysis of the family and spousal violence constituted yet another mode of social dismemberment for Indigenous Peoples.

By classifying family violence as a legal matter within the jurisdiction of Indigenous polities and heralding collective organizing against such violence as the enactment of sovereignty, ONWA also implicitly challenged some First Nations leaders' complicity, which seems to reflect an assumption that (women's) individual rights must be sacrificed for the collective (Fiske 1996). As we've seen, this assumption was demonstrated in the wake of the 1969 White Paper by political leaders' opposition to women challenging their systemic exclusion under the Indian Act through the 1970s and 1980s. ONWA's research made clear that family violence had become "normalized" in many places through a culture of silence and impunity for male perpetrators. In their contributions to the research, social service workers described family violence as "either hidden or tolerated" (ONWA 1989, 57). Alex Gunner, of Payukotayno James and Hudson Bay Family Services in Moosonee, told the researchers, "many women accept their situation because they are told to do so by their parents" (25), indicating the social reproduction of complicity in abuse. Rosalyn Copenace observed, "everyone knows what is going on but the attitude of some was that the women deserve it" (25). ONWA members learned of political leaders thwarting attempts by abused women to leave their Northern fly-in communities. Marlene explained, "They were prisoners in their own community. When they would try to escape a violent situation, they couldn't. They were kept there by Chief running down to the dock and telling the [pilot of the] plane to go: 'You can't take this woman, and if you do, you're going to lose your job,' all kinds of threats" (Pierre 1994). Such actions suggest that some political leaders construed women's right to safety as a threat to the nation and, drawing on Jo-Anne Fiske's (1996) analysis, "the fraternity." Further, as some contributors observed, in smaller reserve and rural communities of just a few hundred people, "the extended family is actually the community itself" (ONWA 1989, 58). This analysis underscores the complexity inherent to disrupting patterns of violence in small communities where every member has an established relationship with the abuser, as well as with those being abused, further evidence for the relevance of ONWA's argument for Indigenous law grounded in kinship networks. The challenge for community members in this social context, then, is how to "protect those we love—from those we love" (Friedland 2018, xv). Aligned with this inclusive and relational framing, ONWA challenges political leaders' complicity by advocating a normative framework for social relations based on Indigenous ethics, one that refuses to sacrifice the well-being of women: "the welfare of any one member of our communities is important to everyone" (ONWA 1989, 18).

Alongside their geopolitical argument that the resurgence of Indigenous legal systems will redress family violence, ONWA also offered a biopolitical analysis of family violence. Recall from the book's introduction that I'm working with an understanding of biopolitics not confined to the workings of state power. Instead, my argument is grounded in the premise that a diverse set of actors engage in political struggles centred on rights to life and health, well-being, and bodily autonomy that play out on the historically significant terrain of biopower, struggles that often involve tactical engagements with the liberal state but are not entirely controlled by state actors (Rabinow and Rose 2006). I argue that ONWA's analysis can be read as biopolitical, first because they advance a new "truth discourse" about Indigenous well-being, one that argues that Indigenous subjectivities, particularly gendered roles and identities, have been shaped through histories of colonial intervention and state neglect in ways that harm both collective and individual life within families and nations, and second, because ONWA advocate for new forms of Indigenous-managed intervention to support healing, understood as new "practices of the self," or "modes of subjectification," which align with the well-being of individuals, families, and nations (Rabinow and Rose 2006, 197).

ONWA's report explains family violence with reference to how Indigenous men have been subjectified under settler colonialism. It describes how colonial interventions undermined traditional masculine gender roles and responsibilities, leading to feelings of "anger and frustration" and erode(d) self-esteem (ONWA 1989, iii); low levels of formal education, poverty, and everyday experiences of racism exacerbate shrinking options for employment; and "a stifling of leadership potential due to a government system that removes all sense of pride for our men" (27). In the vacuum created by the colonial capitalist destruction of livelihoods and linked social systems such as Clan membership, dominant Canadian understandings of masculinity increasingly influenced how Indigenous men perceive themselves and their roles, ONWA argue. Research contributor Linda Sherman, a mental health counsellor at Tikinagan in Thunder Bay, observed that while Indigenous women's family and community roles are changing, "[Indigenous] men are still trying to be head of the household and chief bread winner" (27). They noted that dominant gender roles prescribe that men "must be strong, keep feelings inside, never cry and head the household," and "do not have mental problems because they are in control of the situation" (27).

ONWA also analyze the prevalence of family violence as resulting from settler state neglect of Indigenous people's basic citizenship rights. This explanation is comparable to Treaty 3 Anishinaabeg's earlier analysis of violent and preventable deaths in Kenora in the *While People Sleep* report (discussed in chapter 2), which I also characterized as largely biopolitical, in that both provide powerful evidence of how the systemic denial of basic infrastructure and services to Indigenous communities contribute directly to suffering and loss of life. ONWA point to systemic underfunding of public services and infrastructure on reserves, and in Northern rural communities predominantly inhabited by Indigenous people, as an important contributory factor to the prevalence of spousal violence. Underdevelopment of child care services, primary health care, and social services all intensify the isolation of those suffering family abuse and limit women's opportunities to access essential help and support. A lack of telecommunication and transportation infrastructure creates virtually insurmountable barriers to accessing help: more than twenty Northern reserves in Ontario lack year-round road access, while a much larger number of reserve and rural communities have no access to a public transportation system, and many households lack even a telephone.[40] The settler state's failure to provide such basic infrastructure fosters ongoing social dismemberment.[41]

ONWA's family healing approach centred on new interventions and services is a powerful repudiation of the liberal feminist criminalization model for responding to family violence. The report points to the already disproportionate incarceration of Indigenous men, and the fact that the Canadian criminal justice system is widely perceived as a "foreign bureaucracy" by Indigenous people and itself one of the root causes of family violence (ONWA 1989, 34).[42] Thus, ONWA rejects then-dominant ideas that the male perpetrator should be "responsible to find his own help" and "sacrificed" in the interest of justice, a critique founded on the inconsistency of criminalization with relational personhood (18). Instead, ONWA insist that honouring and repairing family relationships is integral to Indigenous social and political orders. But in offering concrete recommendations for how this can be done, the report devotes much less attention to Indigenous legal resurgence than it does to describing proposed healing interventions for women, children, and male perpetrators, which, the report explains, are meant as adjuncts to ongoing criminalization "until an Aboriginal criminal justice system is developed" (19).[43] While clearly inspired by their research evidence for a lack of functioning socio-legal mechanisms to keep women and children safe in their homes, this disproportionate emphasis seems inconsistent with ONWA's stated goal of community-based justice systems and strong, principled opposition to criminalization as another mode of colonial dismemberment.

How to interpret the disproportionate attention to recommendations for biopolitical interventions compared with geopolitical legal resurgence? ONWA had to reckon with the pragmatics of protecting victims of family violence in the present. Perhaps the underdeveloped discussion of Indigenous law is an implicit acknowledgement that most of the women and service providers surveyed actually supported criminalization of perpetrators, and so more time and effort is needed to build consensus in support of Indigenous legal approaches. The liberal feminist movement for criminalizing spousal violence garnered significant public and political attention during the 1980s and may have influenced the significant proportion of respondents (82%) who supported the principle that an abuser should be charged (ONWA 1989, 19).[44] ONWA members' extensive experience of service delivery may have translated into greater confidence in developing healing programs than articulating a route to the geopolitical transformation entailed in legal resurgence. And tactically, the focus on healing programs enables ONWA to align their vision with the many other Indigenous organizations and governments that "have a great commitment to address family violence" (40) through such interventions. For instance, in Treaty 9 territory, where Chiefs had been silent in the face of Wally McKay's efforts to discuss family violence in 1984 (described in chapter 2), leadership later supported an innovative proposal for male perpetrators, a therapeutic residential program for men to be located within the territory of a First Nation. Although rejected by the federal government the previous year, this project so impressed ONWA that they included a summary in an appendix to the *Breaking Free* report (68–70). They consider how the issue of victim protection might be addressed through careful design of healing interventions, for instance by locating this therapeutic accommodation for male perpetrators in a remote community (16). The proposed healing lodges for women and children can also be read as a pragmatic acknowledgement of the potential obstacles to implementing their recommendation that Bands develop matrimonial property legislation enabling women and children to remain in the family home. These healing lodges are envisioned as supportive sites to "begin to strengthen women and children so they can return to the community, or resume their life in the community, without being ashamed, alienated or stigmatized for being abused" (34).

    In ONWA's vision for healing abused women and children to enable them to withstand ongoing social challenges, we can glean a risk that comes with using biopolitical tactics to address pressing socio-political issues—namely, artificial individuation of collective matters. This vision of healing is predicated on the assumption that an individual *can* become sufficiently strengthened to be immune to the social duress of being shamed, alienated, and stigmatized, which, in the context of a small community with dense kinship ties, seems ambitious. This assumption, I suggest, foreshadows the individuating concept of "resilience" that, in the decades since the publication of *Breaking Free*, has become prominent in international development, mental health, and social services discourse, and is often invoked in the context of services for Indigenous communities. While at first glance the quality of resilience might appear to align with Indigenous ethics around autonomy and the celebration of survivance, its recent currency is partially explained by alignment with neoliberal ideology's emphasis on the *decontextualized* individual: critics point to how a focus on resilience as aspirational individual trait can displace attention to the larger economic, political, and social structures that render members of particular social groups vulnerable in the first place (Boyden and Cooper 2007; Fennell 2012).

Breaking Free's central tenet that individual and collective well-being is interdependent with the resurgence of sovereign Indigenous legal systems challenges the Canadian settler state's own self-proclaimed sovereignty, as well as state actors' long-standing identification as benevolent providers and protectors of Indigenous people. ONWA's critique of the settler state created space for their extensive proposals for Indigenizing biopolitics, but once detached from the assertion of legal sovereignty, offered a therapeutic route forward both less challenging to settler state authority and more vulnerable to state co-option, potentially detracting from the urgency of legal resurgence. As subsequent developments discussed in the next chapter indicate, some of the biopolitical content of ONWA's work proved susceptible to reworking by settler state actors to better align with neoliberal approaches to health and social policy. In particular, ONWA's discourses about colonialism as etiological of social suffering and healing building individual resilience to withstand punishing social environments were eventually taken up by state and some Indigenous leaders alike. Under neoliberal settler colonialism we see the expansion of Indigenous biopolitical tactics, some of which worked to narrow the locus of change from a collective, social, and political process critical of the settler state and society to a model predicated on individual behaviour, while neglecting the contexts crucial to understanding family violence as ONWA compellingly demonstrated.

Coda:
Family Healing Enters Ontario Politics, 1990

During our conversation in Thunder Bay in 2019, Marlene Pierre recalled mixed responses when the *Breaking Free* report was released in January 1990.[45] Ontario Attorney General Ian Scott met with ONWA representatives to receive the report; she thought he seemed receptive to their proposals.[46] The Union of Ontario Indians provided support for a national press launch out of the Chiefs of Ontario office in Toronto. Marlene was pleased with the resulting coverage: articles in the *Globe and Mail* (Fine 1990) and the *Ottawa Citizen* (Eggerston 1990), and a much shorter one in the *Windspeaker* (1990), the only national Indigenous media outlet at that time. All three gave prominence to ONWA's research finding that 80 per cent of Indigenous women experience violence at home; all three devoted less attention to their proposals for change.[47] At home in Thunder Bay, Marlene heard negative comments from some Indigenous men, who felt unfairly condemned by the report.

The social and political climate of the early 1990s created both possibilities and challenges for implementing family healing as envisioned by ONWA members. Neoliberalism was rapidly gaining ground in Canada under Brian Mulroney's federal government (1984–1993), aligning dominant political culture with an ideological emphasis on increasing individual responsibility and reducing public spending. But the period between 1985 and 1995 also saw the rise of social democratic politics in Ontario, for the first time since the 1920s. The election of a centre-left New Democratic Party (NDP) government in 1990 accelerated provincial efforts at dialogue with Indigenous Peoples initiated by the previous minority Liberal government, and created a window for channelling resources to public services, even amid the national ascent of neoliberal social policy.[48] The 1991 Statement of Political Relationship agreed by the NDP government and First Nations leaders went further: it recognized the inherent Indigenous right to self-government, and committed Ontario to respecting Treaty relations, expediting land claims and undertaking constitutional and legislative reforms to enable full implementation of those inherent rights. Although short-lived (the government failed to take steps to enshrine these commitments in law, and the statement was rejected by the subsequent Progressive Conservative government of Mike Harris, a neoliberal populist), this might have been a window for united Indigenous leaders to press for fiscal and legislative supports to re-establish their own legal systems on reserves.

Breaking Free's enduring social and political effects bear little resemblance to the vision expressed in the report. ONWA's groundbreaking work was largely ignored or belittled by male First Nations political leaders. Settler state actors conveniently disregarded the crucial geopolitical argument for transformation of systems and structures, but embraced the biopolitics of Indigenous healing: in Ontario government literature, ONWA's *Breaking Free* report is celebrated as the origin of the 1994 provincial Aboriginal Healing and Wellness Strategy.[49] Marlene has a rather different take on the development of the Aboriginal Healing and Wellness Strategy: she recalls "that was where we got shafted."[50] Resources for new infrastructure and healing programs were allocated mainly to First Nations and the urban Friendship Centres, while Indigenous women's organizations best placed to serve women in reserve and remote rural communities were shortchanged, the urgent imperative to address family violence was marginalized at the expense of a more generic Indigenous healing, and ONWA's goal of resurrecting Indigenous legal systems was excluded from policy discussions. Thus, the opportunity for transformative change represented by the geopolitical dimension of their analysis— their innovative synthesis of legal sovereignty with individual and collective well-being—was missed. "Indigenous healing" has become ubiquitous in public discourse, yet most of the debilitating material conditions and social issues raised in *Breaking Free* remain current today, and are particularly acute in First Nations rural and urban communities in Northern Ontario. In the next chapter, I examine the process by which ONWA's proposals for family healing were taken up and depoliticized in provincial policy and programming, as proponents of urban re-membering employed biopolitical tactics to navigate the growing influence of neoliberalism in the Canadian social and political landscapes.

4

Biopolitical Tactics under Neoliberal Settler Colonialism

Healing as Public Discourse, 1990–2015

IN A PROGRAM TELEVISED in October 1990, nine months after the Ontario Native Women's Association (ONWA) released their *Breaking Free* report, Chief Phil Fontaine foreshadowed the emergence of a new model of Indigenous healing in Canadian public discourse. Fontaine's vision was quite different to ONWA's. Its outline first came into public view during his interview by Canadian Broadcasting Corporation (CBC) veteran reporter Barbara Frum about childhood experiences of sexual abuse at the Catholic Fort Alexander Residential School.[1] Fontaine described long-term, pernicious effects suffered by those who had been sexually abused at the Fort Alexander school, and implied that such past experiences caused pervasive, ongoing abuse and trauma in contemporary Indigenous communities.[2] He concluded with a call for "a healing process, to make our people whole, so that when we talk about the future, that we can talk...as whole people and not as a people that has...many, many individuals with missing parts and pieces and gaps in their being."

Fontaine invoked nationhood, but in contrast to the collectivist understanding foundational to re-membering and ONWA's family healing, his model of healing was more narrowly individuated, focused on repairing damaged components of a whole more than collective relations or systemic change. Perhaps surprisingly, this paradigm proved to align well with neoliberal ideology, which, as infamously articulated by British Prime Minister Margaret Thatcher, explicitly disavows the social.[3] Subsequently, as Grand Chief of the Assembly of First Nations (AFN) for three terms (1997–2000, 2003–2006, 2006–2009), Fontaine led negotiations with the federal government leading to the 2006 Indian Residential Schools Settlement Agreement, which, as I discuss in this chapter, not only redefined Indigenous "healing" in individuated terms very different to earlier re-membering practice but led to further social dismemberment of Indigenous families and nations.

Juxtaposing Fontaine's discourse on healing from residential schools with ONWA's family healing model reveals not only divergent perspectives on the locus of "healing" and its relationship to Indigenous polities and politics, but also divergent understandings of Canadian settler colonialism and how it is etiological of Indigenous suffering in the present. ONWA's report links Indigenous well-being to the transformation of both Indigenous and settler societies and polities, and healing is predicated on strengthening Indigenous socio-legal systems as interdependent with sovereignty, consistent with practices and philosophies I characterize as re-membering. Recall that ONWA's understanding of healing flows from their analysis of gendered and interpersonal violence, itself inspired by decades of women's labour providing care for their communities. Their paradigm conveyed a socially grounded understanding of colonialism as ongoing structure, embedded in the workings of the Canadian criminal justice and child welfare systems and systemic denial of services and infrastructure to Indigenous communities, and a dominant culture that continues to distort masculine subjectivities and normalize family violence. In contrast, Fontaine's account conveys an understanding of colonialism as past event contained by the residential school system as synecdoche, reducing contemporary manifestations to embodiment by individuals traumatized by past abuse in that system. For Fontaine, Indigenous futures are predicated on the rehabilitation of these damaged individuals, a process that decontextualizes this individuated form of suffering while demanding recognition by the settler state.

ONWA and Fontaine advanced different biopolitical arguments about how best to promote and protect Indigenous life, demonstrating how Indigenous actors' biopolitical tactics can reflect divergent visions of Indigenous sovereignty and sociality. This contrast is consistent with the understanding of biopolitics I've advanced as techniques for navigating relations of (bio)power to promote Indigenous life, rather than a fixed political orientation. Thus, differently located actors craft and circulate discourses that may converge with or diverge from a larger geopolitical vision, and create new subjects with potentially profound, sometimes unintended social and political implications. Biopolitical tactics, then, need to be critically examined for their discursive and material effects.

The growing complexity of such tactics from the late twentieth century is due not only to the challenges presented by neoliberal public policy limiting expenditure on services, but the increasing participation in public, academic, and policy discourse of a growing cadre of credentialled Indigenous professionals and researchers in health care, mental health, and social work fields, as well as a growing number of Indigenous workers on the frontlines of health and social services.[4] Credentialled Indigenous biopolitical actors, who must navigate at times conflicting paradigms, values, and responsibilities in their training, practice, and advocacy (Gone 2009), now play influential roles in producing and shaping public discourse on suffering and healing in health research, and national and provincial health and social policy fora, including the Royal Commission on Aboriginal Peoples (RCAP) and the Truth and Reconciliation Commission (TRC), as I discuss below.[5]

In this chapter, I show how Indigenous biopolitical actors advanced increasingly divergent understandings of healing, variably aligned with older ideas of re-membering, as they navigated the shifting terrain of neoliberal settler colonialism. ONWA's and Fontaine's shared premise that colonialism is etiological of contemporary Indigenous suffering gained traction in public policy through the 1990s and 2000s, and informed the establishment of two state-sponsored healing policies that enabled access to new resources for healing projects: the Ontario Aboriginal Healing and Wellness Strategy (AHWS) (in part the outcome of ONWA's advocacy),[6] and the national Aboriginal Healing Foundation.[7] I show how tactical engagements with these new healing policies supported ongoing re-membering and assertions of Indigenous sovereignty over collective well-being, and the endurance of ONWA's collectivist vision among some frontline Indigenous service providers. I also attend to the constraints imposed by these policy developments, including increased pressure to individuate healing under neoliberalism, anticipated by Fontaine and to a lesser extent ONWA, and some unintended effects of these new biopolitical projects and how these played out in Ontario and nationally.

Neoliberal Self-Management, Reconciliation and Extending Biopolitical Tactics

In June 1994, Dalton McGuinty, Liberal opposition leader in the Ontario legislature, expressed his approval for the Aboriginal Healing and Wellness Strategy introduced by the New Democratic Party (NDP) government near the end of its one term in office: "I think we have to capitalize on the expertise, so to speak, of the Aboriginals themselves and to give them more control...in terms of dealing with and addressing their own particular problems" (Legislative Assembly of Ontario 1994). The NDP government's championing of the AHWS was partially motivated by their expressed commitment to respect Indigenous self-determination and cultivate nation-to-nation relationships, discussed in the previous chapter. But both McGuinty's approval and the language used alert us to how the establishment of this policy and its endurance under subsequent, overtly neoliberal Ontario governments can be understood in terms of its alignment with neoliberal rationality. The naturalization of the market inspired state actors to recognize Indigenous people in a new mode: as self-determining economic subjects, suitable for managing their own services informed by their own expertise, as well as "partnering" with resource extraction industries, such as mining, oil, and gas, in pursuit of the overarching neoliberal quest for endless economic growth.[8] This version of self-determination did not extend to the resurrection of Indigenous legal systems, as called for by ONWA (1989) in *Breaking Free*. As summed up by McGuinty, settler state actors' intention to "capitalize" on Indigenous expertise—to mobilize Indigenous knowledge in service delivery, with the goal of reducing public expenditure—aligns perfectly with the neoliberal maxim of reducing both state management and cost of public services. And yet funding under the AHWS enabled the establishment of ten Aboriginal Health Access Centres (AHACs), Indigenous-managed primary health care including both biomedical services and traditional healing, as well as nine Indigenous women's shelters, during the 1990s and early 2000s. I analyze these as Indigenized biopolitical infrastructure: structures and spaces for propagating knowledge, discourses, and practices aimed at promoting and protecting Indigenous life.

Waasegiizhig Nanaandawe'iyewigamig opened in Kenora in 1998 with AHWS funds. Anita Cameron (Ojibway and German) was the organization's executive director from its opening until her retirement in 2021. In a 2011 conversation with me and her colleague Tina Armstrong, she conveyed the significance of the centre as an Indigenous project with wide-ranging implications for Anishinaabe well-being and social and political life. There are similarities with ONWA's early work: an inclusive vision of membership spanning First Nations living both on- and off-reserve and Métis, with women's interests explicitly identified in the development of the project. Also similar to ONWA's work, for those who have led the establishment of the centre, it is understood as a forum for envisioning and enacting self-determined, Indigenous models for collective and individual health and wellness centred on Anishinaabe knowledge. As Anita explained, "for us it was not just having a cultural component in the programming, but how does the *whole organization* reflect the people who own and operate it." While the AHWS policy framework required funded health centres to include a "traditional" component, Anita observes that this component sometimes is reduced to an "add-on" to a health care model shaped primarily by dominant Canadian values. Not so at Waasegiizhig. Tina, a social worker from Bearskin Lake, long-time Kenora resident and program manager for Waasegiizhig, added, "What we're doing (here) is a way of living, it's a way of being, it's about principles, it's about values. We're just a little bit more thorough about appreciating what we have…What we do is very simple, nothing mystical, nothing magical, but it's *everyday*—not just on Sunday, and not scripted."[9]

Still, as Anita acknowledges, what it means to work as an Indigenous health care organization in the settler-colonial context is not always self-evident. She explained that she and others managing the work of the organization are clear on the principles of self-determination, but the substance of the work needs to be figured out as they go. The challenge of how to incorporate both biomedical and Anishinaabe approaches is ever-present and not easily resolved. For instance, while there is a clear commitment to maintaining roles such as "traditional healing coordinator" to enable access to a range of non-biomedical Indigenous care providers and promote Anishinaabe values and lifeways, there are ongoing concerns about how the existence of such positions might absolve other health care workers from doing the work of building relationships with Elders and Healers. In practice, Anita has observed that those trained in biomedicine tend to "default to their comfort zone." Anita recalled an early conversation with Madeline Skead and one of her daughters who was slated to give a presentation on the topic of "integration" of biomedical and traditional healing. Anita remembered Madeline finally blurting out, "you just can't, you just can't integrate." Reflecting on this, Anita explained, "The best we can achieve is some sort of balance, because 'integration' implies everyone does everything. Nurse practitioners who aren't qualified to practice traditional medicine...shouldn't try."[10] This perspective is similar to concern expressed in academic literature about overly simplistic invocations of "integration" that disregard potentially irreconcilable ontologies and epistemologies between Indigenous and biomedical healing systems (Gone 2010).

Waasegiizhig and other centres offer a structure and some resources for relationships and conversations that strive for balanced, collaborative approaches to care. During my visit in May 2011, I met Kathy Bird, a Cree community health nurse and herbalist from Matootoo Lake in Peguis First Nation, central Manitoba, who had been collaborating with Waasegiizhig workers for over a decade. While she relayed her history to me, Kathy was storing medicinal plants in large jars placed on shelves and covered by a cloth. These, she told me, were gathered from all parts of Canada, and would be used to prepare creams and ointments. Trained by a traditional Healer named Pinaukuim, a Blackfoot from Blood reserve, in the 1980s, Kathy now provides training for health professionals at Waasegiizhig and elsewhere. She described increasing demand for both training in plant medicine and her healing practice, which focuses on helping people living with diabetes, maternal and child health needs, and supporting general wellness. She divides her time between the Health Sciences Centre in Winnipeg and her home community. When we met, she had treated sixteen people during her visit to Kenora. Despite the evident popularity and effectiveness of her healing services, she described ongoing struggles with funding, and expressed the wish that Manitoba had a provincial policy for Indigenous health like the Ontario AHWS.[11]

These accounts demonstrate that the Indigenous self-management enabled by the AHWS is a biopolitical tactic that can work to align public resources with the physical and social reproduction of Indigenous societies and healing knowledge.[12] For many of those I spoke with who work in Indigenous-controlled urban service delivery, this infrastructure is a powerful sign of self-determination that neoliberal self-management ideology has enabled, however imperfectly. The growing number of Indigenous service agencies in Ontario cities has in some cases helped to create a critical mass of advocates better able to influence municipal policy. As one contributor to a 2009 review of the AHWS elaborated, "When I came into this position... there wasn't one reference, not one word in their city plan that had anything to do with Aboriginal people. They had a large population in the city, and it was due to the fact that you had strong structures that were able to build and help each other and move forward that we were able to change the city. And it was a very deliberate move to do that. It was our politicking and coming together that made that change" (Joint Management Committee AHWS 2009, 86). These real, material changes—growing Indigenous infrastructure, visibility, employment in public services—are discernable in many Ontario cities and significant to those who have benefitted. However constrained, there is no doubt that these biopolitical tactics enable the persistence of Indigenous lives under challenging conditions.

But the rhetoric of *self-determination* surrounding neoliberal settler state allocations of funds for Indigenous services belies the reality that *self-management* is subject to multiple constraints inhibiting the full realization of Indigenous visions for service delivery (Moreton-Robinson 2009). The tendency for neoliberal setter colonial institutions to reproduce racialized policy that undermines Indigenous well-being is well illustrated by the systematic underfunding of the AHWS. From its outset, funding was below par with comparable public services not focused specifically on Indigenous users, such as Community Health Centres, starkly illustrating that reduced expenditure is the primary goal driving this state recognition of Indigenous self-determining subjects. Successive Ontario governments continued this pattern and thus "capitalized" further on the neoliberal devolution of Indigenous services. By 2008, when the Liberal government under McGuinty had governed Ontario for five years, many AHACs and Healing Lodges were at capacity with waitlists, and there had been no increases to their operating budgets for fourteen years. This meant programs had to be reduced or cut to cover increases in wages, utility costs, building maintenance, and technological updates, while staff diverted time from service provision and community relations to seek new sources of funding (Joint Management Committee AHWS

2009, 7, 68–69). Further, failure of successive provincial governments to allocate capital funding to support increasing demand prevented construction of new facility space for new clients and programs and acquisition of suitable outdoor space for ceremony (104, 105).

Since re-membering entails reciprocal recognition among Indigenous people and often the creation of "irreconcilable spaces of Indigeneity" (Garneau 2016, 23), it is also problematic that the self-management ethos driving the creation of AHACs didn't translate into significantly increased employment of Indigenous health professionals. This was due at least in part to the lack of parity with the dominant health care system. In 2010 and 2011 workers from AHACs in Ottawa, Kenora, and Hamilton described to me an entrenched racialized division of labour: all non-accredited and paraprofessional staff identified as Indigenous, but virtually all clinical professionals were non-Indigenous. Perhaps most ironically given McGuinty's previous public expression of commitment to Indigenous knowledge, conditions of long-term state neglect have led to exploitation of knowledge holders such as Elders and traditional Healers, many of whom live in poverty while providing services. One Elder quipped, "My gas tank is full of tobacco" (Joint Management Committee AHWS 2009,103). When the ceremony of gifting the sacred plant of tobacco in appreciation of knowledge is carried out under such conditions, can this still be characterized as re-membering in the sense of social repair and resurgence enabled by traditional knowledge? Or does this amount to systematic capitalizing on and undermining of Indigenous social relations and knowledge systems under the auspices of care?

Another way these new healing projects may work against re-membering is the urban-centric distribution of AHACs, reflecting the long-standing jurisdictional division of responsibilities for Indigenous health care between the provincial and federal governments. One of the unintended consequences of the AHWS, then, may be to exacerbate inequities and social stratification within Indigenous nations and communities, and inadvertently reinforce the mid-century settler-colonial notion that Indigenous relocation from reserves to urban spaces is both desirable and inevitable. Eight of the ten provincially funded AHACs are in urban centres, and while clinicians at some centres, including Waasegiizhig, will visit patients on reserves, most primary health care on reserves continues to be organized by the federal government and undermined by high staff turnover and inconsistent availability. In Treaty 3 territory, more than half a century after the 1965 march demanding better services and infrastructure, there is still no public transportation between the Treaty 3 reserves and Kenora. What *has* changed is that many families on reserves now own cars, reducing the impetus to advocate for equitable transportation services. For those whose income level, disability, or age prevents car ownership, there are limited options for getting to town to access services: pay an unaffordable fee to a neighbour or taxi company for a ride, fake a medical emergency to access free transportation, or spend an entire day walking. Those living in a fly-in First Nation in Treaty 9 territory further north lack even these limited options.

For all of the challenges encountered by the AHACs, they have fared better than interventions addressing family violence, which Indigenous community leaders who participated in the development of the AHWS had expected to offer a meaningful response to ONWA's (1989) *Breaking Free* report.[13] Several well-placed commentators spoke about this imbalance in 2009, pointing out that while health interventions are relevant to alleviating family violence, they are far from sufficient: "This is a real failing because they've not really focused any resources towards [addressing family violence], and just throwing money generally into mental health isn't going to do it. I think there needs to be a concerted systemic change to focus on this particular issue" (Joint Management Committee AHWS 2009, 83). Another noted, "our vision [was] to specifically address family violence. However, because family violence is not hot, not a pleasant topic, it's controversial, people have watered it down somewhat and are preferring to do other services. Although everything they're doing may assist them with family violence, they're not truly addressing the violence issues" (83). At the same time, the sensitivity and complexity of the issue makes it more challenging to monitor the impact of even existing AHWS services in preventing and responding to family violence, limiting availability of quantified data demonstrating cost-effectiveness demanded by neoliberal policymakers.

Organizers of Indigenous women's shelters not funded by the AHWS also struggled during this period. In 1993 two Indigenous social workers established Minwaashin Lodge in Ottawa, the federal capital of Canada located on traditional Algonquin territory, to provide shelter and healing for women and children. Castille Troy, who began working at Minwaashin as a volunteer and later became executive director, recalled that they nearly closed on two occasions due to insufficient funds.[14] Despite their best efforts at adapting proposals to suit trending interests among non-governmental donors such as the United Way and the Trillium Foundation, it took fourteen years to secure core funding for the shelter. After the provincial government under Premier Mike Harris publicly declared that they would not fund addiction services, creating an addictions counsellor position became virtually impossible.

In oral history shared with me in 2010, Corene Cheeseman reflected on the changes she'd witnessed over the course of her long history of involvement with the Hamilton Regional Indian Centre: first as a board member, later, after completing her college education, as an employee. She described how activities at the centre shifted from predominantly informal social gatherings, such as playing pool, quilting, and seniors' lunches, to a host of structured interventions aimed at specific ends, such as Native Basic Job Readiness.[15] Recall that for Charles Copenace and other founders of the Ne-Chee Friendship Centre in Kenora in the 1970s, one of its main purposes was to offer a "space for visiting," asserting the value of a vibrant Indigenous society in the midst of ongoing racism, exclusion, and violence in urban centres. Under neoliberal settler colonialism, the very success of some Indigenous organizations in attracting program funding by aligning themselves with self-management and other neoliberal priorities may have squeezed out re-membering as revitalization of Indigenous social relations, as understood by earlier advocates.

Informal social spaces enable everyday interpersonal interactions that help individuals to constitute a sense of connection and belonging, including spontaneous practices of re-membering. As Indigenized urban biopolitical infrastructure has expanded, such space for reciprocal, relational subjectification has apparently shrunk in many Ontario cities. Instead, many of the structured programs attracting funding under neoliberalism are linked to state actors' goals of subjectifying Indigenous people as more efficient, responsible economic actors and managers of their own health and well-being. Compared with the 1970s and 1980s, services in subsequent decades are more likely to have extensive reporting requirements and be delivered by workers with higher or professional education credentials. These shifts have led to a more stratified relationship between those providing and those using services. In earlier models discussed in chapters 1 and 2, we saw how re-membering through state-sponsored programs worked to assert the relational subjectivity of workers and challenge the dominant model whereby service providers subjectify service users as problems. The Ne-Chee Street Patrol valued life experience and language skills as important worker qualifications, and workers such as Charles could end up as service users. Indigenous self-management under neoliberalism suffered the increasing pressures of accreditation, performance indicators, and audit culture, which alongside economic modes of subjectification created new constraints to re-membering.

Alongside neoliberalism, long-standing Indigenous advocacy for publicly funded healing gained traction through a second global shift in dominant political ideology: the rise of reconciliation politics aimed at redressing historic injustices. The proliferation of national reconciliation projects in the late twentieth century can be linked to intensifying socioeconomic and political inequities caused by neoliberal ideology's global dominance (Blackburn 2007; Feldman 2002; Sundar 2004; R.A. Wilson 2003). As Nandini Sundar notes, reconciliation politics hold out a particular appeal for neoliberal states because "in the process of attributing culpability to others, including their *past* selves, through apologies and truth commissions, powerful states often conceal their own culpability in the present" (2004, 157). For the settler society whose collective conscience is haunted by the illegitimacy of their existence, reconciliation politics extend the promise of national redemption without requiring transformative social and political change. As a neoliberal incarnation of the politics of recognition, settler state actors' expressions of sympathy for Indigenous people in the name of reconciliation flow along the unchallenged racialized hierarchy underlying colonization, reasserting the authority of the settler state to define Indigenous suffering as legitimate or otherwise. It's unsurprising therefore to encounter multiple Indigenous critiques of how reconciliation has played out in Canada. Of particular relevance for the history of re-membering is the critique that Canada's reconciliation policy has prioritized the reconciliation of Indigenous Peoples with Canada over restoration of relations within Indigenous families and communities (Corntassel and Holder 2008), precisely what I've been describing as re-membering. I elaborate on this problematic below with reference to the Indian Residential Schools Settlement Agreement.[16]

Such well-founded critique of reconciliation politics can be counterbalanced with acknowledgement that the reciprocal recognition at the heart of Indigenous re-membering was not entirely displaced by state recognition, mainly because of support from the Aboriginal Healing Foundation. Indeed, while the AHF was created under the *Gathering Strength* policy (Department of Indian Affairs and Northern Development 1997), the settler state's first foray into reconciliation politics and a response to legal threats and the Royal Commission on Aboriginal Peoples (discussed further below), it is also the culmination of many years of Indigenous advocacy well beyond organizing focused on justice for residential school Survivors. My conversations with federal policymakers confirmed that the residential school legal cases and RCAP's report were not the only antecedents to the creation of the AHF: Indigenous advocates had for years been inundating First Nations and Inuit Health Branch with demands to fund community-based, collective healing programs. Prior to *Gathering Strength*, Mike DeGagné executive director of the AHF, recalled in our conversation, Health Canada bureaucrats were flummoxed by proposals centred on the work of Elders and holistic approaches to healing that excluded accredited health professionals: "they had no idea what to do with [those proposals that] didn't fit the criteria for either addiction or mental health, so they put them in a big pile and...there was nothing we could do."[17] According to Al Garman at First Nations and Inuit Health Branch, prior to the establishment of the AHF, Health Canada officials had intended to press Cabinet to commit six or seven million dollars towards long-term professional mental health care for on-reserve Indigenous communities; these funds were eventually reallocated to the AHF. Garman speculated that the work of the AHF may have "in a sense offset the need for professional services."[18]

At Minwaashin Lodge in Ottawa, whose focus on supporting Indigenous women fleeing violence and often struggling with addictions does not align well with neoliberal funding priorities, the AHF funded four positions, including an Elder and traditional Healer, beginning in 2000. Re-membering through reconstructing intergenerational relations among women has been a focus of the AHF-supported work there. A healing circle for residential school Survivors facilitated by an Elder from Whitefish River First Nation enabled women to visit that community and participate in various ceremonies, and later construct their own Sweat Lodge on land outside of Ottawa. Having learned about their role as grandmothers, including responsibilities towards their families and communities, they became known as the Grandmothers Group. Many members went on to become respected community leaders and Elders in their own right, some working in their home reserve communities, others in Ottawa. Irene Lindsay, a Cree Elder and Healer, was one of the original members of the group. When we met in 2010, she was working at Minwaashin Lodge. Irene described the focus of her work as supporting other grandmothers to assume their traditional roles as teachers and advisors to younger women, "extended grandmothers in the community." She also worked directly with younger women, many descendants of residential school Survivors, through talking circles, individual counselling, and crafting sessions. Irene has observed that relationships between older and younger women often develop spontaneously during shared activities, such as crafting powwow regalia and jewellery, echoing accounts shared in chapters 1 and 2 of re-membering decades earlier when Indigenous social connections were rekindled during informal conversations around the Drum and teaching of traditional crafts.[19] Indigenous actors have demonstrated their persistence in navigating the shifting terrain of liberal settler colonialism, including the rise of reconciliation politics, to enact long-standing commitments to restore intergenerational relations. But consistent with the goal of "closure" central to reconciliation politics, AHF funding for Minwaashin Lodge and thousands of other healing projects was time-limited, as I discuss further below.

Individuation as Biopolitical Tactic

In 1965, when civil rights to a comprehensive set of public services was still a dominant framework in Canadian politics, it made sense for Treaty 3 Anishinaabeg to demand public transportation services between Kenora and reserves, as described in chapter 1. But in over a decade of visiting, since 2011, I've not heard anyone mention lack of public transportation services as a social and political issue, not because safe and affordable transport is no longer needed but because, as a public service, it has become virtually unthinkable in the current neoliberal context.[20] Prior to the 1990s, urban Indigenous actors could sometimes successfully (re)claim public resources to develop services for their communities because of the then-dominant Keynesian liberal orthodoxy that framed universal public services as smart economic policy. Under late twentieth-century neoliberalism, state provisions once understood as basic citizenship entitlements were "reconfigured as temporary gifts" (Strakosch 2015, 39). Like others seeking to claim public resources managed by a neoliberal state, Indigenous actors were compelled to adapt their biopolitical tactics to this new policy context. But for Indigenous Peoples, these new tactics carry particular social and political risks because of potential alignment with long-standing modes of settler-colonial domination, including paternalism and social dismemberment through individuation.

In this section, I show how during the 1990s and early 2000s, Indigenous biopolitical actors in Ontario increasingly adapted quests for healing resources to align with at least one of two tactical pathways: first, an economic rationality, also described as "responsibilization," whereby services aim to subjectify users as self-managing economic actors, such as employment readiness, child development, and certain mental health programs; and second, irrefutable moral claims that render particular categories of victim worthy, even amidst austerity, by appealing to liberal humanitarianism and "compassionate conservatism" (Berlant 2004; Fassin 2012). Both pathways are predicated on individuation, by which I mean creating subjects who are perceived (and may come to perceive themselves) as fully autonomous actors detached from a collective, and instilling an exaggerated sense of an individual's ability to act in their own self-interest to transcend structural barriers. Neoliberal responsibilization is predicated on a different understanding of individual responsibility than that contained in some Indigenous teachings on healing and well-being that focus on the individual's responsibilities in the context of relationships within the collective, such as the work of the late Métis psychologist Joseph Couture (2013), or men's discussions about gendered and other interpersonal violence in the 1970s, depicted in chapter 1. I analyze the emergence of individuation as an Indigenous biopolitical tactic as a reaction against two significant developments in 1990s public policy and linked discourse: massive neoliberal cuts to collective services, and increasingly salient moralistic rhetoric vilifying those most in need, particularly the unhoused and those dependent on welfare income and/or struggling with addictions.

    A racialized version of this vilification is demonstrated by research on homelessness in the Ontario city of Sudbury in 2001. This analysis describes the significant over-representation of Indigenous people among the homeless while explaining homelessness as resulting from personal problems of substance use, interpersonal conflict, and economic poverty, rather than state failure to ensure an adequate supply of affordable housing (Menzies 2005). Discourse framing homelessness as individual moral failure has significant social and political effects, including channelling public resentment towards the unhoused as scapegoats, legitimating cuts to public services previously understood as basic entitlements of citizenship, and diverting attention from state culpability—in this case, successive federal governments who shirked responsibility for housing provision, leading to decades of under-investment in housing stock. When neoliberal vilification is applied particularly to Indigenous people, as was often the case in Canada during the 1990s, it discursively reinvigorates old racist tropes of Indigenous dysfunction. In this climate of neoliberal morality legitimating austerity, urban service providers struggled to provide care for the growing number of unhoused Indigenous people in Ontario cities.

I argue that a discourse on colonialism as etiology of Indigenous suffering—the invocation of histories of colonization to explain contemporary social suffering—emerged in part as a tactic to deflect this intensifying, paternalistic blame and vilification under neoliberal public policy. ONWA's *Breaking Free* report, Fontaine's CBC interview in 1990, and the AHWS introduced into public discourse the understanding that Indigenous histories of colonization are important for making sense of health and social issues in the present. This analysis held out the promise of perhaps attracting public resources in the increasingly threatening climate created by neoliberal policy and overt anti-Indigenous racism in political and populist discourse of the early 1990s. Such increasingly blatant racism was nationally apparent in media coverage of the Kanehsatà:ke Resistance (aka Oka Crisis) in 1990, and again in 1993, when the right-wing federal Reform Party, whose members freely used racist language, attracted significant voter support.[21]

In the early 1990s, Anishnawbe Health Toronto developed a street patrol to serve the growing number of Indigenous people living on the street in the city, with limited funding pieced together from municipal and provincial sources, "largely run on volunteer time, with donated vehicles," as long-time Executive Director Joe Hester explained to me.[22] The street patrol was pivotal in enabling access to primary health care for vulnerable people, many struggling with alcohol, solvent, or drug abuse as well as lack of housing. But by the late 1990s, given the growing number of people in need, Anishnawbe

Health Toronto leadership were considering how to move beyond harm reduction and crisis management towards a permanent resolution of Indigenous homelessness. Increasingly salient government and public discussions of mental health suggested a possible path forward, one that might lead to funding. They recognized this opportunity and began work on a mental health strategy. Joe recalled, "It was *very difficult*. We had to make a wholesale change, from helping people survive on the street, to helping them escape homelessness—to do this we needed to respond to individual addictions and mental health issues."[23] Indigenous service organizations were at the leading edge of discourse advancing an understanding that many people with an addiction also live with mental illness, often undiagnosed, and that their addiction is partially driven by their efforts to cope with the mental illness (sometimes described as "self-medicating"), as expressed by the growing circulation of concepts of "concurrent disorders," "dual-disordered," and "co-morbidity" in mental health care discourse.

I argue that it isn't a coincidence that Indigenous and allied actors in health and social services started to embrace mental health discourse in this period, amidst growing socioeconomic inequities and massive government cuts to services once providing safety nets for the most vulnerable, some of which were Indigenous-managed and supported re-membering. Clearly, this was a savvy response to the significant withdrawal of funding, particularly from addiction services. But the growing number of people reporting problems with mental health at multiple urban Indigenous agencies needs to be analyzed as the result of not only massive historical trauma but also intensified structural violence under neoliberal settler colonialism in the late twentieth century.

Growing public discussion of residential school experiences in the 1990s often included the deleterious mental health effects on Survivors. Social worker Leslie Saunders recalled a gradual reframing of addiction as symptomatic of underlying mental illness among members of the marginally housed Indigenous community she worked with in downtown Toronto during this period: "Prior to that it was... like everyone was pretending that everything was okay, you know.

And it was just about drinking and having fun. 'Maybe we drink too much,' they would sort of describe, but it was never connected to anything. It was never described as a method of making oneself feel better. Today, they talk very freely about 'This is what I do to feel better.' So there's an acknowledgement that something has happened that you need to feel better about. You need to sooth yourself."[24] When the Ontario government made funds available for Aboriginal mental health several years later, Anishnawbe Health Toronto management was poised to implement their mental health strategy, enabling them to expand services delivered by traditional Healers, Elders, psychiatrists, and psychologists, and establish a residential treatment site.

The availability of this funding for Anishnawbe Health Toronto and other service providers is at least partially explained by how the idea of colonialism as etiological of contemporary suffering can align with neoliberal logic, reducing the complex issue of Indigenous homelessness and mental illness in the context of *ongoing* settler-colonial dismemberment to a narrow focus on changing individual behaviour, summed up by Joe as "helping people manage their lives better."[25] This analysis locates the origins of Indigenous mental illness in historic colonial structures, specifically experiences of residential schools, but does not address the effects of ongoing, neoliberal settler colonialism. Loss of affordable secure housing and basic social supports, for instance, can make the difference between a vulnerable person on a low income eking out a modest but meaningful life in the city, or ending up acutely unwell and self-medicating on the streets, at risk of incarceration or other institutionalization (Hopper 1988). For Indigenous people, even more than this was at stake in the decimation of Indigenous-managed housing that supports re-membering: in the words of one administrator, "preservation and promotion of our languages and culture, and our proper social relations" (National Aboriginal Housing Committee 1993, 7, quoted in Menzies 2005, 47). In the 1990s the federal government terminated two major Indigenous housing programs: the Rural and Native Housing Program that had enabled Indigenous ownership of almost nine thousand homes in towns and cities over nearly thirty years, and the Urban Native Housing Program, which enabled construction of over ten thousand units (Menzies 2005, 43, 47). More than an early example of devolved service delivery, Indigenous-administered housing programs were often foundational to creating urban spaces for re-membering. As discussed in chapter 3, Marlene Pierre and other women in Thunder Bay were able to establish Beendigen in 1978 because they could access shelter through the Native People of Thunder Bay Development Corporation, the non-profit housing corporation launched by activists working out of the Friendship Centre in 1973. When healing discourse centres an understanding of a past colonialism as individually embodied without simultaneously attending to ongoing social dismemberment resulting from contemporary public policy, such as massive cuts to Indigenous housing, it individuates and thus depoliticizes Indigenous social suffering in the present.

The pattern of individuating interventions displacing established programs enabling re-membering continued in the domain of Indigenous children's services. In 1995 the Li'l Beavers program for children run by Friendship Centres was cancelled by the incoming Ontario Progressive Conservative government of Mike Harris, whose populist "common sense revolution" platform emphasized cutting state expenditure. Since the mid-1970s Li'l Beavers had focused on re-membering and relational subjectification: cultivating children's social relations with their peers and respected adult members of their communities, including Elders, Friendship Centre workers, and knowledge keepers, and offering meaningful recreation activities (Ontario Federation of Indigenous Friendship Centres 2015). A decentralized program structure encouraged individual Friendship Centres to autonomously develop activities consistent with their local communities' expertise and priorities, which translated into significant community support and participation by parents and caregivers. The Ne-Chee Friendship Centre in Kenora was one of the early sites where Li'l Beavers was established, around the same time as the Street Patrol discussed in chapter 2. It is noteworthy that of sixteen Li'l Beavers programs in urban centres across Ontario, most were north of North Bay, in regions where Indigenous people make up a much larger proportion of the population and smaller urban centres are situated close to many First Nations reserves.

By the time Li'l Beavers was eliminated by Harris's provincial government, the Ontario Federation of Indigenous Friendship Centres had already navigated new funding opportunities for child services. These emergent opportunities resulted from the neoliberal re-emergence of the "child development" paradigm, which synthesized assumptions about the inherent "culture of poverty" (associated with the Head Start paradigm from 1960s United States social policy) with the implicit, neoliberal goal of subjectifying children as future self-managing economic subjects who will be minimally reliant on public services.[26] Sylvia Maracle, former executive director of the Ontario Federation of Indigenous Friendship Centres, described conversations about healing among Indigenous leadership in Ontario in the early 1990s, in which mental health, child development and cost-effectiveness rhetoric became entangled:

> There were a few meetings that I participated in [where we discussed] how good would this be for our kids, how amazing would it be for children to be raised in homes where there wasn't addictions, where there wasn't family violence, where there wasn't issues in terms of related behaviours, of criminal justice and things like that. And so, that seemed to be a very powerful motivator, and maybe it was sort of articulated too well. And the fact of the matter is that's what Cabinet did grab on. So we're trying to say, there are all these savings to the system if we look at treating people from a mental health perspective, and I remember using the analogy of...the onion, you peel back one thing and it's the next, you peel back, you peel back, let's get right to the core of some of these things and try to deal with them.[27]

The Ontario Federation of Indigenous Friendship Centres took tactical advantage of federal interventions addressing children and mental health, which included the Community Action Program for Children, the Canada Prenatal Nutrition Program, as well as Brighter Futures for First Nations children on reserves. As Sylvia explained to me, she was fully cognizant of the cynical political motivations of the federal government's focus on children: "it was a way for a government that remember had come in, had made *massive* cuts, slashes [to redeem themselves]." Her comment is consistent with analyses of the heightened significance of state actors' moral claims under neoliberalism, including the ascent of reconciliation politics (Sundar 2004). A federal-provincial agreement enabled the Ontario NDP government, who "wanted to put their own brand on things," to select agencies that would receive this federal money, and the province agreed to allocate 30 per cent of the funds to urban Indigenous communities. Sylvia recalled how the Friendship Centre in Sudbury dramatically expanded their services through being designated as a "Better Beginnings" pilot centre: "the Friendship Centre had twenty staff one day and fifty staff the next day. And they were doing this school-community liaison... getting kids ready to be in school, and dealing with families who were having problems with CAS [Children's Aid Society, i.e., child welfare services], and addictions...believing that if we could give these children better beginnings...they would be able to perform better, and be better."[28]

In my analysis, I want to both acknowledge the political savvy of Indigenous leaders who navigated the neoliberal fiscal climate to successfully channel resources to expand services and employment in their communities, and raise questions about unintended consequences that these individuating healing interventions may entail for Indigenous societies, polities, and futures. It is unsurprising that Indigenous community leaders championing healing would seek to access funds for child development programs. Theoretically, asserting Indigenous control over programs for children powerfully challenges settler colonialism, given that children were (and continue to be) the targets of some of the most egregious interventions aimed at dismembering Indigenous societies, including the residential schools and the ongoing child welfare system. Further, adults' healing trajectories are entangled with children's well-being in complex ways: many children were (and continue to be) apprehended by child welfare authorities while parents were drinking, while adults entering residential addiction treatment programs risk losing their children because of challenges in arranging long-term alternate child care.

But I argue that deep skepticism is warranted regarding the motivations of neoliberal settler state actors "investing" in Indigenous children, and that the child development paradigm can provide cover for contemporary modes of biopolitical dismemberment. Child development is predicated on normative models of growth and learning with the explicit goal of making Indigenous children "perform better," not as members of their families and nations, but within the dominant education system and ultimately as workers and consumers. This goal is pursued through surveilling not only children but their caregivers through early childhood development programs, in which workers are encouraged to identify, correct, and report emergent behavioural problems, potentially marking families for further state intrusion. Former participants have noted critically that unlike the Li'l Beavers program, the new child development programs "target or label" children as "at-risk or high-risk" (Ontario Federation of Indigenous Friendship Centres 2015). Despite the best efforts of workers, dominant values and goals influence program directions in ways that may contradict community priorities, for instance by presuming parenting deficiencies and excluding extended family members, as ethnographic research on child development programs for Indigenous families has demonstrated (Miskimmin 2007, 2012). Neoliberal ideology is explicitly opposed to public resources supporting long-term, collective services, precisely the conditions that enabled earlier Indigenous community organizers to cultivate re-membering at the margins of the welfare state. Under neoliberal settler colonialism, terminating a popular and well-established community-initiated program like Li'l Beavers, which focused on relational subjectification of children as *members* of urban

Indigenous kinship networks and communities, is entirely consistent with individuation as a mode of social dismemberment.

When "Healing" Becomes Social Dismemberment

In 2005 white physician Jill Murray (a pseudonym) was hired to work as a general practitioner physician at Wabano Centre for Aboriginal Health in Ottawa, one of the AHACs established under the Ontario AHWS. She and other members of the clinical team (all but one non-Indigenous) received minimal formal training on Indigenous health, but Jill recalled that one of the first things she was told after being hired was that as a general practitioner, "You have to know about residential schools."[29] What the Wabano clinicians were expected to know is now common knowledge in Canada: that the residential school system, run by Christian churches on behalf of the Canadian government from 1867 to 1996, constituted sites for the attempted forced assimilation of thousands of Indigenous children, who suffered multiple forms of violence and neglect at the hands of the priests and nuns who ran the schools.

In the remainder of this chapter, I consider how and why a particular Indigenous experience of settler colonialism—trauma resulting from sexual and physical abuse in residential schools—became such a salient focal point for Indigenous and settler state biopolitical actors during the 1990s and 2000s. I trace the emergence and trajectory of a discourse on Survivors' singular embodiment of residential school histories through various national fora and policies at the interface of Indigenous biopolitical tactics and the settler state: the RCAP (1991–1996), the 1998 federal *Gathering Strength* policy, the negotiation of the Indian Residential Schools Settlement Agreement finalized in 2006, and the important work and untimely termination of the AHF (1998–2014). I argue that in Canadian public discourse, the figure of the traumatized residential school Survivor became a powerful synecdoche for a settler colonialism imagined as past event. I link the ascent of this synecdoche with Indigenous biopolitical tactics employing neoliberal tropes and rhetoric, including individuated victimhood and the marketization of suffering; systemic obstacles that prevented Survivors from advancing collective claims; and the alignment of this representation of Indigenous suffering with reconciliation politics and its appeals to many neoliberal state actors.

In a national forum held in Vancouver in 1993 as part of the RCAP, we can discern the trend for prominent Indigenous biopolitical actors and settler allies to advance discourse that describes suffering in individuated categories of victimhood and capitulates to the neoliberal discourse on scarce public resources. Most of the eighty-plus participants in the National Roundtable on Health and Social Issues were Indigenous health professionals (physicians, nurses, community health representatives, social workers, and administrators), alongside four Elders, Indigenous and non-Indigenous academics, and non-Indigenous health professionals (RCAP 1993), hosted by the RCAP commissioners.[30] RCAP was established by Brian Mulroney's Conservative government in 1991 at a historical moment when ongoing conflict between Indigenous Peoples and the settler state came into sharp relief for national and global audiences, via the Kanehsatà:ke Resistance, failure of the constitutional Meech Lake Accord, and mounting global criticism of Canada's Indigenous human rights violations.

A narrative shared early in the roundtable proceedings indicates that the expansion of Indigenous biopolitical tactics to include individuation was driven by neoliberal funding constraints. Anthropologist John O'Neil, the rapporteur for the roundtable, noted an emerging consensus among participants: "'colonialism' as a central explanation for current Aboriginal health conditions may have limited applicability" (RCAP 1993, 28). He bolstered this point by recounting a previous argument at a workshop in Australia between an unnamed anthropologist and Cree leader Eric Shirt, co-founder of two influential healing institutions that were among the first examples of late twentieth-century Indigenous biopolitical infrastructure in Canada, the Nechi Institute and Poundmaker's Lodge.[31] According to O'Neil, Shirt argued forcefully in favour of individualistic treatment programs for Indigenous alcohol abuse, against the anthropologist's social-historical perspective. Shirt's rationale was that governments are reluctant to fund programs based on a broad etiological model highlighting colonization's social effects because such programs have no clear endpoint. It's unclear whether Shirt's argument signalled an understanding that settler colonialism is ongoing in the present but this fact is unacceptable to settler state policymakers as a premise for programming. Perhaps he was invoking the challenges of providing quantified evidence of impact of interventions aimed at supporting complex social change, during a period when public funding was increasingly conditional on such evidence. What is clear is an implicit acknowledgement that neoliberalism had displaced the older, Keynesian model of lifelong entitlement to public services; so, to attract public funding, proponents of healing programs would be compelled to present their peoples' suffering as an individual phenomenon amenable to short-term interventions to align with neoliberal political ideology. In other words, both anthropologist O'Neil and Shirt, a long-standing leader in Indigenous healing programs, argued that the older, relational, collectivist understanding of re-membering was unlikely to gain traction in the neoliberal funding climate. New tactics were needed.

In apparent alignment with this doctrine, and a strikingly explicit process of discursively constructing biopolitical subjects, roundtable participants identified five groups whose needs "require targeted attention and specific policy frameworks" (RCAP 1993, 23). These were "victims of residential schools," "victims of sexual abuse and domestic violence," "children with fetal alcohol syndrome" (23), Indigenous people with AIDS, and those with disabilities. "Wounds inflicted by residential schools" (23) in need of healing were wounds of trauma: the ongoing psychic consequences of experiences endured many years before. As the rapporteur summarized, "Although the impact of residential schools on Aboriginal society must be considered in broader terms than health consequences, many [roundtable participants] linked their own and others' experiences in the residential schools to problems of alcohol abuse, suicide, and family violence in Aboriginal communities today" (23).

The shift from collectivist to individuating approaches to healing demonstrated by this list of prioritized categories of victims suggests a tacit acceptance of the neoliberal doctrine of scarcity—the false notion that wealthy liberal nations can't afford to provide basic services for all—and recourse to a discourse of innocent victimhood as a moral basis for claiming public resources. Echoing Phil Fontaine's CBC interview three years earlier, participants were primarily concerned with residential school experiences as etiological of individual trauma, foreshadowing a focus now hegemonic in public discourse. It is instructive to read this framing alongside the other classifications, given that the first three categories all underscore victims' innocence by explicit or implicit reference to a perpetrator: "victims of residential schools," "victims of sexual abuse and domestic violence," and "children with fetal alcohol syndrome" (implicitly, the victims of addicted mothers). Such representations of innocent victimhood invoke affective public responses associated with the "compassionate conservatism" of neoliberal morality (Berlant 2004), indicating Indigenous leaders' awareness that affectively compelling victimhood enables access to public resources during a period of fiscal austerity. As I discuss below, this tactic proved effective in leveraging state funds because of its alignment with dominant morality, Canadian torte law, and reconciliation politics. But it has had the unintended effect of partially displacing collective social and political analyses, meaning the experiences of families and nations are marginalized in favour of a narrow focus on individuated Survivors, understood as uniquely impacted by the residential schools, alongside a broader, increasingly pervasive understanding of colonialism as individually embodied, rather than embedded in Canadian structures and culture and continuing in the present. Representations of individuated Indigenous victims embodying a past colonialism now circulate widely in policy and public discourse, not only on residential schools but also Missing and Murdered Indigenous Women and Girls, and in the child welfare and criminal justice systems.

In the mid-1990s, some Indigenous commentators publicly disagreed with this emergent model of individual traumatized victims of residential schools as a category to be singled out for healing interventions, and expressed concerns about how this new paradigm might undermine collective struggles for well-being. Even the AFN produced a report that made the important argument that "Being traumatized is a deeply wounding experience [but] it does not mean that a child who attended residential school belongs to a distinct category of people... Drawing a distinction between those who attended residential school and those who did not trivializes the complexity of the experience of living as a First Nations person and of the impact of residential school" (1994, 79–81). Indigenous mental health professionals also urged caution about the implications of trauma as a central concept for Indigenous healing. Métis psychologist Joseph Couture (1994) refused to lend his authority to the emerging definition of Indigenous people as victims of colonialism and healing as primarily about ameliorating the suffering of individuated victims. He noted that trauma could be relevant for explaining symptoms experienced by some Indigenous people, including the incarcerated men with personal histories of long-term abuse with whom he had worked for many years.[32] But he is vociferous about the limitations of the trauma paradigm given its inattention to individual agency, which, he argues, is of great relevance to clinical work with Indigenous people. Couture does not dispute the relevance of recognizing Indigenous histories of "decades of colonial, oppressive control and damaging manipulations, compounded by overt and covert systemic racism" (5–6). However, he suggests that the Eurocentric paradigm of traumatized victimhood is inconsistent with "unequivocal traditional teachings regarding personal responsibility, for one's actions and their consequences, as these guide the maintenance of essential life-giving and restoring connections" (5–6). Couture insisted on the Indigenous moral principle that individuals should not be isolated from their relational social context, meaning that they are responsible for their actions and need to accept this responsibility as a prerequisite to healing. Similarly, Haudenosaunee psychologist Roland Chrisjohn, also writing in the mid-1990s with co-author Sherri Young, condemned both the focus on trauma in discourse on the residential schools and what he describes as "a therapy-driven approach to residential schooling" (Chrisjohn, Young, and Maraun 2006, 258).[33] He argued that the prevalent focus on trauma and individual psychological problems obscures recognition of the broader political context and the fact that the residential school system "was an assault on First Nations ways of life as a whole" (258). In a prescient note, he also problematized individual legal redress for residential school experiences: "isolating the experience removes the First Nations complainant and his or her complaint from an ideologically meaningful context" (259).

Couture's and Chrisjohn's critiques of trauma as definitive of Indigenous experience are consistent with older understandings of healing as re-membering: individual well-being as mutually determinant with Indigenous relationships and the social life of the collective. As Couture points out, this understanding of Indigenous life is predicated on reciprocity among all, and the expectation that individuals enact their own social and spiritual responsibilities as part of this process. Applying a universalized category like trauma as a basis for diagnosing and treating an individual removes them from this context, thus becoming a contemporary mode of social and cultural dismemberment. Chrisjohn's critique also points to the depoliticizing and de-historicizing effects of trauma discourse. The narrow focus on individual experiences of abuse as the most nefarious manifestation of the residential school system diverts attention from how this system was the expression of the foundational goal of settler state actors and allied missionaries to destroy Indigenous societies. This sleight of hand is particularly ironic, not just because this settler state goal endures in contemporary liberal form, but because state actors' purposeful undermining of collective approaches to healing precisely aligns with this goal.

The ascent of the trope of individuated embodiment of colonialism, advanced by RCAP and fuelled by trauma discourse, was also enabled by the Canadian legal system's core ethos predicated on liberal individualism: this system proved incapable of acknowledging complex, collective losses of family ties, language, and place-based Indigenous knowledge. Residential school Survivors using legal channels to pursue fair compensation for extensive social and cultural losses found that their suffering was artificially individuated and reified by the court as sexual assault (Blackburn 2012). Survivors may have initially hoped that their claims would be recognized on the basis of then-recent Indigenous legal victories in sovereignty claims during the 1970s and 1980s, such as the successful challenge to Eurocentric definitions of land ownership in *Calder v. Attorney-General of British Columbia* (1973). But litigation for residential school experiences differed from territorial sovereignty claims given the emphasis on injury and loss and consequent reliance on tort law, which narrows the conditions of recognition for injury (Blackburn 2012). Under the Canadian system, socio-cultural losses were considered legally significant only to the extent that they "aggravated the negative psychological effects of the abuse...suffered" (Blackburn 2012, 293), while the legal currency of childhood sexual abuse is predicated on the assumption that this form of suffering derives from universalized psychological effects, devoid of historical and political particularity. As of 2001, the only successful cases brought by Survivors were those in which the litigants had previously established in a criminal trial that sexual abuse had occurred (Lewellyn 2002). These legal proceedings constituted epistemological violence, dismissing the value of Indigenous histories, societies, and knowledge, and reinforcing the primacy of Canadian legal culture in defining Indigenous loss and suffering.

  The federal *Gathering Strength* policy, launched in January 1998, provided early evidence for the effectiveness of the emergent biopolitical tactic of individuating healing. Settler state actors embraced reconciliation politics with a new public discourse proclaiming their benevolence towards Indigenous victims embodying colonial pasts. Against the backdrop of mounting residential school court cases and demands for an overdue federal response to the RCAP report, Minister of Indian Affairs and Northern Development Jane Stewart (1998) delivered a "Statement of Reconciliation" at the launch of *Gathering Strength*. In this statement, she heralded residential school Survivors as citizens uniquely deserving of public sympathy and resources, and committed her government to work on a "healing strategy." Consistent with Canadian legal paradigms, Minister Stewart's statement established sexual and physical abuse as the benchmarks by which the settler state would recognize only certain Survivors of residential schools as legitimate victims worthy of public resources. She acknowledged, briefly, that the school system separated children from families and communities and prevented the transmission of Indigenous languages and knowledge, but it was only "the victims[,]... those individuals who experienced the tragedy of sexual and physical abuse," to whom she apologized on behalf of the Government of Canada: "To those of you who suffered *this tragedy* at residential schools, we are deeply sorry" (my emphasis). Like Prime Minister Stephen Harper's subsequent apology on June 11, 2008, Stewart's did not acknowledge state and church culpability.

Gathering Strength also established the AHF, an Indigenous-managed institution with a similarly constrained mandate to support "healing to address the legacy of physical and sexual abuse at residential schools" (Stewart 1998). As Mike DeGagné, the foundation's executive director, explained to me, this unequivocal directive narrowed the scope of fundable interventions: "We were limited to a very specific type of trauma, and a very specific type of program to deal with that trauma." In fact, AHF administrators were obliged to reject most of the proposals for healing projects submitted by Indigenous nations and community groups, which lacked this explicit prescribed focus. As Mike elaborated, "Even some basic things, like language programs and the very important role of language and culture, had to be left out, because that wasn't an acceptable part of our mandate...This was a way to limit [public expenditure]."[34] In this way, the biopolitics of funding "trained" Indigenous community organizers to reconceptualize healing as a narrow response to individuated experiences of past trauma.

Settler state actors were clearly motivated by their felt imperative to contain a massive legal threat while minimizing costs. The residential schools abuse reports also presented an opportunity to (re)assert paternalistic authority over Indigenous lives while striking a moral, caring stance. State forays into Indigenous healing under the banner of reconciliation appeared as liberal assertions of sympathy for Indigenous people, but translated into new modes of domination.

This slippage from care to control isn't without precedent: it was innovated by imperial humanitarians in settler colonies in the nineteenth century who claimed to be protecting vulnerable Indigenous people by containing them in missions and reserves, a moral stance subsequently leveraged by nascent settler states to assert their own fitness and responsibility to govern (Lester and Dussart 2014). I analyze this dynamic as settler humanitarianism (Maxwell 2017). Critics of the late twentieth-century global revival of humanitarian ideology point to how a singular focus on suffering victims aligns with neoliberal morality by diverting attention from the structural causes of suffering, while the process of parsing victims of certain kinds of suffering who should be entitled to public resources from those who should not constitutes another form of domination and violence (Fassin 2012; Petryna 2002; Ticktin 2011). Consistent with this book's premise that collective Indigenous well-being is a paradox in the liberal settler colony, we should not be surprised to find that contemporary liberal interventions under the banner of concern for Indigenous suffering continue to implicitly align with settler colonialism's enduring goal of eliminating Indigenous Peoples as distinct societies and polities.

Despite the establishment of the AHF, Minister Stewart's apology, and her plea to "negotiate not litigate," the volume of court actions brought by residential school Survivors against the government and the churches continued to grow. Between 2001 and 2006, negotiations toward an out-of-court settlement provided a site where political actors affiliated with the settler state, Indigenous governments, and the legal professions reformulated Indigenous healing in neoliberal and settler-humanitarian discourse (Maxwell 2017). These negotiations, led by the AFN under Chief Phil Fontaine, resulted in the controversial Indian Residential Schools Settlement Agreement, which solidified the terms by which the settler state would recognize "victims of residential schools."

The discourse used by the AFN in these negotiations continues the individuation inherent to the trauma paradigm, and runs counter to the ethos of Indigenous re-membering in several respects.[35] Collective experiences of social dismemberment and re-membering continue to be excluded, as they were under *Gathering Strength*.[36] Neoliberal market logic underpins the AFN's arguments, which advance a cost-effectiveness rationale and advocate for cash payments as healing, reproducing an understanding of human relationships as reducible to market values. And they make an explicit appeal to the national self-interest of the settler state, which, while perhaps an effective negotiating tactic, explicitly creates a central role for paternalistic settler actors in Indigenous healing. Heralding the imminent restoration of Canada's "reputation as a leader in the world for the respect of human rights" and the "health of the (Canadian) nation" through the paternalistic healing of Indigenous victims, the AFN leadership promised that cash reparations will enable Canadians to put closure to their reckoning with settler colonialism, reduced in this discourse from a structure and national culture continuous with the present to a singular past "experiment" (AFN 2004, 7, 17). In this "healing" intervention, the same state whose earlier incarnation authorized the residential school system became the adjudicator of those who suffered this system.

Unsurprisingly, many residential school Survivors experienced the interventions that flowed from the Indian Residential Schools Settlement Agreement—the assessment process, cash payments as compensation, even the work of the TRC—as new forms of colonial social dismemberment. They and other commentators have observed that to describe the process governed by the Indian Residential Schools Settlement Agreement as "healing" is an egregious misnomer. In a survey of Survivors conducted by the AHF, only about one-quarter of recipients described cash payments in terms suggesting the possibility for positive transformation, such as a meaningful symbol of public recognition of their suffering, admission of government wrongdoing, or an important step towards reconciliation (Reimer 2010a). Many rejected the assumption that cash payments would be healing, instead equating the payments with capitulation to dominant interests, while some concluded that "to settle for individual monetary compensation was misguided and insufficient" (Reimer 2010a, 93–94). Such critiques continued to be expressed during TRC hearings, with many commentators noting the "retraumatizing and dehumanizing" effects of the Independent Assessment Process for those who sought compensation for sexual and physical abuse (Molema 2016, 141).[37]

Even prior to the TRC hearings, extensive evidence of compelling need for ongoing support for Survivors, their families, and communities was presented to successive Liberal and Conservative federal governments, who further undermined Indigenous re-membering by refusing to support the continuation of the AHF.[38] In 2009 an evaluation report commissioned by the AHF to assess progress in healing since the settlement agreement concluded "healing from trauma experienced at residential schools has just started. Communities require long-term funding, more training for staff in the communities, more service providers to deal with increased demand, and additional accessible facilities" (Reimer 2010b, iv).[39] The year before AHF was terminated, an independent evaluation by Indian and Northern Affairs Canada (INAC) (2009) strongly recommended an extension. Like previous reports, INAC's described the many successes of the organization, and that the Common Experience Payment and Independent Assessment Process, far from inherently "healing," had the effect of increasing the need for supportive programs. INAC officials reasonably anticipated that yet more demand would be generated through the work of the forthcoming TRC. TRC Chair Justice Murray Sinclair publicly stated that the AHF should continue to function for the duration of the TRC, at a minimum (CBC News 2010). The INAC report also described the very limited prospects of AHF-supported programs securing funding from other sources, given a lack of funding agencies with overlapping mandates. The Harper government not only excluded new funding for the AHF from its March 2010 budget; they deliberately withheld from Parliament INAC's evaluation report recommending an extension of funding until March 5, 2010, the day *after* the budget when new funding might have been approved.[40] Rather than extend the AHF's mandate, the government allocated $65.9 million towards Health Canada programs for former residential school students and their families (CBC News 2010).

The systemic underfunding and premature termination of the AHF is evidence that the re-membering and Indigenous intellectual production it supported challenged the settler-colonial order, while the Harper government's reassignment of the healing mandate from a highly effective Indigenous-managed institution to a settler state bureaucracy is a "therapeutic strategy" (Humphrey 2005, 205) to belittle Indigenous Peoples' capacity to care for their own by reasserting illegitimate settler state sovereignty over Indigenous lives. These accounts reinforce the critique that state interventions under the rubric of reconciliation prioritized relations between Indigenous Peoples and Canada over restoration of relations within Indigenous families and communities (Corntassel, Chaw-win-is, and T'lakwadzi 2009), but don't diminish the significance of what the AHF accomplished during its absurdly constrained sixteen years. As well as channelling scarce resources to grassroots Indigenous re-membering in a diverse range of settings, as discussed above, the AHF produced an important series of publications, including multiple research reports on the healing process (Reimer 2010a, 2010b; Waldram 2008), and collected commentaries on healing and reconciliation by prominent Indigenous and other intellectuals, many explicitly critical of settler state policy (Mathur, Dewar, and DeGagné 2011; Younging, Dewar, and DeGagné 2009). Hard and electronic copies were distributed free of charge.[41] In their final years of operation, the AHF continued to respond to emerging issues of importance to Indigenous Peoples. The sensitive and challenging issue of historical lateral violence among students at the residential schools was raised in testimony at the TRC and reports from the Independent Assessment Process.[42] In January 2012 AHF leadership initiated discussions with residential school Survivors, Elders, and health professionals on this topic, leading to a preliminary research project led by Dr. Amy Bombay, Anishinaabe psychologist from Rainy River First Nation in Treaty 3 territory (Bombay, Matheson, and Anisman 2014). This research report was one of the last AHF publications. Unsurprisingly, it echoes some of the themes raised in ONWA's *Breaking Free*.

Indigenous Healing and Biopolitics in the Twenty-First Century

"Healing" became a focal point for Indigenous biopolitical tactics around the turn of the twenty-first century. The analysis shared in this chapter points to biopower as a terrain or matrix within which divergent, even irreconcilable, analyses of Indigenous social suffering and visions for sovereign futures are expressed, enacted, and challenged. Rather than uncritically celebrate the growing ubiquity of "Indigenous healing" in public discourse from the 1990s, I've analyzed its expansion as a set of discourses, institutions, and interventions emanating from the interface of Indigenous (bio)political agency and tactics, on the one hand, and on the other, the changing terrain of the (neo)liberal political and moral economy shaping the settler state's distribution of resources. I've acknowledged Indigenous actors' skill and perseverance at pursuing healing infrastructure and services; attended to the significant constraints they labour under; and explored possible unintended consequences of Indigenous biopolitical work, which, as we have seen throughout this chapter, is always vulnerable to (re)assertions of settler state sovereignty and the resurrection of old, dehumanizing tropes of Indigeneity.

Perhaps the most significant shift in Indigenous healing discourse I've documented is the increasingly dominant (mis)representation of colonialism as embodied past event, which I have shown to be increasingly ubiquitous in public discourse. I've argued that this discourse works to individuate and depoliticize healing by advancing a superficial acknowledgement of colonial histories inspired by reconciliation politics, which then rapidly pivots to a focus on contemporary Indigenous dysfunction and the need for state intervention. My analysis has considered how an embodied past colonialism is conveyed through the discursive figure of the residential school Survivor, and parallel processes discernible in discussions of housing, mental health, and child development services. Previously (2017), I've argued that the TRC's analysis of the ongoing disproportionate removal of Indigenous children in the name of child welfare rests on this same trope of individual embodiment of colonialism: the TRC report explains contemporary child apprehension as "a result or legacy of the way that Aboriginal children were treated in residential schools" (2015, 135). In other words, the embodied effects of parents' and grandparents' experiences of residential school result in families mistreating their children who are then (it is implied) necessarily and reasonably apprehended by state authorities. This account attributes the contemporary apprehension of Indigenous children to dysfunction inherent in Indigenous families, rather than the ideology of Indigenous family dysfunction inherent in and still propelling settler statecraft. Other scholars have offered comparable analyses. Les Sabiston (2021) discusses how the TRC's analysis of fetal alcohol spectrum disorder and associated disability similarly (mis)represents this condition as the individual embodiment of a past colonialism, disregarding critical analyses of how the diagnosis has been socially produced and applied in problematic and racializing ways (see also Briggs 2012; Oldani 2009; Tait 2009). As Sabiston observes, this uncritical medicalization works to naturalize fetal alcohol spectrum disorder as the primary cause of disproportionate Indigenous incarceration, thus obscuring attention to how ongoing settler colonialism criminalizes Indigeneity.

In one sense, this discourse on individuated embodiment of history and the concurrent displacement of dominant, contemporary systems and cultures as the cause of Indigenous suffering is not new. In fact, it is disturbingly reminiscent of older tropes of Indigenous pathology that work to "biologize dispossession as natural" (Kolopenuk 2020a, 16), from paradigms of innate vulnerability to tuberculosis and alcohol abuse, to the "thrifty gene" theory of diabetes (Belcourt 2018; Daschuk, Hackett, and MacNeil 2006; Hay 2018, 2021; Lux 1998; Genosko and Thompson 2009; Waldram 2004). But there are also significant differences with this contemporary version of embodied colonialism that warrant careful attention: the credibility lent through participation by the growing number of credentialled Indigenous biopolitical actors, increasing grassroots circulation through the growth of Indigenous biopolitical infrastructure and social media, and in the wake of reconciliation politics, a new impetus and opportunities for liberal settler actors to gain political capital by responding to Indigenous suffering. In the absence of countervailing analyses, such as what I offer in this book, these conditions foretell the potential for the trope of Indigenous embodiment of colonialism to gain further reach and influence.

Conclusion

Towards an Indigenized Politics of Life

I'VE ARGUED that understanding Indigenous healing as a paradox affords a useful conceptual tool for analyzing the entanglement of collective well-being and politics in the liberal settler colony. To conclude, I want to consider how the idea of healing as paradox might help to align future research on Indigenous health, well-being, and care with ongoing sovereignty struggles and the dismantling of settler colonialism. Recall from the book's introduction Ghassan Hage's (2015) argument that "anti-politics" and "alter-politics" are the complementary constituents of transformative social movements, encompassing opposition to the dominant order and a vision for radical change, respectively. Paradox as analytic concept for Indigenous healing can support both, because it is simultaneously oriented to critique (aligned with anti-politics) and investigations of alternative ways of being, doing, and relating (alter-politics). E. Summerson Carr (2023) points to the socio-cultural work paradox does to not only manage but also *disguise* difference, and defuse conflict inherent to irreconcilable differences. In an account that parallels my discussion of healing's metaphoric capacity in this book's introduction, Carr describes the "productive pleasure of paradox" (51), by which she means, paradox can be usefully manipulated towards diverse outcomes: should keeping the "both/and" of a given paradox in the frame become untenable in a given context, social actors can work with paradox to temporarily align with its more politically expedient side. Building on Carr's insight, we can interpret some dominant actors' invocations of "Indigenous healing" as working to obscure and defuse an ultimately irreconcilable difference between the restoration of healthy, vibrant Indigenous polities whose well-being is interdependent with that of the land and water and other-than-human beings, on the one hand, and, on the other, continuing liberal capitalist commitments to endless economic growth and accumulation of obscene wealth for some, predicated on environmental destruction. In this book, I've aimed to heighten awareness of such discursive manipulations by pointing to how liberal state interventions into Indigenous health and healing often claim benevolent motivations and effects while actually furthering social dismemberment and shoring up the illegitimate authority of the Canadian settler state.

This line of critique bolsters anti-politics, but attending to the paradox of Indigenous healing simultaneously encourages us to consider how the coexistence of multiple realities, potentially incommensurable but not necessarily mutually unintelligible, enables alter-politics.[1] I've focused on re-membering to emphasize the persistence of Indigenous ways of knowing and relating often at odds with dominant models of health and social care. Collective approaches to care and healing at the margins of the welfare state and beyond can be read as alter-politics, and recent literature, especially at the interface of academic and activist work, shows that such work continues (K. Anderson et al. 2018; Downe 2021; Van Styvendale et al. 2021). Grassroots community organizing in response to Missing and Murdered Indigenous Women and Girls, and Indigenous legal studies scholarship, has sustained public conversations about healing and justice as intertwined, first initiated by the Ontario Native Women's Association in 1989 (K. Anderson et al. 2018; Chartrand 2022; Friedland 2018; Nielsen and Jarratt-Snider 2023). Notably, recent literature has addressed difficult discussions of lateral violence (Friedland 2018; Innes and Anderson 2018) and challenged the smuggling of patriarchal, heteronormative, and anti-queer ideas into traditional stories and teachings (L. Simpson 2018; A. Wilson 2018) and academic Indigenous studies (Belcourt 2016; D. Hunt 2023).

Empirically rich research methods, such as social history and ethnography, can support alter-politics by revealing how radically other ways of being not only exist but infiltrate dominant modes of being in demonstrable ways (Hage 2015). This book has provided multiple examples of how Indigenous social actors have circumnavigated institutional, financial, political, and social constraints to advance re-membering of societies and nations and knowledge in a wide range of settings. These accounts depict hopeful possibilities for transformative change and fuel alter-politics by challenging narratives about the inevitability of dominant ways of being, since, in fact, alternate ways of being are already practiced, as Hage points out. Further, Hage argues, dominant Euro-American societies have *always* contained a multiplicity of realities, although prevailing modes of thought would have us believe otherwise, suggesting a potential for fruitful alignments between Indigenous sovereignty struggles and other alter-politics. Again, ethnographers are well situated to study such relationships and their potential to challenge the dominant order.[2] Ethnographic and social-historical research centred on Indigenous well-being, health, and social care can complement and extend current research on Indigeneity and biopolitics dominated by political and literary theorists, which tends to be theoretically rich but empirically thin, and productively "confront theory with the world it would explain" (Li 2007, 30).[3] And as this book has shown, there is value in seeking out sites within state-sponsored institutions and programs to identify where and how Indigenous relational subjectification persists, and identify supports and threats to this work. Paying attention to tactical engagements with the settler state and what ensues can disrupt misrepresentations of settler-colonial power as totalizing and omnipotent, fostering hope for change and pointing to where dominant structures are vulnerable to reworking. But even (and especially) in the face of significant gains in Indigenous-managed health and social programming, and Indigenous participation in the health and social work professions training, the healthy suspicion expressed by Mary's sister in the introduction remains warranted. Critique is still needed. Liberal inclusion of Indigenous professionals and superficial engagement with Indigenous knowledge and ceremony must not be misread as decolonization (A. Simpson 2011; Watts 2016).

In 2011, speaking at a federal Status of Women Committee hearing in Thunder Bay, Marlene Pierre reflected on the conditions of Indigenous women's and children's lives in Northern Ontario and concluded that they hadn't improved over the four decades since she helped to establish Beendigen women's shelter (Pierre 2011). She angrily denounced the regional and national Indigenous women's organizations she'd previously led, Ontario Native Women's Association and Native Women's Association of Canada, alongside the Canadian settler state and Indigenous political leaders, for abandoning Northern women and their families. When Marlene and I met in Thunder Bay in 2019, she reiterated this profound frustration, and illustrated the failure to adequately transform health and social services by pointing to a single change: rather than the traditional, settler-led Children's Aid Societies, it was now Indigenous-managed family service organizations removing their children. Under Marlene's leadership in the 1980s, members of the Ontario Native Women's Association organized to demand social and political change of First Nations and the settler state as an organic extension of their frontline caring labour. As discussed in chapter 4, expansion of Indigenous biopolitical tactics under neoliberalism was partially enabled by the diversion of Indigenous organizations once committed to advocacy into expanded service delivery roles that often involve more self-management than self-determination. Unsurprisingly, Marlene felt betrayed by organizations that developed from extensive grassroots support but no longer prioritize advocacy demanding political and social transformation to meet the needs of women and children in Northern communities. The success of biopolitical tactics at channelling state resources means that Indigenous-managed healing services expanded, but so have social stratification and individuation in Indigenous societies and, at least in Ontario, the underdevelopment of Indigenous healing resources in Northern, reserve, and rural settings. I've argued that analyzing these tactics as biopolitics and asking what kinds of Indigenous subjects are being created through the ensuing interventions helps to draws critical attention to their unintended social and political effects as well as political actors' savvy. As Marlene's testimony conveys, biopolitical tactics can lead to conjunctures misaligned with the priorities of the collectivities one intends to serve.

Mobilizing healing as paradox as analytical tool might deepen critical analysis in Indigenous health and social services research by directing purposeful attention to how liberalism and colonialism are intertwined, enabling more rigorous critiques of contemporary relations of power. Invocations of colonial "legacy" and racism, increasingly prevalent in the Indigenous health literature, are insufficient for analyzing complex problems of co-option and unintended effects of seemingly benevolent intervention, increasingly under Indigenous management. As we've seen repeatedly, the Canadian welfare state simultaneously offers opportunities for Indigenous tactical engagements and reproduces liberal values of individuation, productivity, and universalism, often in irreconcilable tension with Indigenous aspirations such as re-membering to strengthen the collective. Conceptual and methodological tools aligned with critique (or "anti" politics) are needed to analyze the production, circulation, and effects of knowledge of Indigenous health and social relations produced by state-authorized experts. Foucault's concept of power/knowledge (*le savoir-pouvoir*) expresses how these are inextricably linked, and is central to biopolitics. Critical ethnographic and related qualitative investigations informed by this perspective are attentive to both discourse and action, revealing the complexities and contradictions that characterize Indigenous experience as lived and the micro workings of power, and challenging assumptions that the knowledge and practice of health sciences is beyond the social and political.[4] Leslie Sabiston's (2021) ethnographic research on fetal alcohol spectrum disorder (FASD) illustrates the value of ethnography for critical analysis of the politics of healing, and particularly for demonstrating the entanglement of liberalism and settler colonialism often overlooked in the Indigenous health literature. Discussed briefly in chapter 4 of this book, Sabiston's ethnography follows circulating FASD discourse and the experiences of those assigned this diagnosis across the child welfare system, social services, policy debates, media representations, and the criminal justice system. The breadth and depth of his scrutiny enable Sabiston to show that far from a compassionate explanation for Indigenous disability and diagnostic entry point for care and support, FASD is easily absorbed into the settler-colonial equation of Indigeneity with inherent disfunction, and may actually work to deny diagnosed individuals opportunities for rehabilitation, since state-authorized experts widely judge them unresponsive to treatment. In a particularly striking illustration, the Gladue legal system, a hallmark of contemporary Canadian liberalism that purports to incorporate considerations of colonial context to redress inequities in the criminal justice system's treatment of Indigenous people, is revealed by Sabiston to be another mechanism of colonial disciplinary power, which functions to reinforce an understanding of settler colonialism as an embodied effect explaining Indigenous dysfunction and criminality.

    I suggest an Indigenized biopolitical approach synthesizes such much-needed critical analyses of dominant systems with the attentiveness to Indigenous political agency and alter-politics that I've called for above and tried to demonstrate throughout this book. In particular, this approach offers a useful critical framework for navigating the coexistence of divergent modes of knowledge of Indigenous health and well-being under liberal settler colonialism. In the remainder of this conclusion, I briefly discuss two contemporary trends in Indigenous health research to demonstrate the need for

Indigenized biopolitical analysis: the incorporation of the Indigenous onto-epistemology "Two-Eyed Seeing," and the biologization of Indigenous suffering and healing as "reconciliation project," using the example of epigenetic science.[5]

I first encountered Two-Eyed Seeing in a presentation by settler biologist Cheryl Bartlett many years ago as a graduate student attending a Network Environment for Aboriginal Health Research gathering in Halifax, where most participants (many Indigenous) were students of health sciences, and I was one of a small minority in critical social science and humanities.[6] Two-Eyed Seeing is a translation of the Mi'kmaq word *Etuaptmumk*, and describes a principle affirming the value and practice of incorporating multiple perspectives to enrich an analysis, offered by Bartlett's collaborators Mi'kmaw Elders Albert Marshall and Murdena Marshall as part of their advocacy for the continuing importance of Indigenous knowledge. Murdena Marshall explains the origins of Two-Eyed Seeing with a teaching previously shared by the late Healer and Chief Charles Labrador of Acadia, who directed learners to observe the relationship among trees illustrated by the intertwining of their root systems: "the gift of multiple perspectives" (Marshall, Marshall, and Bartlett 2018, 45–46). Etuaptmumk therefore suggests an approach for analyzing Indigenous people's pursuit of well-being in the context of multiple systems of knowledge. At the time, I was struck by both the promise of Two-Eyed Seeing for challenging dominant ethnocentric perspectives in health research, and how (at least in this presentation) the concept did not extend to an understanding of the production of biomedical knowledge as an inherently social and political process. Instead, it seemed to implicitly reinforce the positivist or post-positivist paradigm prevailing in most Canadian health research, which represents knowledge as a set of empirical truths awaiting discovery by the objective scientist, even while acknowledging the possibility of a plurality of knowledges.

In the intervening years, the Two-Eyed Seeing concept has gained significant traction among academic researchers seeking to collaborate with Indigenous Peoples, particularly in health and environmental science.[7] Many scholars claim that using a Two-Eyed

Seeing approach enables "decolonization" of research. Certainly, Two-Eyed Seeing advances important principles for the respect of Indigenous knowledge in the context of collaborative work, and there is evidence that it can be effective at this in small-scale projects where all sides are genuinely open to learning from others (Reid et al. 2021). But I maintain my initial reservations about how it is being used in the burgeoning field of Indigenous health because, in published research, Two-Eyed Seeing teachings are largely silent on the colonial context of knowledge coexistence. This is not to say that Albert Marshall and Murdena Marshall are oblivious to the colonial context, but as principle or approach to knowledge production, Two-Eyed Seeing apparently does not offer tools for incorporating relations of power into analysis. Two recent reviews of health and fisheries research, respectively, bear out this concern (Reid et al. 2021; Roher et al. 2021). Roher and colleagues' fine-grained analysis of how Two-Eyed Seeing has been used in Indigenous health research publications found that the same researchers who claim decolonizing effects for their work with Two-Eyed Seeing repeatedly neglect two important dimensions of the principle: spirituality and relations with other-than-human knowledge systems—that is, understanding humans as part of a larger natural world, a foundational premise. Reid et al. (2021) note the principle's effectiveness in redressing power imbalances between Indigenous and scientific expertise in small-scale collaborative projects, but argue that in larger policymaking processes, state actors' expressed commitments to genuine collaboration and meaningful implementation of Indigenous knowledge are only enacted to the extent that they align with Western scientific analysis. Importantly, these authors conclude that failure to address how these knowledge systems are imbricated with colonialism, past and present, enables continued marginalization of Indigenous knowledge systems in policymaking. These critiques align with Brendan Hokowhitu and colleagues' (2022) argument, discussed in the introduction, that mobilizing Indigenous philosophy as conveyed through pre-contact concepts may be insufficient to challenge the continuing dominance of settler-colonial systems of knowledge production in the context of

Indigenous health research, and their conclusion that an Indigenous biopolitics is needed for this purpose.

Indigenized biopolitical theory could also support critical analyses of contemporary trends in the biologization of Indigenous suffering and healing. As discussed briefly in chapter 4, this trend is particularly evident in health and related discourse around trauma and FASD, often fuelled by the burgeoning bioscientific field of epigenetics. Despite long-standing opposition to genetic research by many Indigenous Peoples, Emma Kowal and Megan Warin (2018) report that many Indigenous health professionals, researchers, and other commentators describe an "affinity" between Indigenous ontologies and epigenetics, which theorizes biological mechanisms by which environmental causes of poor health can not only permanently alter cells but transmit those alterations across generations. In Australia, many influential Indigenous and allied health advocates have embraced epigenetics as a lever for improved services, including maternal and early childhood health, and a route to enhanced collective health (Warin, Kowal, and Meloni 2020). Warin and colleagues analyze the proliferation of epigenetics discourse in Indigenous health research and policy as both a politics of hope and a new mode of biopolitics predicated on a strategic environmental determinism. But as they note, the hype generally attached to epigenetics outpaces the science. Notably, two assumptions about epigenetics foundational to Indigenous interest—intergenerational transmission and the potential for sustainable reversal of epigenetic changes—are yet to be robustly proven (Warin, Kowal, and Meloni 2020). Beyond this problem, Warin, Kowal, and Meloni point to the social and political risks that Indigenous epigenetics engenders, including intensified settler state-driven interventions into Indigenous lives, dooming certain people as "irredeemable" (already happening to some individuals diagnosed with FASD in the legal system, as documented by Sabiston), and the return of a "nurturist eugenics" that could enable a reinvigorated racialist biology (101–103).

Writing in the North American context, Joseph P. Gone and Laurence Kirmayer (2020) express similar concerns regarding speculation that epigenetic mechanisms underlie the intergenerational transmission of trauma in Indigenous families. Gone and Kirmayer note that some researchers of Indigenous trauma allocate excessive explanatory power to still preliminary epigenetic models for intergenerational transmission, and, especially in Canadian research, equate residential school attendance with both trauma and its intergenerational transmission in a way that flattens the complexity and range of Indigenous histories, including the significance of other colonial interventions. This critique echoes those expressed by some Indigenous mental health professionals decades ago, described in chapter 4, about how residential school experience has become a dominant trope for representing Canadian settler colonialism in ways that foreclose more complex understandings of actual Indigenous experiences, past and present, and are inconsistent with Indigenous ethics. Further, Gone and Kirmayer point to the challenge of disentangling the contemporary effects of historical experiences from experiences of ongoing settler colonialism, and ultimately question whether this "biologization of distress" (242) aligns with Indigenous Peoples' priorities. In earlier work (Maxwell 2014), I similarly questioned the social, political, and potentially depoliticizing implications of the emergent biosociality shaped by the concept of embodied intergenerational trauma that some young Indigenous people are adopting, in which their sense of self and belonging is shaped by the belief that trauma is genetically encoded and inherited and therefore an inevitable condition of their lives.

The social histories shared in this book show that providing care to one's people while dominant actors aim to destroy you as a People is an inherently political act, and the quest to re-member while settler colonialism continues is neither an oxymoron nor peripheral to resurgence politics and sovereignty struggles. I've argued that we need to understand the pursuit of re-membering via the welfare state as part of a larger politics of Indigenous life. This perspective emphasizes that health and social care discourse and interventions can powerfully (re)shape how individuals perceive themselves and their relationships, processes of subjectification that can align with re-membering and socio-cultural and political resurgence or, conversely, enable individuation and social stratification, undermining collective well-being. In this conclusion, I've pointed to some current dynamics in Indigenous health research that warrant critical analysis through an Indigenized biopolitics lens, but all aspects of Indigenous health and social care—research, training, and education; advocacy and policy development; design, delivery, and use (or refusal) of services—are potentially significant sites for social and political (re)visioning and transformation, often coming up against new assertions of settler-colonial dominance. These biopolitical struggles and their outcomes significantly shape contemporary Indigenous experience, but, of the phenomenal intellectual work produced under the rubric of Indigenous studies in North America since the 2010s, only a small portion is directed to issues of collective health, well-being, and healing. "Turning away" from engagements with the state, as urged by some proponents of Indigenous liberationist thought, risks obscuring the everyday caring labour and biopolitical tactics, often carried out by women, to support and protect Indigenous life. The ongoing Indigenization of biopolitics deserves more attention and support from scholars and intellectuals committed to resurgence, decolonization, anti-colonialism, and other Indigenous liberationist thought and struggles.[8]

Appendix

Methods and Sources

THE RESEARCH that informed this book was conducted in two main phases, the first during my PhD (2005–2010), the second after that (2011–2021). As discussed in the preface and introduction, my research focus shifted over time, and my use of methods and selection of sources reflect those shifts. I initially spent significant time attempting to trace the genealogy of the then-ascendant discourse on "Aboriginal mental health" in public policy records at Library and Archives Canada and the Archives of Ontario; this work afforded some useful background knowledge, and some of that research made its way into my PhD thesis, but very little is cited in these pages. Reports from the archives of the Centre for Addiction and Mental Health produced during the former Addiction Research Foundation's work in Kenora (1960s–1980s) were particularly relevant as my focus shifted to Indigenous social histories of healing, and are cited extensively in chapter 1.

I identified potential research contributors first by asking my existing contacts, Dr. Peter Menzies, Vern Harper, and Grafton Antone, then Elder in Residence at First Nations House, University of Toronto, to recommend knowledgeable people, and then asking the same of those people (snowballing). Grafton was also the first person to instruct me in the importance of ceremony to research relations (S. Wilson 2008), and helped me understand more deeply the significance of a tobacco offering as an opener, a first step towards building a trusting relationship and a way to convey respect for the knowledge to be shared. In a few cases, I directly approached people in public-facing positions whose work seemed relevant to my research questions. Of the thirty-five people I invited to contribute to the project, thirty agreed. (Two declined, two did not respond to emailed invitations, and one was willing to participate but cancelled two scheduled interviews at the last minute, after which I abandoned my attempts.) In three cases, the person I initially approached to participate delegated the invitation to another person within the same organization.

Contributors to this phase of the research may be grouped into two broad categories based on their location in relation to the settler state: first, those currently or previously working mainly with or within the federal government and civil service, including First Nations and Inuit Health Branch of Health Canada (formerly Medical Services Branch), the Aboriginal Healing Foundation, leaders of national and provincial Indigenous organizations, Indigenous and settler scholars involved in national policymaking, and psychiatrists and psychologists working on reserves; and second, those primarily involved in Indigenous healing as part of urban health and social services (some in senior positions are also involved in provincial advocacy and policymaking): Elders, directors and staff of Indigenous agencies (Friendship Centres, women's shelters, and Aboriginal Health Centres), and other health and social service providers serving many Indigenous people, and psychiatrists and psychologists. This book focuses mostly on the second set of experiences grounded in urban settings. With the exception of one visit to a home on a reserve, I conducted oral history and qualitative interviews in person in Ottawa, Toronto, and Hamilton between September 2008 and April 2010, usually at the person's workplace, sometimes at another location such as a café or hotel lobby, or at the home of Elders with limited mobility. The questions or prompts I worked with varied significantly, as I tailored my preparation for each meeting and my questions shifted over time in response to my growing understanding. For instance, I initially used the language of mental health and addictions. An interview with Castille Troy, executive director of Miinwaashin Lodge in Ottawa, in which she explained "we just call it healing," alerted me to the need to adapt my terms. The structure and flow of conversations also varied considerably, as some contributors offered lengthy narratives that spontaneously addressed many of my topics of interest and meant I didn't need to speak much, while others were less forthcoming, meaning that I ended up directing the conversation more. Most of the oral history interviews were digitally recorded with permission and professionally transcribed. In three cases, contributors gave permission for me to take notes instead, which I later word-processed. This component of the research was reviewed and approved by the University of Toronto Health Sciences Research Ethics Board.[1]

The second phase was very different, encompassing extensive learning through participation in formal and informal community social and political events, often under the auspice of my other major research project on Anishinaabe histories of kinship and child welfare sovereignty (still ongoing at the time of writing). Individual contributions included extensive oral histories shared by three people over two or more meetings, and more informal conversations and interviews with several others. Early in this phase of the research, I learned more about the role of ceremony: some of my Anishinaabe interlocutors requested that tobacco (and sometimes other offerings) be made not only to the direct contributors, but also for those who have passed and will feature in the histories being discussed, such as Don Morrison, Joseph Morrison, and other members of the Lake of the Woods Powwow Club. This component of the research was reviewed and approved by the University of Toronto Social Sciences, Humanities and Education Research Ethics Board.[2]

Notes

PREFACE

1. These trips were part of research on histories of Anishinaabe kinship and challenges to the child welfare system, ongoing at the time of writing.
2. My first two degrees (in anthropology and biology, and medical anthropology) were completed in England, where we read Talal Asad's *Anthropology and the Colonial Encounter*, but didn't discuss the intertwined histories of anthropology and settler colonialism in North America. My PhD was completed in Canada in an interdisciplinary social science and health program (with a historian as primary supervisor).

INTRODUCTION

1. With this distinction, I don't intend to imply that settler colonialism in the past was somehow separate from or less violent than British imperialism at large; the settler colonies were politically, economically, and culturally intertwined with global imperialism and the transatlantic trade in Black African slaves.
2. These settler nations have featured most prominently in comparative discussions of Indigenous experiences of settler colonialism including North America; scholars have also applied the settler colonialism concept in other settings, including some parts of East Asia and sub-Saharan Africa, and Israel/Palestine.
3. See also reports of recent provincial investigations into anti-Indigenous racism in health care, including the coroner's report on the torment and death of Joyce Echaquan in a Quebec hospital (Kamel 2020) and a review commissioned by the British Columbia Ministry of Health in response to pervasive racism in hospitals in that province (*In Plain Sight* 2020).
4. Anthropologist James Waldram (2004b) notes the significance of healing as metaphor spanning individual, social, cultural, and political change in Indigenous usage, prior to its wide uptake by settler state actors.
5. An extended discussion of this wide-ranging literature is beyond the scope of this introduction. Some useful starting points include ethnographic works by Naomi Adelson (2000, 2001), Michelle M. Jacob (2013), Craig Proulx (2003), James Waldram (1997, 2008); historiography including Mary-Ellen Kelm (1998) and Kristin Burnett (2010); the interdisciplinary collection focused on mental health and addictions edited by Laurence Kirmayer and Gail Valaskakis (2009); critical work of psychologist Joseph P. Gone (2010, 2021), and the earlier work of psychologist Joseph Couture (2013); on Indigenous feminist perspectives, collections edited by Kim Anderson and Bonita Lawrence (2003) and Kim Anderson, Maria Campbell, and Christi Belcourt (2018); on healing, literature, and the arts, Jo-Ann Episkenew (2009), and collections edited by Dylan Robinson and Keavy Martin (2016) and Nancy Van Styvendale, J.D. McDougall, Robert Henry, and Robert Alexander Innes (2021).
6. See Pasternak (2015) for an extended critical discussion of Flanagan's work.
7. See also Jacob (2013) on Yakama healing as "decolonizing praxis."

8. See Tuck and Yang (2012) on decolonization as metaphor.
9. Alongside various interventions with potentially individuating effects, I discuss the Indian Residential Schools Settlement Agreement negotiated by the Canadian government and Assembly of First Nations, claimed by both parties to be "healing" but condemned by many as intrusive and retraumatizing.
10. Million (2013) points to the Australian example whereby earlier calls for healing the Indigenous trauma resulting from experiences of settler-colonial violence later transmuted into state legitimations for intensified interventions into Indigenous communities in the Northern Territory intervention.
11. Matthews et al. (2023) provide a compelling discussion of Pauingassi and Little Grand Rapids First Nations, where few people attended residential school due to the inaccessibility of their communities on the upper Berens River. Nevertheless, these communities have suffered excess apprehension of their children by the child welfare system and incarceration of adults in the criminal justice system, inequities commonly explained—for instance by the Truth and Reconciliation Commission of Canada's final report—with reference to histories of residential school internment.
12. These earlier research experiences include research on young gay men's experiences of sexual health and HIV prevention in London during the early days of the AIDS epidemic (Maxwell 1997b); Black health and racialization in the British National Health Service (Maxwell 1997a; Maxwell, Streetly, and Bevan 1999); and several unpublished research projects addressing access to primary health care in Benue State, Nigeria.
13. Social histories shared with me suggest that the English term *healing* was widely taken up in urban Indigenous community organizing and social services in Ontario from the 1990s. Given the breadth of its meaning and its frequent association with recovery from the effects of colonization, my working assumption from a few conversations with Anishinaabemowin speakers is that this term doesn't correspond neatly with any single older term in that language, which includes multiple terms for a range of expertise and practices linked to health and wellness spanning different ceremonies, plant-based medicine, bone-setting, midwifery and reproductive health, and so on.

14. Ngũgĩ wa Thiong'o's discussion of a schism between the African diaspora and educated elite on the continent regarding relations with "memory and means of memory," especially the use of Indigenous languages (2009, 51), illustrates this sort of analysis, but he is less attentive to how the profoundly gendered effects of colonialism have important implications for contemporary (post)colonial subjects.

15. In my observation, some contemporary non-Christian traditionalists in Northern Ontario First Nations similarly take tactical advantage of multiple opportunities offered by Christian missionaries ranging from on-reserve pedicures to children's overnight summer camps.

16. Marisol de la Cadena (2015) employs the concept of extension of knowledge in her analysis of Quechua community leaders' navigations of worlds beyond their own.

17. For comparable analyses of Lekwammen and other Indigenous women's tactical adaptation of new crafts and other domestic skills, see Lutz (1999) and Carter (2002), cited in Burnett (2010).

18. In the late nineteenth century, state involvement in Indigenous health care was minimal, restricted to the work of Indian agents, also designated as "health officers" (although their expertise in health care varied widely), and occasional interventions by the North West Mounted Police, who employed some physicians (Waldram, Herring, and Young 2006).

19. Arthur Kleinman defines a health care system as "socially organized responses to disease that constitute a special cultural system…of symbolic meanings, anchored in particular arrangements of social institutions and patterns of interpersonal interactions" (1980, 24).

20. This division between ontology and epistemology is, of course, itself artificial and a reflection of a particular, Eurocentric worldview. For discussions of Indigenous ontologies that critique dominant social theory and have implications for collective well-being in the context of continuing settler colonialism, see Nadasdy (2007) and Watts (2013, 2020).

21. See Janelle Taylor (2003) on biomedicine's "culture of no culture."

22. Although the concept of disciplinary power is elaborated most extensively in Foucault's earlier *Discipline and Punish*, his later work (1990, 261–62) suggests that disciplinary power forms one axis of biopower corresponding to the institutional control of the human body, which he

also described as "anatomo-politics," while the second axis is constituted by biopolitics, which works through regulation of human subjects at the level of population.

23. These fears and experiences of surveillance and repression, including missionaries burning confiscated ceremonial items, were reported to me in oral histories from both Southern and Northern Ontario. See also Kinew (1995).

24. The Potlatch and West Coast winter dances were outlawed in 1884, the Sundance in 1895 (Kelm and Smith 2018). These prohibitions were lifted as part of the 1951 revisions to the Indian Act, inspiring a revival of Giveaway ceremonies across Canada (Dickason and McNab 2009).

25. Occasions of Indigenous Christians burning ceremonial items have been described to me by interlocutors from Treaty 3 and Treaty 9 (Nishnawbe Aski Nation) territories. See also Dombrowski (2001).

26. Windigo (pl. Windigowag) is understood by Anishinaabeg and Cree as a condition of insanity expressed as lateral violence, including cannibalism, posing a serious threat to the well-being of the collective (Borrows 2010; Friedland 2018).

27. This commentary is in response to the 1857 Gradual Civilization Act passed by the Assembly of United Canadas, the first to contradict the earlier British policy of supporting Indigenous self-governance (Milloy 1983).

28. Imperial liberal rhetoric's emphasis on universal liberties and rights was belied by nineteenth-century liberal political actors' continued attachment to social hierarchies organized by class, gender, and race, with property-owning white men at the pinnacle of society.

29. The process of usurping Indigenous definitions of membership to impose patrilineal values through legislation began with the 1869 Gradual Enfranchisement Act, the provisions of which excised women entirely from their home community if they married a non-status man. This gendered discrimination continued in subsequent legislation and wasn't effectively challenged until 1985. The Enfranchisement Act also undermined women's influence by excluding them from voting or standing for office in the imposed Band Council system of governance. On the contemporary social implications of late nineteenth- and twentieth-century gendered political dismemberment, see Lawrence (2004), A. Simpson (2014), and Cannon (2019).

30. For varied interpretations of how liberalism shaped the residential school system, see McKay (2000) and Brownlie (2019). It is noteworthy that the report of the Truth and Reconciliation Commission does not engage with how liberal ideology influenced the system.
31. Notably, several former patients and Indigenous health workers spontaneously likened the hospitals to the residential schools in oral histories cited by Lux (2016, 109).
32. *Subjectification* refers to the social process of remaking individuals and is central to the workings of biopolitics in Foucault's analysis. The term describes how individual social actors (subjects) come to understand themselves as biosocial beings and are "brought to work on themselves" (Lemke 2011, 120) in ways intended to optimize well-being, in alignment with particular norms and values. Some translations use *subjectivation*.
33. The National Indian Brotherhood was the precursor of the contemporary Assembly of First Nations.
34. Settler state actors' intentions to render Indigenous people suitable for Canadian citizenship were cemented in policy by 1950, when Indian Affairs branch, the institution centrally involved in the everyday governance of those deemed "Indians" under the Indian Act, moved from the Department of Mines and Resources to the newly created Department of Citizenship and Immigration (Peters 2001, 60).
35. Older youth were usually still required to leave home and seek board in the nearest urban centre to attend high school; even today, young people from most Nishnawbe Aski Nation communities, Treaty 9 territory (Northern Ontario) must do so, in Thunder Bay (Talaga 2017).
36. Butler uses the term "subjection."
37. Carolyn Rouse (2021) describes as "antibiopolitics" the trend in recent anthropological literature to oversimplify the relationship between state power and social suffering and neglect the extent to which the workings of biopolitics can and do benefit the lives of large numbers of people, through access to health care and the oversight of public health systems. In my observation, there is a similar trend in Indigenous and settler-colonial studies, which works to obscure Indigenous political agency and sidesteps the material challenges of implementing Indigenous sovereignty over health and health care.
38. Too vast to summarize here, this literature spans the history of science and medicine, medical anthropology, medical sociology, science and

technology studies, and the emerging field of Indigenous science and technology studies. One of the earlier publications is the collection by Wright and Treacher (1982).

39. McCallum (2014) notes that the opportunity to be close to relatives was one motivation for Indigenous people seeking employment in the hospitals.

40. See McCallum (2014) for a comprehensive history of the first decade of the CHR program. The program was driven in part by the globally ascendant community development paradigm, which emphasized autonomy and participation, and aligned with the new Liberal government's priorities of increasing Indigenous "self-sufficiency," reducing welfare expenditure and increasing provincial government involvement in providing service to Indigenous people (Shewell 2004).

41. Women's Institutes were community-based organizations first established by rural white women in Ontario in the late nineteenth century.

42. Among the first social welfare interventions initiated by the settler state, by 1956 there were 178 Homemakers' Clubs in reserves across the country (Harris and McCallum 2012).

43. By the late 1940s, many policymakers perceived the transition from wardship to citizenship as an urgent mission, as reflected by the relocation of Indian Affairs in 1949 from the Department of Mines and Resources to the newly formed Department of Citizenship and Immigration. During the 1960s, Citizenship Branch within the same department was increasingly involved in sponsoring research and programming around Indigenous people in urban centres, and eventually funded the Friendship Centres (Peters 2001).

44. This gap may be partially explained by Kim TallBear's (2016) critique of Indigenous studies as disinterested in science and technology research, which she argues is central to contemporary governance and sovereignty for Indigenous Peoples, as much as for settler nation-states. TallBear suggests this disinterest is explained by Indigenous studies scholars' enduring attachments to humanities disciplines of literary studies and nineteenth-century history, which were foundational to the establishment of the field and continue to dominate, and the misguided idea that science is somehow more inherently colonial than the humanities.

45. For a critical anthropological discussion of the limitations of the concept of citizenship in the context of First Nations politics, see Nadasdy (2017).

46. See, for example, Warwick Anderson's (2006) historical analysis of biomedical citizenship in Australia and the US-occupied Philippines. As well as the limitations of the conceptual framework, such historiography may also inadvertently obscure Indigenous social and political agency by relying solely on colonial archival sources.
47. In his later work on biopower, Foucault "distanced himself from the view that such power over life is unambiguously nefarious" (Rabinow and Rose 2006, 200). This attentiveness to the malleability of biopolitics distinguishes Foucault's approach, and mine, from that of much recent work on biopolitics in anthropology, Indigenous studies, and settler-colonial studies, often inspired by Giorgio Agamben's work on biopower, which departs significantly from Foucault's.
48. Jeffries argues that to "Re-Member power" requires full acknowledgement of what was done to survive historically, including tactical conversion to Christianity and denial of one's Indigenous identity: "the Indian closet" (2015, 173).
49. For example, work by historian Kim Anderson (2011), psychologist Joseph P. Gone (2014, 2021), and many Indigenous legal studies scholars (Borrows 2010; Friedland 2018; Snyder, Napoleon, and Borrows 2015).
50. See also Corntassel (2012); Daigle (2019); and L. Simpson (2017).
51. For other arguments on the theme of Indigenous Peoples turning away from the settler state, see Taiaiake Alfred (2009a, 2009b) and Audra Simpson (2014); for critiques of dualistic thought in Indigenous political theory, see Sarah Hunt's (2015) Indigenous feminist response to Coulthard's analysis, and Paul Nadasdy's (2017) work on sovereignty.
52. Reciprocal Indigenous recognition can also be considered a prerequisite to the formation of "irreconcilable spaces of Aboriginality," Indigenous-only social spaces for reasserting collective identity beyond the gaze and domineering frameworks of settlers, which David Garneau (2016, 26–30) argues are essential to a meaningful transformation of Indigenous and settler relations beyond the limitations of the reconciliation paradigm.
53. For a range of perspectives on resurgence compared to reconciliation politics, see the edited collections by Asch, Borrows, and Tully (2018) and Stark, Craft, and Aikau (2023).
54. Foucault developed this argument in his lectures at the Collège de France (1975–1976), later published as *"Society Must Be Defended"* (2003), in an analysis focused on Europe.

55. See Nadi Abu El-Haj (2010) for a comparable argument about the Israeli state's treatment of Palestinians.
56. Such purposeful deprivations have been imposed on collectives and individuals. Examples of the former include nineteenth- and early twentieth-century policies of deliberate starvation of Indigenous Peoples (Daschuk 2012; Fiddler and Stevens 1985), and ongoing failures to ensure safe drinking water or fund adequate housing in First Nations reserve communities, or to regulate retail pricing of essential foods in Northern First Nations and Inuit communities (Burnett and Hay 2023; Galloway 2017). State actors deliberately withholding essential shelter from individuals is illustrated by the notorious police practice known as "starlight tours," the apprehension of Indigenous people, typically in an urban setting, and their subsequent abandonment in remote locations under freezing conditions where they risk death from exposure, widely associated with Saskatoon but rumoured to occur countrywide (Comack 2012; Razack 2015). See also the short film *Redlights* (2023), directed by Eva Thomas (2023).
57. See National Inquiry into Missing and Murdered Indigenous Women and Girls (2019).
58. The public inquiry investigating the killing of Dudley George by an Ontario Provincial Police (OPP) officer during the Kettle and Stony Point First Nation's occupation of Ipperwash Provincial Park in September 1995 identified racist discourse by political leaders as contributing directly to this murder and condemned its subsequent celebration in police culture (Linden 2007).
59. In an infamous example in Saskatchewan in 2018, white settler and farmer Gerald Stanley was acquitted by a jury of shooting and killing the young Cree man Colten Boushie after Boushie and his friends drove onto Stanley's property seeking help in August 2016 (Starblanket and D. Hunt 2020). University of Saskatchewan Indigenous studies scholar Robert Innes reported that many local settlers expressed support for Stanley on social media: "some farmers are blaming First Nations people for rural crime. Their mentality is to protect their property…there's this real fear and contempt towards indigenous men by many white people, to the point where they will shoot before asking questions" (CBC News 2016). See also the documentary film by director Tasha Hubbard (2019), *nîpawistamâsowin: We Will Stand Up*.

60. The theory of primitive accumulation refers to the violent dispossession of collectively held land and resources to enable capitalist exploitation, driving the creation of the proletariat, or working class.
61. Coulthard cites testimonies at the 1970s Mackenzie Valley Pipeline inquiry that conveyed not only vigorous opposition to capitalist accumulation and resource extraction but also the persistence of distinct Indigenous ethics of reciprocity and relationality (2014, 62–63). Coulthard's concept for these persistent ethics, drawing on the work of Taiaiake Alfred, is "grounded normativity."
62. Because the researcher is in effect an instrument in this sort of research, it is important to discuss not only the academic context but also the social and relational context including one's own positionality, as I've done in the preface.
63. For an overview of treaties in Ontario, see Linden (2007), volume 2, chapter 3, "Treaty Relations in Ontario." For a history of the numbered treaties, including Treaties 3 and 9, see Talbot (2009); a more extensive account of Treaty 9 is provided by Long (2010).

1 | GIIZHIIGANANG AND ANISHINAABE RE-MEMBERING, 1965–1980

1. Joseph Morrison, oral history shared with author, November 28, 2009, Hamilton, ON.
2. Over one hundred Anishinaabeg from Treaty 3 territory volunteered (Treaty #3 Achievers Project Committee 2000).
3. Carol Yawney, "The Kenora Report," 1967, 5, unpublished manuscript, box 42-22, Addiction Research Foundation fonds, Centre for Addiction and Mental Health Archives, Toronto.
4. This is an important distinction from the Sioux's relationship with their drum, which accompanies the Grass Dance, a secular object not given the same attention and significance (Vennum 2009).
5. This historical knowledge has been shared with me by several Anishinaabeg in casual conversation; it is also documented by scholars. An account shared by traditional drum maker William Bineshi Baker Sr. with Thomas Vennum (2009) centres on Tailfeather Woman, a Dakota Sioux woman who escaped a massacre by US soldiers and, while hiding,

received a vision about the need to construct a ceremonial dance Drum, the playing of which would induce the white soldiers to cease their attacks. Sharing the Drum with other Tribes would enable the spread of peace.

6. This oral history contributor requested that I describe him in this way in my writing; henceforth, simply "the Old Guy."
7. The Old Guy, oral history shared with author, March 7, 2017, Toronto.
8. Here I refer to indigenous people globally, so the term is not capitalized as would be conventional for peoples in a named territory.
9. Borrows and Tully (2018) make a similar argument about postcolonial studies literature more broadly.
10. As elaborated in the introduction, the process of subjectification is central to the workings of biopolitics theorized by Foucault.
11. These are the words of white ally, Toronto-based lawyer Alan Borovoy.
12. Scott Rutherford (2017, 170) suggests that journalist Peter Gzowski, reporting on North Battleford, Saskatchewan in 1963, was the first to use this analogy. It is also worth noting that Black American civil rights activist and scholar Daniel G. Hill, the first director of the Ontario Human Rights Commission, was among the Toronto-based supporters of the Kenora march.
13. See also Treaty #3 Achievers Project Committee 2000, 23.
14. Old Guy, oral history, March 7, 2017.
15. My basic understanding of these interrelationships between livelihoods, territory, humans, and other-than-humans comes particularly from conversations with the late Adolphus Cameron, as well as oral histories shared by Elders in Wabaseemoong about how the erosion of fishing and trapping by late twentieth-century environmental destruction and colonial regulation undermined community well-being. See also ethnographic accounts of forced sedentarization and destruction of Northern peoples' livelihoods, including the Cree nation of Eeyou Istchee (Northern Quebec) (Tanner 2009) and the Innu (Samson 2009).
16. There were five residential schools in Treaty 3 territory.
17. Old Guy, oral history, March 7, 2017.
18. Christian suppression of Indigenous ceremony, including public burnings of ceremonial items, recurred in some Indigenous communities throughout the twentieth century, sometimes with participation of Indigenous Christians, causing painful ruptures within families and communities.

19. Joseph Morrison, oral history, November 28, 2009.
20. B. Scully, "Kenora 1965–1974: A Report on the Development of ARF's Work in Kenora and Its Current Status," 1974, 2, unpublished manuscript, box 45-49, Addiction Research Foundation fonds, Centre for Addiction and Mental Health Archives, Toronto.
21. G.W. Mercer, "The Kenora Waystation," 1970, unpublished manuscript, box 41-03, Addiction Research Foundation fonds, Centre for Addiction and Mental Health Archives, Toronto.
22. Yawney, "Kenora Report."
23. Mercer, "Kenora Waystation," 7. During the period corresponding to the first 23 months of the Waystation's operations, Mercer reported that there were 1,486 alcohol convictions involving 249 people.
24. As reported to me by a white woman who grew up in Kenora in this period, also confirmed in Yawney's "Kenora Report."
25. Scully, "Kenora 1965–1974."
26. Mercer, "Kenora Waystation," 3.
27. Mercer, "Kenora Waystation," 3.
28. Joseph Morrison, oral history shared with author, November 26, 2010, Toronto.
29. The Liquor Control Board of Ontario developed an elaborate system for monitoring and restricting Indigenous alcohol consumption and didn't lift its racial prohibition on sales in stores until 1959 (Genosko and Thompson 2009).
30. That year it was struck down by the Supreme Court as racially discriminatory and contrary to the Canadian Bill of Rights.
31. See Anna Willow (2011, 2012) on the history of activism against clearcutting by members of Asubpeeschoseewagong (Grassy Narrows) First Nation.
32. Joseph Morrison, oral history, November 26, 2010.
33. Mercer, "Kenora Waystation"; Scully, "Kenora 1965–1974."
34. Scully, "Kenora 1965–1974."
35. Joseph Morrison, oral history, November 26, 2010.
36. Don Morrison letter to Joseph Morrison, March 4, 1967, Morrison family archive, copy in author's possession.
37. Mary Alice Smith, personal communication with author, March 3, 2020. See also Basil Johnston (1982).

38. Don's letter was found among Joseph's papers by his widow, Mary Alice Smith, several years after the latter's death. As Mary Alice observed, the fact that Joseph kept this letter safely for decades signals its significance to him.
39. Mercer, "Kenora Waystation," 6.
40. Don screened this film dozens of times during visits to reserves in the mid-1970s, as documented in a ledger he kept to record his visits and meetings across Treaty 3 territory between 1971 and 1978, Morrison family archive, copy in author's possession (hereafter "Don's ledger").
41. Treaty 3 Anishinaabeg have emphasized the importance of this perspective to me in multiple conversations; its significance is also demonstrated by the safekeeping of the Paypom Treaty, a copy of notes taken during the Treaty negotiations recording Anishinaabe perspectives (Daugherty 1986).
42. Mercer, "Kenora Waystation," 13.
43. Yawney, "Kenora Report," 22, 26–27. Yawney's 1967 "Kenora Report" is based on observational field research she conducted in Kenora, May 28 to July 31, 1966.
44. Yawney, "Kenora Report," 13.
45. Yawney, "Kenora Report," 12.
46. Yawney, "Kenora Report," 12.
47. Mercer, "Kenora Waystation," 3, 8, 9.
48. Mercer, "Kenora Waystation"; Scully, "Kenora 1965–1974."
49. Scully, "Kenora 1965–1974."
50. Scully, "Kenora 1965–1974."
51. According to ARF records, approximately 25,000 individual user visits per year were documented, including "approximately 300 hard core chronic alcohol abusers who used the place most frequently and were usually in a state of considerable intoxication" (Scully 1974, 3).
52. Scully, "Kenora 1965–1974," 3.
53. Lecture notes titled "To a people in trouble comes this message of love," (hereafter "Don's lecture notes"), preserved with Don's ledger.
54. I don't claim more than a superficial grasp of these aspects of Anishinaabe cultural knowledge. I encourage interested readers to seek relevant texts written by Anishinaabemowin speakers such as Basil Johnston (1982) and John Borrows (2010).
55. According to oral history sources, as well as the text of this speech.

56. Cindy Piche (née Skead), personal communication with author, March 2017; Scully, "Kenora 1965–1974," 3.
57. Old Guy, oral history, March 7, 2017.
58. Don's ledger; Mary Alice Smith, personal communication.
59. Gail Skead and Cindy Piche, personal communication with author, March 2017.
60. Anishinaabe powwows as practiced in Treaty 3 territory in the latter part of the twentieth century centred on the Grandfather Drum, synthesized the late nineteenth-century dance form associated with the gifted Sioux Peace Drum with older Anishinaabe traditions, including family, Clan, and broader social gatherings, Midewiwin and Wabanowin ceremonies (Berbaum 2000). For a detailed account of the gifting of the drum, see B. Johnston (1982).
61. Old Guy, oral history, March 7, 2017.
62. Elder Ann Wilson, Rainy River First Nation, oral history and teaching, as told to Mary Alice Smith, 1992, transcription in the author's possession.
63. Anishinaabe scholar and powwow dancer Karen Pheasant-Neganigwane (2020) makes a similar observation about the importance of powwows to restoring kinship relations in the autobiographical components of her beautifully rendered book for young people.
64. Prior to the mid-1970s, this group hosted some gatherings at the Presbyterian Church in Kenora. Andy White, oral history shared with author via telephone, December 21, 2023.
65. Colin Wasacase, former principal of Cecelia Jeffrey residential school, personal communication with author (telephone), April 23, 2020.
66. Don Morrison attended Cecelia Jeffrey for ten years from 1928, after the death of his mother; Ada Morrison attended from 1931; their son Joseph attended for s a shorter period in the late 1940s, while Ada was in the tuberculosis sanitorium. Doug Skead also attended the school; Madeline did not.
67. Don's ledger.
68. Andy White, oral history, December 21, 2023.
69. Cindy Piche, oral history shared with author, March 22, 2017.
70. Bev Williamson, oral history shared with author, March 22, 2017.
71. Joseph Morrison, oral history, November 28, 2009.
72. Old Guy, oral history shared with author via telephone, March 23, 2020.

73. Old Guy, oral history, March 7, 2017.
74. Old Guy, oral history, March 23, 2020.
75. Old Guy, oral history, March 7, 2017.
76. Old Guy, oral history, March 23, 2020.
77. Adolphus Cameron, oral histories shared with author, April 4, 2017, Toronto; April 19, 2020, telephone.
78. Adolphus Cameron, oral history, April 4, 2017.
79. Adolphus Cameron, oral history, April 19, 2020.
80. Adolphus Cameron, oral history, April 19, 2020. Adolphus opines that the alignment of AA and Anishinaabe knowledge reflects the former's origins in AA co-founder Bill W's study of Indigenous spiritual systems.
81. Adolphus Cameron, oral history, April 19, 2020.
82. Adolphus Cameron, oral history, April 19, 2020.
83. Adolphus's long-term sobriety and knowledge of traditional teachings equipped him to assume a series of significant leadership roles at Wabaseemoong and beyond; in his later years he was instrumental in beginning to implement Abinoojii Inakonigewen (child care law).
84. It is ironic that because the Grandfather Drum is traditionally considered a men's domain among Treaty 3 Anishinaabeg, its central role in re-membering and resurgence partially reproduces the gender segregation imposed by the residential school system and other interventions aimed at proselytization. Women participated in the Drum and powwow resurgence as dancers and (less often) singers, and contributed extensive labour, but are excluded from many of the conversations and relationships formed around the Drum. In recent decades, women at Asubpeeschoseewagong (Grassy Narrows) in Treaty 3 territory have established their own Drum, and Indigenous women elsewhere in Ontario have challenged their exclusion from the Drum (Deerchild 2003). See also Karen Pheasant-Neganigwane's (2020, 56–57) discussion of the gender politics of the Drum in different Indigenous nations.
85. Don's lecture notes.
86. Don's lecture notes.
87. Sam McKegney's (2012) insights are drawn from his analysis of a story shared by Mohawk Elder Tom Porter.

2 | RE-MEMBERING AND BIOPOLITICS IN URBAN ONTARIO, 1973-1980S

1. The report's full title is *While People Sleep: Sudden Deaths in Kenora Area: A Study of Sudden Deaths amongst the Indian People of the Kenora Area, with Primary Emphasis on Apparent Alcohol Involvement*. The research was supported by the University of Manitoba's Centre for Settlement Studies.
2. Timelines for histories of AIM and Red Power conventionally begin in 1969 with the occupation of Alcatraz, but Glen Coulthard (2019) provides an account of earlier organizing north of the border by the Native Alliance for Red Power, formed in Vancouver in 1967.
3. There were, of course, exceptions, such as Madeline Skead, whose role is documented in chapter 1. For a contemporary analysis of women's experience in Indian Act governance, see Kim Anderson's (2009) report of research with twelve female Chiefs.
4. The Kenora-based group of Anishinaabeg and white allies who initiated this work, named in the report as the Concerned Citizens Committee, was an offshoot of the Kenora Social Planning Council, which began meeting in 1970, and another group known as the Red and White Committee. Membership fluctuated over time, but involved white professionals (including staff of the Children's Aid Society) and Anishinaabe participation, according to oral history provided by a white former member who asked to remain anonymous. This group should not be confused with the similarly named Committee of Concerned Citizens in Kenora, which organized in opposition to the occupation of Anicinawbe Park (Rutherford 2010).
5. See Making Kenora Home, "Appendix: Kenora Fellowship Centre Hostel History" (2015).
6. Joseph Morrison, oral history shared with author, November 28, 2009, Hamilton, ON.
7. Scott Rutherford (2010) documents a total of twenty-five distinct grievances and articulated demands.
8. Joseph Morrison, oral history, November 28, 2009.
9. For further discussion of the politics of Black- and Indigenous-led street patrols in North America, see Maxwell (forthcoming).
10. Charles Copenace, oral history shared with author, March 22, 2017, Kenora, ON.

11. Charles Copenace, oral history, March 22, 2017.
12. Joseph Morrison, oral history, November 28, 2009.
13. Joseph Morrison, oral history, November 28, 2009.
14. Charles Copenace, oral history, March 22, 2017.
15. The office later moved to a more central shopfront in downtown Kenora.
16. G.K. Hamilton, *Kenora Native Street Patrol: First Interim Evaluation Report: November 1978–September 1979*, prepared for the Ministry of Community and Social Services, December 1979.
17. Hamilton, *Kenora Native Street Patrol*.
18. Charles Copenace, oral history, March 22, 2017.
19. Charles Copenace, oral history, March 22, 2017.
20. Hamilton, *Kenora Native Street Patrol*.
21. In Australia, the Community Development and Employment Project introduced in the Northern Territory in 1977 similarly encompassed flexible work conditions so that workers could fulfill family and community responsibilities including participation in ceremony, and became the main employer of Indigenous people in the region. It was abolished in the mid-2000s under the legislation enabling the infamous Northern Territory intervention (Stringer 2007).
22. Hamilton, *Kenora Native Street Patrol*.
23. The Native Canadian Centre in Toronto was the third Friendship Centre to be established in Canada, following those in Winnipeg and Vancouver (Howard 2009).
24. This judgemental moral stance is suggested particularly by a quotation from Millie Redmond relaying her conversation about the women with a Salvation Army Major (Native Canadian Oral History Project 1983b, 29, cited in Howard 2004, 158).
25. Vern Harper, oral history shared with author, November 4, 2008, Toronto. In his 1979 book *Following the Red Path: The Native People's Caravan, 1974*, Vern describes tensions within the movement around gender politics, and his own and others' efforts to challenge enduring misogyny and gender hierarchy in the Red Power movement.
26. Over one thousand Indigenous children were "in care" in Ontario during any given year during the 1970s, hundreds were adopted by non-Indigenous families, and Indigenous children constituted the large majority of those in the care of Children's Aid Societies in Northern Ontario (P. Johnston 1983). Surveys in various parts of Canada have

identified the over-representation of Indigenous people who have been through the child welfare system or non-Native adoptions amongst Indigenous inmates, street kids, and residents of homeless shelters. For example, Suzanne Fournier and Ernie Crey (1997, 90) report the results of a survey in Prince Albert penitentiary where over 95 per cent of Indigenous prisoners had been through the child welfare system. See also Menzies (2005).

27. Native Sons was a mutual support program for Indigenous men incarcerated in the provincial prison system, linked to the Native Brotherhood in the federal system (Reasons 1975; Waldram 1997).
28. Leslie Saunders, oral history shared with author, March 18, 2010, Toronto.
29. James Waldram's (1997) analysis of the work of Elders in prisons similarly points to the significance of political consciousness in both personal trajectories and healing work.
30. Leslie Saunders, oral history, March 18, 2010, Toronto.
31. As described in chapter 1, members of the Lake of the Woods Powwow Club reclaimed the site of the former Cecilia Jeffrey residential school as a powwow ground in 1974, enacting re-membering at this site of recent social dismemberment.
32. These experiences have been relayed to me in oral histories documented as part of my ongoing research project on histories of Anishinaabe kinship and the child welfare system in Treaty 3 territory.
33. Lisa Stevenson (2014) identifies anonymous care as a hallmark of Canadian biopolitics, as typified by the treatment of Inuit in southern sanatoria and contemporary suicide prevention interventions in Nunavut.
34. As discussed in the introduction, in the first half of the twentieth century Canada's own Indian hospital system was likewise conceived as a set of segregated institutions, while the education system was in effect also segregated through most of the twentieth century.
35. As recounted in multiple oral histories shared with me; see also Peters (2001).
36. Vern Harper, oral history shared with author, May 5, 2009, Toronto.
37. As Vern Harper (oral history, May 5, 2009) recalled, the other activists included Art Solomon, an Elder from Sudbury and former mine worker and union activist; Pauline Shirt; Jim Dumont; and Roger Obonsawin,

executive director of the Native Canadian Centre from 1974 to 1981 and first president of the National Association of Friendship Centres.

38. Native American organizers in Los Angeles established similar programs—known as the Indian Men's Lodge and Indian Women's Lodge—during the early 1970s (Weibel-Orlando 1999).
39. *Pedahbun Lodge Inc. Policies*, Nechi Institute part 3, file 851-11, vol. 3041, Record Group 29, Library and Archives Canada.
40. *Pedhabun Lodge Native Alcohol Abuse Program Quarterly Report*, July 1–August 31, 1978, vol. 5, file 850-11, vol. 3045, record group 29, Library and Archives Canada.
41. A culture of silence and complicity around men's violence against female partners in Northern First Nations is further evidenced by women using services, health professionals, and social workers consulted by Timpson et al. (1987). The broader issue of male Indigenous leaders prioritizing territory, natural resources, and economic development over social relations and well-being is a long-standing concern of Indigenous women across North America, well documented in academic and activist literature.
42. Indigenous women had organized against sexism in the Indian Act since the 1950s, asserting women's equal entitlements to the belonging and benefits that came with Status and Band membership (Carlson, Steinhauer, and Goyette 2013; K. Jamieson 1978).
43. For more thorough discussions of Indigenous women's social and political organizing in the 1970s and 1980s, see Barker (2008); Carlson, Steinhauer, and Goyettte (2013); Fiske (1990, 1996); K. Jamieson (1978); and Weaver (1993).
44. Other early publications in this genre include Lee Maracle's *Bobbi Lee Indian Rebel* (1975, 1990), Beatrice Mosionier's *In Search of April Raintree* (1983), Jeannette Armstrong's *Slash* (1985), and Ruby Slipperjack's *Honour the Sun* (1987). More recent autobiographical publications (Chacaby 2016; A. Wilson 2018) have extended the genre by documenting Two-Spirit experiences.
45. This was the first collection of Indigenous women's creative works published in North America, featuring over sixty women from forty nations. First published as a special issue of the lesbian feminist journal *Sinister Wisdom*, the collection—including poetry, short stories, autobiography, drawings, and sculpture—was republished by Toronto Women's Press

in 1988 as a book called *A Gathering of Spirit: A Collection by North American Indian Women*.

46. For an analysis of Brant's work focused on sexuality, see Womack (2009).

3 | "FAMILY VIOLENCE IS WEAKENING OUR NATIONS"

1. Although this report is a historical document, I deliberately use present tense in discussing its content to emphasize its contemporary relevance.
2. For a historical analysis of the uptake of the historical trauma concept by Indigenous social actors, see Maxwell (2014).
3. The Special Committee of the House of Commons on Indian Self-Government's (1983) *Indian Self-Government in Canada* (aka the Penner report) named justice and law among the many domains in which First Nations government should hold jurisdiction (Jackson 1988).
4. Readers who are interested to learn more about Marlene Pierre's life history and groundbreaking social and political organizing work are encouraged to seek out her autobiography, with Damien Lee, *Fighting Inertia: 40 Years of Indigenous Women's Organizing in Canada*, in preparation at the time of writing.
5. Marlene Pierre, oral history shared with author via telephone, November 10, 2019.
6. In addition to her work with ONWA, Marlene participated in founding local and national Indigenous women's organizations, and served terms as president of Thunder Bay Anishinabequek, ONWA (1976–1978; 1995–1997), and the Native Women's Association of Canada (1980–1981).
7. Marlene Pierre, oral history shared via telephone, November 10, 2019.
8. The Fort William reserve is next to what is now the city of Thunder Bay, formed in 1970 from the amalgamation of two smaller cities, Fort William and Port Arthur.
9. Marlene Pierre, oral history shared with author, October 16–17, 2019, Thunder Bay, ON.
10. Marlene Pierre, oral history, October 16–17, 2019.
11. Like the smaller city of Kenora further northwest, discussed in chapters 1 and 2, Thunder Bay is surrounded by First Nations. Those in the immediate vicinity are signatories to the 1850 Robinson-Superior Treaty; to the northeast, Treaty 9 (1905–1906); to the northwest, Treaty 3 (1873);

and further north, the 1929 adhesion to Treaty 9. The second-largest urban area in Northern Ontario after Sudbury, Thunder Bay is a service hub for citizens of more than twenty Anishinaabe, Cree, and Oji-Cree First Nations lacking year-round road access, who must travel to the city to access services, including secondary and tertiary health care, high school education, and the criminal justice system.

12. As discussed in the introduction, provincial child welfare agencies' aggressive apprehension of Indigenous children from homes both on and off reserves became a significant new mode of social dismemberment during the 1960s. By 1981, 85 per cent of the children in the "care" of the Kenora Children's Aid Society were Indigenous, an over-representation of about 400 per cent (P. Johnston 1983). Most of these children would be adopted by white families and given no information about their birth family and nation of origin; some were even taken out of Canada (P. Johnston 1983).

13. Nancy Janovicek (2009) presents a more critical account of the role of the Thunder Bay Friendship Centre in the history of Beendigen and Anishinabequek. Drawing on oral history shared by Audrey Gilbeau and Bernice Dubec, Janovicek argues that women's voices were not always listened to within the Friendship Centre movement and reports a certain apathy towards action to address women's experiences of violence (2009, 61–62).

14. Anduhyaun was established in 1969 through a collaboration between the Toronto Native Canadian Centre and the YWCA (Howard 2004).

15. In 1973 activists working out of the Friendship Centre established the Native People of Thunder Bay Development Corporation, one of six urban Indigenous non-profit housing corporations established across Canada in the early 1970s (Belanger, Head, and Awusoga 2012). The corporation accessed funds through the Ontario non-profit housing program to purchase properties for rent to Indigenous people in the city. At the time when Marlene left to focus on work with ONWA, she recalls that the corporation owned 120 housing units.

16. Marlene Pierre, oral history, October 2019.

17. Thanks to Dorothy Cameron (Taajii), Anishinaabemowin instructor, for this translation.

18. By 1981 there were thirty-four Anishinabequek local chapters affiliated with ONWA, spanning small reserve communities, such as Shoal Lake

in Treaty 3 territory in the northwest and Osnaburgh in the northeast, mid-sized cities including Thunder Bay, Sudbury, and Sault Ste. Marie in the mid-north, and the larger southern cities of Ottawa, Toronto, London, and Hamilton. Ontario Native Women's Association, *ONWA Resource Manual*, May 1981, personal collection of Marlene Pierre.

19. Marlene Pierre, oral history, October 16–17, 2019. Janovicek (2009) also makes this point.
20. Marlene Pierre, oral history, October 16–17, 2019.
21. Research conducted by Indigenous women's organizations in both Alberta and Quebec in the 1970s similarly found that most Indigenous women and men had little knowledge of the Indian Act; 49 per cent of those surveyed in Quebec hadn't heard of it at all (K. Jamieson 1978, 92).
22. Marlene Pierre, oral history, October 16–17, 2019.
23. Grand Council of Treaty 9 was renamed Nishnawbe Aski Nation in 1983. The meeting also included Attorney General Roy McMurty,
24. Marlene Pierre, oral history, October 16–17, 2019.
25. Specifically, section 15 of the Canadian Charter of Rights and Freedoms prohibits "discrimination based on race, national or ethnic origin, colour, religion, sex, age, or mental and physical disability."
26. The other important development contributing to the passage of C-31 was the 1981 ruling against Canada by the United Nations Human Rights Committee, in support of the right of Sandra Lovelace, a Maliseet woman who had lost status under the Indian Act when she married a non-Indian, to live on her home reserve (Cannon 2019; Lawrence 2004).
27. For considered discussions of the social effects of Bill C-31, see Cannon (2019); Innes (2013), particularly chapter 6; Lawrence (2004), and A. Simpson (2014, 56–63).
28. Similarly, in academic literature on Indigenous politics and settler colonialism in North America, colonial violence is often defined in terms of territory, governance, and structural violence, leaving intimate, interpersonal, lateral, and other everyday experiences of violence under-analyzed. See S. Hunt (2015).
29. For example, ONWA's research on women's experiences of spousal violence was supported by the Ontario Women's Directorate; an earlier collaboration between Indian Rights for Indian Women and the National Advisory Council on the Status of Women enabled the 1978 publication *Indian Women and the Law in Canada: Citizens Minus*,

by Kathleen Jamieson, a rigorous, historical analysis of the gendered implications of Canadian settler colonialism.

30. Indigenous women's critiques of white-dominated liberal feminism in North America were consistent with those of many other racialized women in the 1970s and 1980s, such as the 1977 "Combahee River Collective Statement" and Chandra Mohanty's (1988) widely cited article "Under Western Eyes: Feminist Scholarship and Colonial Discourses."

31. Reports from social service workers, most of whom identified as Indigenous, indicated that all had encountered family violence among service users within the course of their work; five of the responding agencies reported "over 90% of their cases," regardless of the presenting issue, involved family violence also. Fourteen of the participating organizations "saw family violence as a way of life for some Aboriginal communities" (ONWA 1989, 25).

32. These and related fears continue to stifle discussion among Indigenous people today (Innes and Anderson 2018).

33. Marlene Pierre, oral history, October 16–17, 2019. A slightly higher proportion of respondents (84%) confirmed that family violence occurs in their community; a further 15 per cent were "unsure" about this. Of course, there are many reasons to believe that spousal violence among Canadian women at large was significantly underreported.

34. Those living off-reserve, like other women in Canada, can in principle obtain an interim occupancy order in cases of spousal violence, guaranteeing their right to shelter in their own home.

35. The National Action Committee on the Status of Women condemned the Supreme Court rulings and called for amendment to the Indian Act (Turpel 1991, 36n57).

36. Some First Nations leaders welcomed the decisions as underscoring "the need for Indian self-government," as did sympathetic commentators advocating for the protection of already circumscribed powers of Band Councils, whose authority to allocate reserve lands was "the most, and perhaps the only, significant power accorded a band council under the Indian Act" (Bartlett 1986, 193).

37. Thirty-five years after *Breaking Free* was published, the issue of matrimonial property rights on reserves remains unresolved, despite the passage of Bill S-2, Family Homes on Reserves and Matrimonial Rights or Interest Act, on June 19, 2013, which includes a mechanism for First

Nations to implement their own laws governing matrimonial real property on reserves. For a summary of Indigenous critiques, see the Ontario Women's Justice Network (n.d.). At the time of writing, only seventeen First Nations have enacted their own laws under this mechanism, while forty have changed laws under the Land Code from a different framework agreement.

38. The authors of *Breaking Free* analyze the reasons for non-intervention, but do not directly critique First Nations leadership for inaction on violence against women and children. Accounts of Chiefs' and Councillors' inaction against spousal violence on reserves were provided by Indigenous counsellors working out of the Sioux Lookout Hospital in Northern Ontario in 1987 (Timpson et al. 1987); evidence was also documented by the 1991 Manitoba Justice Inquiry (Fiske 1996, 84).

39. Friedland understands historical Cree and Anishinaabe values around Windigo as legal principles, and analyzes how those principles were undermined by the Canadian state's prosecution and harsh and degrading treatment of Indigenous leaders for Windigo killings in the late nineteenth and early twentieth centuries.

40. Nearly one-third of ONWA's respondents reported their lack of access to transportation needed to reach support services; 15 per cent did not have access to a telephone with which to seek advice (1989, 7).

41. See also the New Democratic Party Task Force on Northern Health Issues's report—*First Come, Last Served: Native Health in Northern Ontario*—published the same year as *Breaking Free*.

42. The authors describe the five-fold over-representation of Indigenous people who, as 2 per cent of the Canadian population, constitute 10 per cent of the prison population, and in some provinces make up more than one-third of the prison population, citing the Canadian Bar Association report *Locking Up Natives in Canada* (Jackson 1988). Indigenous women were and are also significantly over-represented in the prison population.

43. ONWA's research had confirmed very low rates of court-mandated abuser participation in any form of treatment (1989, 79).

44. Among interviewed service providers, Josephine Mandamin, executive director of Beendigen in Thunder Bay, advocated that ONWA should pressure judges to sentence perpetrators of spousal violence more harshly

(OWNA 1989, 29), consistent with a trend among providers of women's shelter services at large to support criminalization (MacLeod 1987).
45. Marlene Pierre, oral history, October 16–17, 2019.
46. Scott was also minister responsible for Native affairs and minister responsible for women's issues at that time.
47. The *Ottawa Citizen* doesn't detail any of the proposals; *Windspeaker* mentions the proposed healing lodges only; the *Globe and Mail* alone mentions Indigenous justice systems.
48. The previous minority Liberal government (1985–1990) was supported by an accord with the NDP.
49. See, for example, the ten-year anniversary edition of the Aboriginal Healing and Wellness Strategy newsletter, *In the Spirit of Healing & Wellness* (2004).
50. Marlene Pierre, oral history, October 16–17, 2019.

4 | BIOPOLITICAL TACTICS UNDER NEOLIBERAL SETTLER COLONIALISM

1. Fontaine was one of the first Indigenous political leaders to speak publicly about his residential school experiences. Previously Chief of Sagkeeng First Nation, he was elected Grand Chief of the Assembly of Manitoba Chiefs in 1991.
2. In Fontaine's (1990) words, it produced "distortion of (the victim's) sense of morality"; "the abused becomes the abuser...acting out what has been done to you."
3. A 1987 interview with Thatcher conveys the intensified individuation that is the hallmark of neoliberalism: "I think we have gone through a period when too many children and people have been given to understand 'I have a problem, it is the Government's job to cope with it!' or 'I have a problem, I will go and get a grant to cope with it!' 'I am homeless, the Government must house me!' and so they are casting their problems on society and who is society? There is no such thing! There are individual men and women and there are families and no government can do anything except through people and people look to themselves first."
4. The growing number of Indigenous professionals and paraprofessionals during this period was the result of increased Indigenous access to

higher education from the 1970s onward, particularly for those in urban centres and southern territories, which continues to be highly uneven.

5. Warin, Kowal, and Meloni (2020) provide a very helpful account demonstrating the value of biopolitical analysis for understanding these complex relations of power in their analysis of how Indigenous and allied health policymakers and researchers have tactically embraced epigenetic science as a "politics of hope."

6. For a comprehensive account of the development of the AHWS, see Dudziak (2000).

7. The AHF was established as part of the federal government's *Gathering Strength* policy, which responded to the work of the RCAP and residential school Survivors' legal cases, as well as long-standing grassroots advocacy for the federal government to support healing programs.

8. Even the United Nations Declaration on the Rights of Indigenous Peoples, the first draft of which was approved the same year that AHWS was passed in Ontario, presents an understanding of Indigenous self-determination as primarily enacted through economic development, reflecting the global influence of neoliberal ideology (Howard-Wagner, Bargh, and Altamirano-Jiménez 2018).

9. Anita Cameron and Tina Armstrong, personal communication with author, May 31, 2011, Kenora, ON.

10. Anita Cameron, personal communication with author, May 31, 2011, Kenora, ON.

11. Kathy Bird, personal communication with author, May 31, 2011, Kenora, ON.

12. Indigenous Peoples in other settings, notably Māori, have similarly taken tactical advantage of this shift in settler state ideology to assume management of social services for their people (Bell 2018; O'Sullivan 2018).

13. The AHWS policy resulted from the merger of two previously distinct provincial policy development processes, one focused on family violence, prompted by ONWA's *Breaking Free* report, and a second focused on Indigenous health (Dudziak 2000).

14. Castille Troy, oral history shared with author, February 19, 2009, Ottawa, ON,

15. Corene Cheeseman, oral history shared with author, March 24, 2010, Hamilton, ON.

16. A similar critique has been levelled at the National Inquiry into Missing and Murdered Indigenous Women and Girls (2016–2019) and national organizing around this issue for the inadequate involvement of family members (Livingston and Hunt 2018).
17. Mike DeGagné, oral history shared with author, September 17, 2008, Toronto, ON.
18. Al Garman, oral history shared with author, November 13, 2008, Ottawa, ON.
19. Irene Lindsay, oral history shared with author, June 15, 2010, Ottawa, ON.
20. This shift is further evidenced by the fact that this period saw the cancellation of two important bus services, the Greyhound service between Winnipeg and Thunder Bay via Kenora and the local service between Kenora and Fort Frances. After several years without these essential services, at the time of writing they have recently been restored by the provincial Crown agency Ontario Northlands, operating a Winnipeg–Thunder Bay service, including stops at Kenora, Fort Frances, and several smaller towns in Treaty 3 territory.
21. This famous stand-off between the Canadian military and Mohawk warriors under the direction of their women leaders unfolded in response to the municipality of Oka's planned authorization of a golf course on traditional Kanehsatà:ke territory. For critical analyses of media coverage, see Orsini (2010) and Valaskakis (2005).
22. Joe Hester, oral history shared with author, March 21, 2010, Toronto.
23. Joe Hester, oral history, March 21, 2010.
24. Leslie Saunders, oral history shared with author, March 18, 2010, Toronto.
25. Joe Hester, oral history, March 21, 2010.
26. See Miskimmin (2012) for a critical ethnography of how the Head Start model of child and family services has been used to target Indigenous families in Canada.
27. Sylvia Maracle, oral history shared with author, April 17, 2009, Toronto.
28. Sylvia Maracle, oral history, April 17, 2009.
29. Jill Murray (pseudonym), personal communication with author, June 13, 2008, Ottawa.
30. The RCAP was overseen by seven commissioners, of whom four were Indigenous: Paul Chartrand, Co-chair Georges Erasmus, Viola Robinson, and Mary Sillett.

31. Both institutions were funded from the 1970s via the federal government's National Native Alcohol and Drug Addictions Program.
32. In this 1994 report for Corrections Canada, Couture quotes influential trauma theorist Judith Herman's argument regarding commonalities between survivors of multiple forms of trauma, noting that "there seems to be a close parallel, if not a direct analogy, between Aboriginal symptoms of personality disorder and pathology and those of victims of other situations," and that dominant social forces of "acculturation" may induce such symptoms (5, 13). The text of this report is available in the collection of Couture's writing edited by Couture and McGowan (Couture 2013).
33. Chrisjohn was lead researcher with the Cariboo Tribal Council in Williams Lake, British Columbia, and did some of the earliest research on residential schools, which he reported to the RCAP in 1994.
34. Mike DeGagné, oral history shared with author, September 17, 2008, Toronto.
35. This analysis focuses on the text of the AFN's 2004 *Report on Canada's Dispute Resolution Plan to Compensate for Abuses in Indian Residential Schools*, which responded to the 2003 *Dispute Resolution Plan* produced by Indian Residential Schools Resolution Canada, a new federal department established in 2001 under the deputy prime minister with the mandate to negotiate an out-of-court settlement.
36. AFN negotiators did achieve at least implicit recognition by the settler state of the harm caused by simply attending the schools, a reversal of the earlier government position and a political victory for the AFN.
37. Arie Molema's (2016) ethnographic account of TRC hearings includes several examples of public expressions of such critiques. I've also heard several personal accounts of the various harms that flowed directly from participation in the Independent Assessment Process, including increased suicides, deaths from overdoses, and financial exploitation of Survivors.
38. From its inception, AHF leadership requested to function as a foundation subject to fewer restrictions (an option also proposed in the subsequent 2009 INAC evaluation), and to be allocated a longer time frame to allow for investment of funds. The then-Liberal government denied these requests. They also pressed for the Indian Residential Schools Settlement Agreement to extend the timeline of the AHF, which was not granted in the agreement. Jonathan Dewar, Director of

Research, Aboriginal Healing Foundation, personal communication with author, July 22, 2010.
39. Further evidence of the long-term nature of the healing work supported by the AHF, growing demand for healing services, and how the residential schools settlement enhanced demand for healing services is provided by Indian and Northern Affairs Canada (2009), Kishk Anaquot Health Research (2006), and Reimer (2010b).
40. Jonathan Dewar, personal communication, July 22, 2010.
41. At the time of writing, electronic copies of these publications are available at https://www.ahf.ca/publications.
42. This issue was also raised with me by several frontline workers and Survivors I've spoken with during and after my doctoral research.

CONCLUSION

1. Here I'm again drawing on Hage's (2015) analysis.
2. For a stellar recent example, see anthropologist Anne Spice's (2024) analysis of interrelationships between Indigenous and radical queer political imaginaries in the land defenders' movement.
3. The current shortage of the sort of work I am advocating for under the rubric of Indigeneity and biopolitics is illustrated by the recent collection edited by René Dietrich and Kerstin Knopf (2023), which, while undoubtedly valuable, does not include any oral historical or ethnographic research.
4. Such approaches to research are commonly used by those working in critical social science and humanities studies of science and medicine, including the emergent field of Indigenous science and technology studies, and by some medical anthropologists and medical sociologists.
5. "Reconciliation project" is Alondra Nelson's (2012) concept for characterizing the pursuit of reparative justice for past violations, such as transatlantic slavery, reliant on genetic science such as DNA testing.
6. This program has since been renamed Network Environments for Indigenous Health Research. Supported by the Canadian Institutes of Health Research, the program aims to support Indigenous health research and increase the number of Indigenous-identified health researchers.

7. It has also featured in important federal policy documents, including the Canadian Institutes of Health Research's five-year strategic plan in 2014, and the 2017 Naylor report on science (Roher et al. 2021).
8. And here I want to acknowledge that despite my best efforts, my discussion of existing literature that does have this focus may not be exhaustive.

APPENDIX

1. Protocol reference #21252, approval date August 14, 2008. All participants were given an information sheet describing the project with the initial invitation letter and invited to reread the information prior to signing the informed consent form. Two participants declined to sign the form after reading it; instead we reached verbal agreements regarding their participation in the research, the details of which I noted. Ethical research practice dictates that researchers recognize a participant's discomfort with a written contract and respect preferences for a verbal agreement.
2. Protocol references #26605, approval date July 25, 2011; #36102, approval date April 23, 2018; #37392, approval date February 12, 2019.

References

ORAL HISTORIES AND PERSONAL COMMUNICATION

Armstrong, Tina (with Anita Cameron). Personal communication. May 31, 2011, Kenora.
Bird, Kathy. Personal communication. May 31, 2011, Kenora.
Cameron, Adolphus. Oral history. April 4, 2017, Toronto; April 19, 2020, via telephone.
Cameron, Anita (with Tina Armstrong). Personal communication. May 31, 2011, Kenora.
Cheeseman, Corene. Oral history. March 24, 2010, Hamilton.
Copenace, Charles. Oral history. March 22 and 27, 2017, Kenora.
DeGagné, Mike. Oral history. September 17, 2008, Toronto.
Dewar, Jonathan. Personal communication. July 22, 2010, via telephone.
Garman, Al. Oral history. November 13, 2008, Ottawa.

Harper, Vern. Oral history. November 4, 2008, May 5, and June 2, 2009, Toronto.
Hester, Joe. Oral history. March 19, 2010, Toronto.
Letander, Mary Equay. Personal communication. June 24, 2013, Kenora.
Lindsay, Irene. Oral history. June 15, 2010, Ottawa.
Maracle, Sylvia. Oral history. January 29, March 17, April 17, 2009; January 11 and July 9, 2010, Toronto.
Morrison, Joseph. Oral history. November 28, 2009, Hamilton; February 3, November 26, 2010, Toronto.
"Old Guy" from Naicatchewinin. Oral history. March 7, 2017, Toronto; March 23, 2020, via telephone.
Piche, Cindy. Oral history. March 22, 2017, Kenora.
Piche, Cindy (with Gail Skead). Personal communication. March 2017, via telephone.
Pierre, Marlene. Oral history. October 16 and 17, 2019, Thunder Bay; November 10, 2019, via telephone.
Saunders, Leslie. Oral history. March 18, 2010, Toronto.
Smith, Mary Alice. Personal communication. March 3, 2020, via email.
Troy, Castille. Oral history. February 19, 2009, Ottawa.
Wasacase, Colin. Personal communication. April 23, 2020, via telephone.
White, Andy. Oral history. December 21, 2023, via telephone.
Williamson, Beverly. Oral history. March 22, 2017, Kenora.

ARCHIVAL SOURCES

Hamilton, G.K. 1979. *Kenora Native Street Patrol: First Interim Evaluation Report: November 1978–September 1979*. Prepared for the Ministry of Community and Social Services, December 1979. Morrison family archive. Copy provided to the author by Mary Alice Smith.
Mercer, G.W. 1970. "The Kenora Waystation." Unpublished manuscript, box 41-03, Addiction Research Foundation fonds, Centre for Addiction and Mental Health Archives, Toronto.

Morrison, Don. 1971–1978, Handwritten ledger, Morrison family archive. Copy provided to the author by Mary Alice Smith.

Ontario Native Women's Association. 1981. *ONWA Resource Manual*, May 1981. Personal collection of Marlene Pierre.

Pedahbun Lodge Inc. Policies. Nechi Institute part 3, file 851-11, vol. 3041, record group 29. Library and Archives Canada.

Pedhabun Lodge Native Alcohol Abuse Program Quarterly Report, July 1–August 31, 1978. Vol. 5, file 850-11, vol. 3045, record group 29. Library and Archives Canada.

Scully, B. 1974. "Kenora 1965–1974. A Report on the Development of ARF's Work in Kenora and Its Current Status." Unpublished manuscript, box 45-49, Addiction Research Foundation fonds, Centre for Addiction and Mental Health Archives, Toronto.

Yawney, Carol. 1967. "The Kenora Report." Unpublished manuscript, box 42-22, Addiction Research Foundation fonds, Centre for Addiction and Mental Health Archives, Toronto.

PRIMARY AND SECONDARY SOURCES

Aboriginal Healing and Wellness Strategy. 2004. "AHWS Celebrates Ten Years of Healing and Wellness." *In the Spirit of Healing & Wellness*, newsletter, 1–2.

Adelson, Naomi. 2000. *"Being Alive Well": Health and the Politics of Cree Well-Being*. Toronto: University of Toronto Press.

Adelson, Naomi. 2001. "Reimagining Aboriginality: An Indigenous People's Response to Social Suffering." In *Remaking a World: Violence, Social Suffering, and Recovery*, edited by Veena Das, Arthur Kleinman, Margaret Lock, Mamphela Ramphele, and Pamela Reynolds, 76–101. Berkeley: University of California Press.

Alfred, Gerald Taiaiake. 2009a. "Restitution Is the Real Pathway to Justice for Indigenous Peoples." In *Response, Responsibility, and Renewal: Canada's Truth and Reconciliation Journey*, edited by Gregory Younging, Jonathan Dewar, and Mike DeGagné, 179–87. Ottawa: Aboriginal Healing Foundation.

Alfred, Taiaiake. 2009b. *Wasáse: Indigenous Pathways of Action and Freedom.* Toronto: University of Toronto Press.

Anand, Nikhil, Akhil Gupta, and Hannah Appel. 2018. *The Promise of Infrastructure.* Durham, NC: Duke University Press.

Andersen, Chris. 2014. *"Métis": Race, Recognition, and the Struggle for Indigenous Peoplehood.* Vancouver: UBC Press.

Anderson, Kim. 2009. "Leading by Action: Female Chiefs and the Political Landscape." In *Restoring the Balance: First Nations Women, Community, and Culture*, edited by Gail Guthrie Valaskakis, Eric Guimond, and Madeleine Dion Stout, 99–123. Winnipeg: University of Manitoba Press.

Anderson, Kim. 2011. *Life Stages and Native Women: Memory, Teachings, and Story Medicine.* Winnipeg: University of Manitoba Press.

Anderson, Kim, Tracy Bear, Christi Belcourt, Maria Campbell, Maya Ode'amik Chacaby, Tanya Kappo, Lyla Kinoshameg, et al. 2018. "Epilogue: Sitting in with Sisters." In *Keetsahnak / Our Missing and Murdered Indigenous Sisters*, edited by Kim Anderson, Maria Campbell, and Christi Belcourt, 305–26. Edmonton: University of Alberta Press.

Anderson, Kim, Maria Campbell, and Christi Belcourt, eds. 2018. *Keetsahnak / Our Missing and Murdered Indigenous Sisters.* Edmonton: University of Alberta Press.

Anderson, Kim, and Bonita Lawrence, eds. 2003. *Strong Women Stories: Native Vision and Community Survival.* Toronto: Sumach Press.

Anderson, Warwick. 2006. "States of Hygiene: Race 'Improvement' and Biomedical Citizenship in Australia and the Colonial Philippines." In *Haunted by Empire: Geographies of Intimacy in North American History*, edited by Ann Laura Stoler, 94–115. Durham, NC: Duke University Press.

Anderson, Warwick. 2007. "The Colonial Medicine of Settler States: Comparing Histories of Indigenous Health." *Health and History* 9 (2): 144–54. https://www.jstor.org/stable/40111579.

Anglin, Perry. 1965. "Protest: How They Organized the March that Killed Kenora's Apathy." *Toronto Daily Star*, November 27, 1965, 8.

Antze, Paul, and Michael Lambek, eds. 1996. *Tense Past: Cultural Essays in Trauma and Memory*. London: Routledge.

Asad, Talal, ed. 1995. *Anthropology and the Colonial Encounter*. London: Ithaca Press; Atlantic Highlands, NJ: Humanities Press.

Asch, Michael, John Borrows, and James Tully, eds. 2018. *Resurgence and Reconciliation: Indigenous-Settler Relations and Earth Teachings*. Toronto: University of Toronto Press.

Assembly of First Nations (AFN). 1994. *Breaking the Silence: An Interpretive Study of Residential School Impact and Healing as Illustrated by the Stories of First Nations Individuals*. Ottawa: Assembly of First Nations.

Assembly of First Nations. 2004. *Report on Canada's Dispute Resolution Plan to Compensate for Abuses in Indian Residential Schools*. N.p.: Assembly of First Nations. https://epub.sub.uni-hamburg.de/epub/volltexte/2009/2889/pdf/Indian_Residential_Schools_Report.pdf.

Assembly of First Nations. 2015. "AFN National Chief Perry Bellegarde Supports Rally to Honour 50th Anniversary of 'Kenora Indian March' for First Nations Rights." *Canada Newswire*, November 20, 2015. https://www.newswire.ca/news-releases/afn-national-chief-perry-bellegarde-supports-rally-to-honour-50th-anniversary-of-kenora-indian-march-for-first-nations-rights-552285521.html.

Barker, Joanne. 2008. "Gender, Sovereignty, Rights: Native Women's Activism against Social Inequality and Violence in Canada." *American Quarterly* 60 (2): 259–66. https://www.jstor.org/stable/40068533.

Barker, Joanne. 2018. "Indigenous Feminisms." In *Oxford Handbook of Indigenous People's Politics*, edited by José Antonio Lucero, Dale Turner, and Donna Lee VanCott. Oxford: Oxford University Press. https://doi.org/10.1093/oxfordhb/9780195386653.013.007.

Barkwell, Peter Alan. 1982. "The Medicine Chest Clause in Treaty No. 6." *Canadian Native Law Reporter*, no. 4, 1–23.

Barnett, Michael. 2011. *Empire of Humanity: A History of Humanitarianism*. Ithaca, NY: Cornell University Press.

Bartlett, Richard H. 1986. "Indian Self-Government, the Equality of the Sexes, and Application of Provincial Matrimonial Property Laws." *Canadian Journal of Family Law* 5 (1): 188–95.

Belanger, Yale D., Gabrielle Weasel Head, and Olu Awusoga. 2012. "Housing and Aboriginal People in Urban Centres: A Quantitative Evaluation." *Aboriginal Policy Studies* 2 (1): 4–25. https://doi.org/10.5663/aps.v2i1.17705.

Belcourt, Billy-Ray. 2016. "Can the Other of Native Studies Speak?" *Decolonization: Indigeneity, Education and Society Blog*, February 1, 2016. https://decolonization.wordpress.com/2016/02/01/can-the-other-of-native-studies-speak/.

Belcourt, Billy-Ray. 2018. "Meditations on Reserve Life, Biosociality, and the Taste of Non-Sovereignty." *Settler Colonial Studies* 8 (1): 1–15. https://doi.org/10.1080/2201473X.2017.1279830.

Bell, Avril. 2018. "A Flawed Treaty Partner: The New Zealand State, Local Government and the Politics of Recognition." In *The Neoliberal State, Recognition and Indigenous Rights: New Paternalism to New Imaginings*, edited by Deirdre Howard-Wagner, Maria Bargh, and Isabel Altamirano-Jiménez, 77–91. Canberra: Australian National University.

Berbaum, Sylvie. 2000. *Ojibwa Powwow*. Edited and translated by Michael M. Pomedli. Thunder Bay, ON: Centre for Northern Studies, Lakehead University.

Berlant, Lauren. 2004. *Compassion: The Culture and Politics of an Emotion*. New York: Routledge.

Berry, Nicole. 2010. *Unsafe Motherhood: Mayan Maternal Mortality and Subjectivity in Post-war Guatemala*. New York: Berghahn Books.

Blackburn, Carole. 2007. "Producing Legitimacy: Reconciliation and the Negotiation of Aboriginal Rights in Canada." *Journal of the Royal Anthropological Institute* 13 (3): 621–38. https://doi.org/10.1111/j.1467-9655.2007.00447.x.

Blackburn, Carole. 2012. "Culture Loss and Crumbling Skulls: The Problematic of Injury in Residential School Litigation." *Political and Legal Anthropology Review* 35 (2): 289–307. https://doi.org/10.1111/j.1555-2934.2012.01204.x.

Bombay, Amy, Kim Matheson, and Hymie Anisman. 2014. *Origins of Lateral Violence in Aboriginal Communities: A Preliminary Study of Student-to-Student Abuse in Residential Schools*. Ottawa: Aboriginal Healing Foundation.

Borrows, John (Kegedonce). 2010. *Drawing Out Law: A Spirit's Guide*. Toronto: University of Toronto Press.

Borrows, John, and James Tully. 2018. Introduction to *Resurgence and Reconciliation: Indigenous-Settler Relations and Earth Teachings*, edited by Michael Asch, John Borrows, and James Tully, 3–25. Toronto: University of Toronto Press.

Bourgeois, Robyn. 2018. "Generations of Genocide: The Historical and Sociological Context of Missing and Murdered Indigenous Women and Girls." In *Keetsahnak / Our Missing and Murdered Indigenous Sisters*, edited by Kim Anderson, Maria Campbell, and Christi Belcourt, 65–87. Edmonton: University of Alberta Press.

Boyden, Jo, and Elizabeth Cooper. 2007. "Questioning the Power of Resilience: Are Children Up to the Task of Disrupting the Transmission of Poverty?" Chronic Poverty Research Centre (CPRC) Working paper no. 73. https://dx.doi.org/10.2139/ssrn.1753009.

Brant (Degonwadonti), Beth. 1983. "Introduction: A Gathering of Spirit." In "A Gathering of Spirit: North American Indian Women's Issue," ed. Beth Brant. Special issue, *Sinister Wisdom*, no. 22–23, 5–9. http://sinisterwisdom.org/sites/default/files/Sinister%20Wisdom%2022%20and%2023.pdf.

Brant, Beth, ed. 1988. *A Gathering of Spirit: A Collection by North American Indian Women*. Toronto: Toronto Women's Press.

Briggs, Laura. 2012. *Somebody's Children: The Politics of Transracial and Transnational Adoption*. Durham, NC: Duke University Press.

Brownlie, Robin Jarvis. 2019. "A Persistent Antagonism: First Nations and the Liberal Order." In *Liberalism and Hegemony: Debating the Canadian Liberal Revolution*, edited by Michel Ducharme and Jean-Francois Constant, 298–321. Toronto: University of Toronto Press.

Burke, James. 1976. *Paper Tomahawks: From Red Tape to Red Power.* Winnipeg: Queenston House Publishing Inc.

Burnett, Kristin. 2010. *Taking Medicine: Women's Healing Work and Colonial Contact in Southern Alberta, 1880–1930.* Vancouver: UBC Press.

Burnett, Kristin, and Travis Hay. 2023. *Plundering the North: A History of Settler Colonialism, Corporate Welfare, and Food Insecurity.* Winnipeg: University of Manitoba Press.

Burnett, Kristin, Travis Hay, and Lori Chambers. 2016. "Settler Colonialism, Indigenous Peoples and Food: Federal Indian Policies and Nutrition Programs in the Canadian North since 1945." *Journal of Colonialism and Colonial History* 17 (2). https://doi.org/10.1353/cch.2016.0030.

Butler, Judith. 1997. *The Psychic Life of Power: Theories in Subjection.* Stanford, CA: Stanford University Press.

Canadian Charter of Rights and Freedoms, s 15, Part 1 of the *Constitution Act, 1982*, being Schedule B to the *Canada Act 1982* (UK), 1982, c 11.

Canadian Welfare Council and Canadian Association of Social Workers. 1947. *Joint Submission to the Special Joint Committee of the Senate and the House of Commons Appointed to Examine and Consider the Indian Act.* Ottawa: Canadian Welfare Council.

Cannon, Martin J. 2019. *Men, Masculinity, and the Indian Act.* Vancouver: UBC Press.

Cariou, Warren. 2007. "'We Use Dah Membering': Oral Memory in Métis Short Stories." In *Trope and Territories: Short Fiction, Postcolonial Readings, Canadian Writing in Context*, edited by Marta Dvořák and W.H. New, 210–18. Montreal and Kingston: McGill-Queen's University Press.

Carlson, Nellie, Kathleen Steinhauer, as told to Linda Goyette. 2013. *Disinherited Generations: Our Struggle to Reclaim Treaty Rights for First Nations Women and Their Descendants.* Edmonton: University of Alberta.

Carr, E. Summerson. 2023. *Working the Difference: Science, Spirit, and the Spread of Motivational Interviewing.* Chicago: University of Chicago Press.

Carter, Sarah. 2002. "First Nations Women and Colonization on the Canadian Prairies, 1870s–1920s." In *Rethinking Canada: The Promise of Women's History*, 4th ed., edited by Veronica Strong-Boag, Mona Gleason, and Adele Perry, 135–48. Don Mills, ON: Oxford University Press.

CBC News. 2010. "Residential School Survivors Fear Network End." March 19, 2010. https://www.cbc.ca/news/canada/residential-school-survivors-fear-network-end-1.907879.

CBC News. 2016. "RCMP Respond to FSIN Statement on Fatally Shot Indigenous Man." August 12, 2016. https://www.cbc.ca/news/canada/saskatchewan/rcmp-response-indigenous-man-death-1.3719518.

Chacaby, Ma-Nee. 2016. *A Two-Spirit Journey: The Autobiography of a Lesbian Ojibwa-Cree Elder*. Winnipeg: University of Manitoba Press.

Chartrand, Vicki. 2022. "Unearthing Justices: Mapping 500+ Grassroots Initiatives for the Missing and Murdered Indigenous Women, Girls, and Two Spirit+." *Decolonization of Criminology and Justice* 4 (1): 7–30. https://doi.org/10.24135/dcj.v4i1.34.

Chen, Xiaobei. 2003. "The Birth of the Child-Victim Citizen." In *Reinventing Canada: Politics of the 21st Century*, edited by Janine Brodie and Linda Trimble, 189–202. Toronto: Prentice Hall.

Child, Brenda J. 2014. *My Grandfather's Knocking Sticks: Ojibwe Family Life and Labor on the Reservation*. St. Paul: Minnesota Historical Society Press.

Chrisjohn, Roland D., Sherri Young, with Michael Maraun. 2006. *The Circle Game: Shadows and Substance in the Indian Residential School Experience in Canada*, rev. ed. Penticton, BC: Theytus Books.

Comack, Elizabeth. 2012. *Racialized Policing: Aboriginal People's Encounters with the Police*. Winnipeg: Fernwood Publishing.

Combahee River Collective. 1977. "The Combahee River Collective Statement." Republished on *BlackPast.org*. https://www.blackpast.org/african-american-history/combahee-river-collective-statement-1977/.

Corntassel, Jeff. 2012. "Re-envisioning Resurgence: Indigenous Pathways to Decolonization and Sustainable Self-Determination." *Decolonization: Indigeneity, Education & Society* 1 (1): 86–101. https://jps.library.utoronto.ca/index.php/des/article/view/18627.

Corntassel, Jeff. 2021. "Life beyond the State: Regenerating Indigenous International Relations and Everyday Challenges to Settler Colonialism." *Anarchist Developments in Cultural Studies*, no. 1, 71–97. https://journals.uvic.ca/index.php/adcs/article/view/20172.

Corntassel, Jeff, Chaw-win-is, and T'lakwadzi. 2009. "Indigenous Storytelling, Truth-Telling, and Community Approaches to Reconciliation." *English Studies in Canada* 35 (1): 137–59. https://doi.org/10.1353/esc.0.0163.

Corntassel, Jeff, and Cindy Holder. 2008. "Who's Sorry Now? Government Apologies, Truth Commissions, and Indigenous Self-Determination in Australia, Canada, Guatemala, and Peru." *Human Rights Review*, no. 9, 465–89. https://doi.org/10.1007/s12142-008-0065-3.

Coulthard, Glen Sean. 2014. *Red Skin, White Masks: Rejecting the Colonial Politics of Recognition*. Minneapolis: University of Minnesota Press.

Coulthard, Glen Sean. 2019. "Introduction: A Fourth World Resurgent." In *The Fourth World: An Indian Reality*, edited by George Manuel and Michael Posluns, ix–xxxiv. Minneapolis: University of Minnesota Press.

Couture, Joseph E. 1994. *Aboriginal Behavioral Trauma: Towards a Taxonomy*. Saskatoon, SK: Corrections Canada.

Couture, Joseph. 2013. *A Metaphoric Mind: Selected Writings of Joseph Couture*. Edited by Ruth Couture and Virginia McGowan. Athabasca, AB: Athabasca University Press.

Crandon-Malamud, Libbet. 1991. *From the Fat of Our Souls: Social Change, Political Process, and Medical Pluralism in Bolivia*. Berkeley: University of California Press.

Crowley-Matoka, Megan, and Gala True. 2012. "No One Wants to Be the Candy Man: Ambivalent Medicalization and Clinician

Subjectivity in Pain Management." *Cultural Anthropology* 27 (4): 689–712. https://doi.org/10.1111/j.1548-1360.2012.01167.x.

Daigle, Michelle. 2019. "Tracing the Terrain of Indigenous Food Sovereignties." *Journal of Peasant Studies* 46 (2): 297–315. https://doi.org/10.1080/03066150.2017.1324423.

Daschuk, James. 2012. *Clearing the Plains: Disease, Politics of Starvation, and the Loss of Aboriginal Life*. Regina: University of Regina Press.

Daschuk, J.W., Paul Hackett, and Scott MacNeil. 2006. "Treaties and Tuberculosis: First Nations People in Late 19th-Century Western Canada, a Political and Economic Transformation." *Canadian Bulletin of Medical History* 23 (2): 307–30. https://doi.org/10.3138/cbmh.23.2.307.

Daugherty, Wayne E. 1986. *Treaty Research Report—Treaty Three (1873)*. Gatineau, QC: Indian and Northern Affairs Canada.

de Certeau, Michel. 1984. *The Practice of Everyday Life*. Translated by Steven Rendall. Berkeley: University of California Press.

de la Cadena, Marisol. 2015. *Earth Beings: Ecologies of Practice across Andean Worlds*. Durham, NC: Duke University Press.

Deerchild, Rosanna. 2003. "Tribal Feminism Is a Drum Song." In *Strong Women Stories: Native Vision and Community Survival*, edited by Kim Anderson and Bonita Lawrence, 97–105. Toronto: Sumach Press.

Deloria, Philip J. 2004. *Indians in Unexpected Places*. Lawrence: University Press of Kansas.

Department of Indian Affairs and Northern Development. 1997. *Gathering Strength: Canada's Aboriginal Action Plan*. Ottawa: Department of Indian Affairs and Northern Development. https://files.eric.ed.gov/fulltext/ED450974.pdf.

Dhillon, Jaskiran, and Will Parish. 2019. "Exclusive: Canada Police Prepared to Shoot Indigenous Activists, Documents Show." *The Guardian*, December 20, 2019. https://www.theguardian.com/world/2019/dec/20/canada-indigenous-land-defenders-police-documents.

Dickason, Olive P., and David T. McNab. 2009. *Canada's First Nations: A History of Founding Peoples from Earliest Times*. 4th ed. Oxford: Oxford University Press.

Dietrich, René. 2023. "Introduction: The Bio/Geopolitics of Settler States and Indigenous Normativities." In *Biopolitics, Geopolitics, Life: Settler States and Indigenous Presence*, edited by René Dietrich and Kerstin Knopf, 1–43. Durham, NC: Duke University Press.

Dietrich, René, and Kerstin Knopf. 2023. *Biopolitics, Geopolitics, Life: Settler States and Indigenous Presence*. Durham, NC: Duke University Press.

Dombrowski, Kirk. 2001. *Against Culture: Development, Politics, and Religion in Indian Alaska*. Lincoln: University of Nebraska Press.

Downe, Pamela J. 2021. *Collective Care: Indigenous Motherhood, Family, and HIV/AIDS*. Toronto: University of Toronto Press.

Dudziak, Suzanne. 2000. "The Politics and Process of Partnership: A Case Study of the Aboriginal Healing and Wellness Strategy." PhD diss., University of Toronto. https://hdl.handle.net/1807/14163.

Eggertson, Laura. 1990. "Native Women under Assault." *Ottawa Citizen*, January 19, 1990, A6.

El-Haj, Nadia Abu. 2010. "Racial Palestinianization and the Janus-Faced Nature of the Israeli State." *Patterns of Prejudice* 44 (1): 27–41. https://doi.org/10.1080/00313220903507610.

Episkenew, Jo-Ann. 2009. *Taking Back Our Spirits: Indigenous Literature, Public Policy, and Healing*. Winnipeg: University of Manitoba Press.

Fanon, Frantz. 2004. *The Wretched of the Earth*. Translated by Richard Philcox. New York: Grove Press.

Fassin, Didier. 2012. *Humanitarian Reason: A Moral History of the Present*. Berkeley: University of California Press.

Fassin, Didier, and Richard Rechtman. 2009. *The Empire of Trauma: An Inquiry into the Condition of Victimhood*. Princeton, NJ: Princeton University Press.

Feldman, Allen. 2002. "Strange Fruit: The South African Truth Commission and the Demonic Economies of Violence." *Social Analysis* 46 (3): 234–65. https://doi.org/10.3167/015597702782409248.

Fennell, Catherine 2012. "The Museum of Resilience: Raising a Sympathetic Public in Postwelfare Chicago." *Cultural Anthropology* 27 (4): 641–66. https://doi.org/10.1111/j.1548-1360.2012.01165.x.

Fiddler, Thomas, and James R. Stevens. 1985. *Killing the Shamen*. Moonbeam, ON: Penumbra Press.

Fine, Sean. 1990. "Study of Native Women Says 80% Have Suffered Abuse." *Globe and Mail*, January 19, 1990, A16.

Fiske, Jo-Anne. 1990. "Native Women in Reserve Politics: Strategies and Struggles." *Journal of Legal Pluralism and Unofficial Law* 23 (30–31): 121–38. https://doi.org/10.1080/07329113.1990.10756426.

Fiske, Jo-Anne. 1996. "The Womb Is to the Nation as the Heart Is to the Body: Ethnopolitical Discourse of the Canadian Indigenous Women's Movement." *Studies in Political Economy* 51 (Fall): 65–95.

Fontaine, Phil. 1990. "Phil Fontaine's 1990 Account of Physical and Sexual Abuse at Residential School." *The Journal*, CBC, October 30, 1990. CBC Archives. https://www.cbc.ca/player/play/video/1.3332787.

Foucault, Michel. 1990. *The History of Sexuality*. Vol. 1, *An Introduction*. Translated by Robert Hurley. New York: Vintage Books.

Foucault, Michel. 1995. *Discipline and Punish: The Birth of the Prison*. Translated by Alan Sheridan. New York: Vintage Books.

Foucault, Michel. 2003. *"Society Must Be Defended": Lectures at the Collège de France, 1975–76*. Translated by David Macey. New York: Picador.

Fournier, Suzanne, and Ernie Crey. 1997. *Stolen from Our Embrace: The Abduction of First Nations Children and the Restoration of Aboriginal Communities*. Vancouver: Douglas & McIntyre.

Friedland, Hadley Louise. 2018. *The Wetiko Legal Principles: Cree and Anishinabek Reponses to Violence and Victimization*. Toronto: University of Toronto Press.

Galloway, Tracey. 2017. "Canada's Northern Food Subsidy Nutrition North Canada: A Comprehensive Program Evaluation." *International Journal Circumpolar Health* 76 (1), art. 1279451. https://doi.org/10.1080/22423982.2017.1279451.

Garneau, David. 2016. "Imaginary Spaces of Conciliation and Reconciliation: Art, Curation, and Healing." In *Arts of Engagement: Taking Aesthetic Action in and beyond the Truth and Reconciliation Commission of Canada*, edited by Dylan Robinson and Keavy Martin, 21–41. Waterloo, ON: Wilfrid Laurier University Press.

Genosko, Gary, and Scott Thompson. 2009. *Punched Drunk: Alcohol, Surveillance, and the L.C.B.O., 1927–75*. Black Point, NS: Fernwood Publishers.

Globe and Mail. 1965. "Better Deal in Kenora Demanded by Seven Indian Bands." November 23, 1965, 14.

Gone, Joseph P. 2009. "Encountering Professional Psychology: Re-Envisioning Mental Health Services for Native North America." In *Healing Traditions: The Mental Health of Aboriginal Peoples in Canada*, edited by Laurence J. Kirmayer and Gail Guthrie Valaskakis, 419–39. Vancouver: UBC Press.

Gone, Joseph P. 2010. "Psychotherapy and Traditional Healing for American Indians: Exploring the Prospects for Therapeutic Integration." *The Counselling Psychologist* 38 (2): 166–235. https://doi.org/10.1177/0011000008330831.

Gone, Joseph P. 2014. "Reconsidering American Indian Historical Trauma: Lessons from an Early Gros Ventre War Narrative." *Transcultural Psychiatry* 51 (3): 387–406. https://doi.org/10.1177/1363461513489722.

Gone, Joseph P. 2021. "Recounting Coup as the Recirculation of Indigenous Vitality: A Narrative Alternative to Historical Trauma." *Transcultural Psychiatry*. https://doi.org/10.1177/13634615211054998.

Gone, Joseph P., and Laurence J. Kirmayer. 2020. "Advancing Indigenous Mental Health Research: Ethical, Conceptual and Methodological Challenges." *Transcultural Psychiatry* 57 (2): 235–49. https://doi.org/10.1177/1363461520923151.

Grande, Sandy. 2023. "The Biopolitics of Aging: Indigenous Elders as Elsewhere." In *Biopolitics, Geopolitics, Life: Settler States and*

Indigenous Presence, edited by René Dietrich and Kerstin Knopf, 67–84. Durham, NC: Duke University Press.

Grande, Sandy, and Teresa L. McCarty. 2018. "Indigenous Elsewheres: Refusal and Re-membering in Education Research, Policy, and Praxis." *International Journal of Qualitative Studies in Education* 31 (3): 165–67. https://doi.org/10.1080/09518398.2017.1401144.

Hage, Ghassan. 2015. *Alter-Politics: Critical Anthropology and the Radical Imagination*. Victoria, Australia: Melbourne University Press.

Hard-to-Find Mormon Videos. 2015. *Bitter Wind*, 1963. Posted October 9, 2015, YouTube, 30 min. https://www.youtube.com/watch?v=q5HahApUeMQ.

Harper, Vern. 1979. *Following the Red Path: The Native People's Caravan, 1974*. Toronto: NC Press.

Harris, Aroha, and Mary Jane Logan McCallum. 2012. "'Assaulting the Ears of Government': The Indian Homemakers' Clubs and the Māori Women's Welfare League in their Formative Years." In *Indigenous Women and Work: From Labor to Activism*, edited by Carol Williams, 225–39. Urbana: University of Illinois Press.

Hay, Travis. 2018. "Commentary: The Invention of Aboriginal Diabetes: The Role of the Thrifty Gene Hypothesis in Canadian Health Care Provision." *Ethnicity & Disease* 28 (1): 247–52. https://doi.org/10.18865%2Fed.28.S1.247.

Hay, Travis. 2021. *Inventing the Thrifty Gene: The Science of Settler Colonialism*. Winnipeg: University of Manitoba Press.

Henderson, Jennifer, and Pauline Wakeham. 2013. *Reconciling Canada: Critical Perspectives on the Culture of Redress*. Toronto: University of Toronto Press.

Hightower-Langston, Donna. 2003. "American Indian Women's Activism in the 1960s and 1970s." *Hypatia* 18 (2): 114–32. https://doi.org/10.1353/hyp.2003.0021.

Hokowhitu, Brendan, John Oetzel, Anne-Marie Jackson, Mary Simpson, Stacey Ruru, Michael Cameron, Yingsha Zhang, Bevan Erueti, Poia Rewi, Sophie Nock, and Isaac Warbrick. 2022. "Mana Motuhake, Indigenous Biopolitics and Health."

AlterNative: An International Journal of Indigenous Peoples 18 (1): 104–13. https://doi.org/10.1177/11771801221088448.

Hopper, Kim. 1988. "More than Passing Strange: Homelessness and Mental Illness in New York City." *American Ethnologist* 15 (1): 155–67. https://www.jstor.org/stable/645491.

Howard, Heather A. 2004. "Dreamcatchers in the City: An Ethnohistory of Social Action, Gender and Class in Native Community Production in Toronto." PhD diss., University of Toronto.

Howard, Heather A. 2009. "Women's Class Strategies as Activism in Native Community Building in Toronto, 1950–1975." In *Keeping the Campfires Going: Native Women's Activism in Urban Communities*, edited by Susan Applegate Krouse and Heather A. Howard, 105–24. Lincoln: University of Nebraska Press.

Howard-Wagner, Deirdre, Maria Bargh, and Isabel Altamirano-Jiménez. 2018. "From New Paternalism to New Imaginings of Possibilities in Australia, Canada and Aotearoa / New Zealand: Indigenous Rights and Recognition and the State in the Neoliberal Age." In *The Neoliberal State, Recognition and Indigenous Rights: New Paternalism to New Imaginings*, edited by edited by Deirdre Howard-Wagner, Maria Bargh, and Isabel Altamirano-Jiménez, 1–39. Canberra: Australian National University Press.

Hubbard, Tasha, dir. 2019, *nîpawistamâsowin: We Will Stand Up*. National Film Board. https://www.nfb.ca/film/nipawistamasowin-we-will-stand-up/.

Huhndorf, Shari M., and Cheryl Suzack. 2010. "Indigenous Feminism: Theorizing the Issues." In *Indigenous Women and Feminism: Politics, Activism, Culture*, edited by Cheryl Suzack, Shari M. Huhndorf, Jeanne Perreault, and Jean Barman, 1–17. Vancouver: UBC Press.

Humphrey, Michael. 2005. "Reconciliation and the Therapeutic State." *Journal of Intercultural Studies* 26 (3): 203–20. https://doi.org/10.1080/07256860500153492.

Hunt, Dallas. 2023. "(Ad)dressing Wounds: Expansive Kinship Inside and Out." In *Indigenous Resurgence in an Age of Reconciliation*, edited by Heidi Kiiwetinepinesiik Stark, Aimée Craft, and Hōkūlani K. Aikau, 66–78. Toronto: University of Toronto Press.

Hunt, Nancy Rose. 1999. *A Colonial Lexicon of Birth Ritual, Medicalization, and Mobility in the Congo*. Durham, NC: Duke University Press.

Hunt, Sarah. 2015. "Violence, Law and the Everyday Politics of Recognition: Comments on Glen Coulthard's *Red Skin, White Masks*." Paper presented at the Native American and Indigenous Studies Association, June 6, 2015, Washington, DC.

Hunt/Tłaliłila'ogwa, Sarah, and Leanne Betasamosake Simpson. 2023 "Thinking through Resurgence Together: A Conversation between Sarah Hunt/Tłaliłila'ogwa and Leanne Betasamosake Simpson." In *Indigenous Resurgence in an Age of Reconciliation*, edited by Heidi Kiiwetinepinesiik Stark, Aimée Craft, and Hōkūlani K. Aiku, 129–42. Toronto: University of Toronto Press.

Indian and Northern Affairs Canada. 2009. *Evaluation of Community-Based Healing Initiatives Supported through the Aboriginal Healing Foundation*. Ottawa: Indian and Northern Affairs Canada. https://www.rcaanc-cirnac.gc.ca/eng/1100100011405/1547572026320.

In Plain Sight: Addressing Indigenous-Specific Racism and Discrimination in B.C. Health Care. 2020. Addressing Racism Review, Full report, November 2020. https://engage.gov.bc.ca/app/uploads/sites/613/2020/11/In-Plain-Sight-Full-Report-2020.pdf.

Innes, Robert Alexander. 2013. *Elder Brother and the Law of the People: Contemporary Kinship and Cowessess First Nation*. Winnipeg: University of Manitoba Press.

Innes, Robert Alexander, and Kim Anderson. 2018. "The Moose in the Room: Indigenous Men and Violence against Women." In *Keetsahnak / Our Missing and Murdered Indigenous Sisters*, edited by Kim Anderson, Maria Campbell and Christi Belcourt, 175–92. Edmonton: University of Alberta Press.

Innes, Robert Alexander, and Kim Anderson, eds. 2015. *Indigenous Men and Masculinities: Legacies, Identities, Regeneration*. Winnipeg: University of Manitoba Press.

Irlbacher-Fox, Stephanie. 2009. *Finding Dahshaa: Self-Government, Social Suffering, and Aboriginal Policy in Canada*. Vancouver: UBC Press.

Ivison, John. 2010. "Can Property Rights Heal Native Reserves?: Tom Flanagan Makes the Case in New Book." *National Post*, March 24, 2010.

Jackson, Michael. 1988. *Locking Up Natives in Canada: A Report of the Committee of the Canadian Bar Association on Imprisonment and Release*. Ottawa: Canadian Bar Association.

Jacob, Michelle M. 2013. *Yakama Rising: Indigenous Cultural Revitalization, Activism, and Healing*. Tucson: University of Arizona Press.

Jamieson, Kathleen. 1978. *Indian Women and the Law in Canada: Citizens Minus*. Ottawa: Ministry of Supply and Services Canada.

Jamieson, Wanda. 1987. "Aboriginal Male Violence against Aboriginal Women in Canada." MA thesis, University of Ottawa.

Janovicek, Nancy. 2009. "'Assisting Our Own': Urban Migration, Self-Governance, and Native Women's Organizing in Thunder Bay, Ontario, 1972–1989." In *Keeping the Campfires Going: Native Women's Activism in Urban Communities*, edited by Susan Applegate Krouse, and Heather A. Howard, 56–75. Lincoln: University of Nebraska Press.

Janzen, John M. 1978. *The Quest for Therapy: Medical Pluralism in Lower Zaire*. Berkeley: University of California Press.

Jeffries, Marshall. 2015. "Re-Membering Our Own Power: Occaneechi Activism, Feminism, and Political Action Theories." *Frontiers: A Journal of Women Studies* 36 (1): 160–95. https://www.jstor.org/stable/10.5250/fronjwomestud.36.1.0160.

Johnston, Basil. 1982. *Ojibway Ceremonies*. Toronto: McClelland & Stewart.

Johnston, Patrick. 1983. *Native Children and the Child Welfare System*. Ottawa: Canadian Council on Social Development.

Joint Management Committee AHWS. 2009. *Phase 3 Longitudinal Study: Final Report*. Aboriginal Healing and Wellness Strategy, Ontario Ministry of Health, Toronto.

Kamel, Gehane. 2020. *Investigation Report. Law on the Investigation of the Causes and Circumstances of Death. For the Protection of Human Life. Concerning the Death of Joyce Echaquan* (translated from the original French). Bureau du coroner, Gouvernement du Québec. https://www.coroner.gouv.qc.ca/fileadmin/Enquetes_publiques/2020-06375-40_002__1__sans_logo_anglais.pdf.

Kauanui, J. Kēhaulani. 2016. "'A Structure, Not an Event': Colonialism and Enduring Indigeneity." *Lateral: Journal of the Cultural Studies Association* 5 (1). https://csalateral.org/issue/5-1/forum-alt-humanities-settler-colonialism-enduring-indigeneity-kauanui/.

Kelm, Mary-Ellen. 1998. *Colonizing Bodies: Aboriginal Health and Healing in British Columbia, 1900–1950.* Vancouver: UBC Press.

Kelm, Mary-Ellen, and Keith D. Smith. 2018. *Talking Back to the Indian Act: Critical Readings in Settler Colonial Histories.* Toronto: University of Toronto Press.

Kenora and District Social Planning Council and Concerned Citizens Committee. 1973. *While People Sleep: Sudden Deaths in Kenora Area: A Study of Sudden Deaths amongst the Indian People of the Kenora Area, with Primary Emphasis on Apparent Alcohol Involvement.* Kenora, ON: Grand Council Treaty #3.

Kilroy-Marac, Katie. 2019. *An Impossible Inheritance: Postcolonial Psychiatry and the Work of Memory in a West African Clinic.* Oakland: University of California Press.

Kinew, Kathi Avery. 1995. "Manito Gitigaan Governing in the Great Spirit's Garden: Wild Rice in Treaty #3: An Example of Indigenous Government Public Policy Making and Intergovernmental Relations between the Boundary Waters Anishinaabeg and the Crown, 1869–1994." PhD diss., University of Manitoba.

Kirmayer, Laurence J., and Gail Guthrie Valaskakis. 2009. *Healing Traditions: The Mental Health of Aboriginal Peoples in Canada.* Vancouver: UBC Press.

Kishk Anaquot Health Research. 2006. *Final Report of the Aboriginal Healing Foundation.* Vol. 2, *Measuring Progress: Program Evaluation.*

Ottawa: Aboriginal Healing Foundation. https://ehprnh2mw03.
exactdn.com/wp-content/uploads/2021/01/final-report-vol-2.pdf.

Kleinman, Arthur. 1980. *Patients and Healers in the Context of Culture: An Exploration of the Borderland between Anthropology, Medicine, and Psychiatry.* Berkeley: University of California Press.

Kleinman, Arthur. 2012. "Medical Anthropology and Mental Health: Five Questions for the Next Fifty Years." In *Medical Anthropology at the Intersections: Histories, Activisms, and Futures*, edited by Marcia C. Inhorn and Emily A. Wentzell, 116–28. Durham, NC: Duke University Press.

Kolopenuk, Jessica. 2020a. "Power and Echoes: Colonial Relations of Re/iteration and their Genomic Indigeneities." PhD diss., University of Victoria.

Kolopenuk, Jessica. 2020b. "Provoking *Bad* Biocitizenship." *Hastings Center Report* 50 (S1): S23–S29. https://doi.org/10.1002/hast.1152.

Konishi, Shino. 2019. "First Nations Scholars, Settler Colonial Studies, and Indigenous History." *Australian Historical Studies* 50 (3): 285–304. https://doi.org/10.1080/1031461X.2019.1620300.

Kowal, Emma, and Megan Warin. 2018. "Anthropology, Indigeneity, and the Epigenome." *American Anthropologist* 120 (4): 822–25. https://doi.org/10.1111/aman.13141.

Krouse, Susan Applegate, and Heather A. Howard, eds. 2009. *Keeping the Campfires Going: Native Women's Activism in Urban Communities.* Lincoln: University of Nebraska Press.

Kuppers, Petra, and Margaret Noodin. 2021. "*Minobimaadiziwinke* (Creating a Good Life): Native Bodies Healing." In *The Arts of Indigenous Health and Well-Being*, edited by Nancy Van Styvendale, J.D. McDougall, Robert Henry, and Robert Alexander Innes, 177–93. Winnipeg: University of Manitoba Press.

Kyriakides, Theodoros. 2018. "Tactics of Association." *Social Anthropology* 26 (4): 471–86. https://doi.org/10.1111/1469-8676.12579.

Ladner, Kiera L. 2009. "Understanding the Impact of Self-Determination on Communities in Crisis." *Journal of Aboriginal Health / Journal de la santé autochtone* 5 (2): 88–101. https://jps.library.utoronto.ca/index.php/ijih/article/view/28984/23937.

Lambek, Michael. 1996. "The Past Imperfect: Remembering as Moral Practice." In *Tense Past: Cultural Essays in Trauma and Memory*, edited by Paul Antze and Michael Lambek, 235–54. London: Routledge.

Lambert, Valerie. 2022. *Native Agency: Indians in the Bureau of Indian Affairs*. Minneapolis: University of Minnesota Press.

Langford, Will. 2016. "Friendship Centres in Canada, 1959–1977." *American Indian Quarterly* 40 (1): 1–37. https://www.jstor.org/stable/10.5250/amerindiquar.40.1.0001.

Lawrence, Bonita. 2004. *"Real" Indians and Others: Mixed-Blood Urban Native Peoples and Indigenous Nationhood*. Vancouver: UBC Press.

Legislative Assembly of Ontario. 1994. *Hansard*. Session 35.3, June 20, 1994 (Mr. Dalton McGuinty).

Lemke, Thomas. 2011. *Biopolitics: An Advanced Introduction*. New York: NYU Press.

Lester, Alan, and Fae Dussart. 2014. *Colonization and the Origins of Humanitarian Governance: Protecting Aborigines across the Nineteenth-Century British Empire*. Cambridge: Cambridge University Press.

Lewellyn, Jennifer J. 2002. "Dealing with the Legacy of Native Residential School Abuse in Canada: Litigation, ADR, and Restorative Justice." *University of Toronto Law Journal* 52 (3): 253–300. https://www.jstor.org/stable/825996.

Li, Tania Murray. 2007. *The Will to Improve: Governmentality, Development, and the Practice of Politics*. Durham, NC: Duke University Press.

Li, Tania Murray. 2010. "To Make Live or Let Die? Rural Dispossession and the Protection of Surplus Populations." *Antipode* 41 (S1): 66–93. https://doi.org/10.1111/j.1467-8330.2009.00717.x.

Linden, Sidney B. 2007. *Report of the Ipperwash Inquiry*. 4 vols. Toronto: Queen's Printer for Ontario.

Livingston, Ann-Marie, and Sarah Hunt. 2018. "Honouring Elsie: Was She Just a Dream?" In *Keetsahnak / Our Missing and Murdered Indigenous Sisters*, edited by Kim Anderson, Maria Campbell, and Christi Belcourt, 45–62. Edmonton: University of Alberta Press.

Long, John S. 2010. *Treaty No. 9: Making the Agreement to Share the Land in Far Northern Ontario in 1905*. Montreal and Kingston: McGill-Queen's University Press.

Low, Colin, dir. 1960. *Circle of the Sun*. National Film Board. https://www.nfb.ca/film/circle-of-the-sun/.

Lutz, John. 1999. "Gender and Work in Lekwammen Families, 1843–1970." In *Gendered Pasts: Historical Essays in Femininity and Masculinity in Canada*, edited by Kathryn McPherson, Cecelia Morgan, and Nancy Forestell, 80–105. Don Mills, ON: Oxford University Press.

Lux, Maureen. 1998. "Perfect Subjects: Race, Tuberculosis, and the Qu'Appelle B.C.G. Vaccine Trial." *Canadian Bulletin of Medical History* 15 (2): 277–95. https://doi.org/10.3138/cbmh.15.2.277.

Lux, Maureen K. 2016. *Separate Beds: A History of Indian Hospitals in Canada, 1920s–1980s*. Toronto: University of Toronto Press.

MacLeod, Linda. 1987. *Battered But Not Beaten: Preventing Wife Battering in Canada*. Ottawa: Canadian Advisory Council on the Status of Women.

Macoun, Alissa, and Elizabeth Strakosch. 2013. "The Ethical Demands of Settler Colonial Theory." *Settler Colonial Studies* 3 (3-04): 426–43. https://doi.org/10.1080/2201473X.2013.810695.

Mahmood, Saba. 2009. "Agency, Performativity, and the Feminist Subject." In *Pieties and Gender*, edited by Lene Sjørup and Hilda Rømer Christensen, 13–45. Leiden: Brill.

Making Kenora Home. 2015. "Appendix: Kenora Fellowship Centre Hostel History." In *A Way Forward: Housing the Chronically Homeless*, 22–23. http://makingkenorahome.ca/A%20Way%20Forward%20Report%20final.pdf.

Maracle, Sylvia. 2003. "The Eagle Has Landed: Native Women, Leadership and Community Development." In *Strong Women Stories: Native Vision and Community Survival*, edited by Kim Anderson and Bonita Lawrence, 70–80. Toronto: Sumach Press.

Marshall, Murdena, Albert Marshall, and Cheryl Bartlett. 2018. "Two-Eyed Seeing in Medicine." In *Determinants of Indigenous Peoples' Health in Canada: Beyond the Social*, edited by Margo

Greenwood, Sarah de Leeuw, Nicole Marie Lindsay, and Charlotte Reading, 44–53. Toronto: Canadian Scholars.

Mathur, Ashok, Jonathan Dewar, and Mike DeGagné, eds. 2011. *Cultivating Canada: Reconciliation through the Lens of Cultural Diversity*. Ottawa: Aboriginal Healing Foundation.

Matthews, Maureen, Margaret Simmons, Myra Tait, and Lorna A. Turnbull. 2023. "Naanaaba'amii: In the Footsteps of Others." *Storia delle Donne*, no. 18–19, 139–64. https://oaj.fupress.net/index.php/sdd/article/view/15011/11997.

Maxwell, Krista. 1997a. "The Racialized 'Other' and Health Care in Britain: The Case of Sickle Cell Disorders." MA thesis, University of London.

Maxwell, Krista. 1997b. "Towards Targeted HIV Prevention: An Ethnographic Study of Young Gay Men in London." In *AIDS: Activism and Alliances*, edited by Peter Aggleton, Peter Davies, and Graham Hart, 148–66. London: Taylor & Francis.

Maxwell, Krista. 2014. "Historicizing Historical Trauma Theory: Troubling the Trans-generational Transmission Paradigm." *Transcultural Psychiatry* 51 (3): 404–35. https://doi.org/10.1177/1363461514531317.

Maxwell, Krista. 2017. "Settler-Humanitarianism: Healing the Indigenous Child Victim." *Comparative Studies in Society and History* 59 (4): 974–1007. https://doi.org/10.1017/S0010417517000342.

Maxwell, Krista. Forthcoming. "Protecting Indigenous Life: The Ne-Chee Street Patrol, Liberatory Politics, and Humanitarian Tactics." In *Humanitarianism from Below? Universalism and the Politics of Inhumanity*, edited by Till Mostowlansky and Elmira Muratova. London: University College London Press.

Maxwell, Krista, Allison Streetly, and David Bevan. 1999. "Experiences of Hospital Care and Treatment Seeking for Pain from Sickle Cell Disease: Qualitative Study." *British Medical Journal* 318 (7198): 1585–90. https://doi.org/10.1136%2Fbmj.318.7198.1585.

Mbembe, Achille. 2003. "Necropolitics." Translated by Libby Meintjes. *Public Culture* 15 (1): 11–40. https://doi.org/10.1215/08992363-15-1-11.

McCallum, Mary Jane Logan. 2014. *Indigenous Women, Work, and History, 1940–1980*. Winnipeg: University of Manitoba Press.

McCallum, Mary Jane Logan, and Adele Perry. 2018. *Structures of Indifference: An Indigenous Life and Death in a Canadian City*. Winnipeg: University of Manitoba Press.

McGregor, Deborah. 2018. "Reconciliation and Environmental Justice." *Journal of Global Ethics* 14 (2): 222–31. https://doi.org/10.1080/174496 26.2018.1507005.

McKay, Ian. 2000. "The Liberal Order Framework: A Prospectus for Reconnaissance of Canadian History." *Canadian Historical Review* 81 (4): 616–45. https://muse.jhu.edu/article/590654.

McKegney, Sam. 2012. "Warriors, Healers, Lovers, and Leaders: Colonial Impositions on Indigenous Male Roles and Responsibilities." In *Canadian Perspectives on Men and Masculinities: An Interdisciplinary Reader*, edited by Jason A. Laker, 241–68. New York: Oxford University Press.

McKegney, Sam. 2014a. "'Into the Full Grace of the Blood in Men': An Introduction." *Masculindians: Conversations about Indigenous Manhood*, 1–11. Winnipeg: University of Manitoba Press.

McKegney, Sam, ed. 2014b. *Masculindians: Conversations about Indigenous Manhood*. Winnipeg: University of Manitoba Press.

Menzies, Peter M. 2005. "Orphans within Our Family: Intergenerational Trauma and Homeless Aboriginal Men." PhD diss., University of Toronto.

Mihesuah, Devon Abbott. 2001. "Anna Mae Pictou-Aquash: An American Indian Activist." In *Sifters: Native American Women's Lives*, edited by Theda Perdue, 217–35. Oxford: Oxford University Press.

Miller, Robyn. 2021. "Wabano Centre Accused of Mishandling Funds, Workplace Harassment." *CBC News*, June 29, 2021. https://www.cbc.ca/news/canada/ottawa/city-investigates-wabano-center-following-complaints-of-mismanagement-harassment-1.6083171.

Million, Dian. 2013. *Therapeutic Nations: Healing in an Age of Indigenous Human Rights*. Tucson: University of Arizona Press.

Milloy, John S. 1983. "The Early Indian Acts: Developmental Strategy and Constitutional Change." In *As Long as the Sun Shines and Water Flows: A Reader in Canadian Native Studies*, edited by Ian A.L. Getty and Antoine S. Lussier, 56–64. Vancouver: UBC Press.

Mills, Aaron. 2018. "Rooted Constitutionalism: Growing Political Community." In *Resurgence and Reconciliation: Indigenous-Settler Relations and Earth Teachings*, edited by Michael Asch, John Borrows, and James Tully, 133–74. Toronto: University of Toronto Press.

Miskimmin, Susanne. 2007. "When Aboriginal Equals 'At Risk': The Impact of an Institutional Keyword on Aboriginal Head Start Families." In *Words, Worlds, and Material Girls: Language, Gender, Globalization*, edited by Bonnie S. McElhinny, 107–28. Berlin: Mouton de Gruyter.

Miskimmin, Susanne. 2012. "Regulating Risk: Health Canada's Approach to a Pre-School Program for Aboriginal Children." In *Education and the Risk Society: Theories, Discourse and Risk Identities in Education Contexts*, edited by Steven Bialostok, Robert Whitman, and William Bradley, 169–82. Rotterdam: Sense Publishers.

Mohanty, Chandra. 1988. "Under Western Eyes: Feminist Scholarship and Colonial Discourses." *Feminist Review* 30 (1): 61–88. https://doi.org/10.1057/fr.1988.42.

Molema, Arie. 2016. "Errors of Commission: Canada's Legacy of Indian Residential Schools." PhD diss., University of Toronto. https://hdl.handle.net/1807/76569.

Monture-Okanee, Patricia A. 1992. "The Violence We Women Do: A First Nations View." In *Challenging Times: The Women's Movement in Canada and the United States*, edited by Constance Backhouse and David H. Flaherty, 193–200. Montreal and Kingston: McGill-Queen's University Press.

Moreton-Robinson, Aileen. 2009. "Imagining the Good Indigenous Citizen: Race War and the Pathology of Patriarchal White Sovereignty." *Cultural Studies Review* 15 (2): 61–79. https://doi.org/10.5130/csr.v15i2.2038.

Moreton-Robinson, Aileen. 2015. *The White Possessive: Property, Power, and Indigenous Sovereignty.* Minneapolis: University of Minnesota Press.

Morgensen, Scott Lauria. 2011. *Spaces between Us: Queer Settler Colonialism and Indigenous Decolonization.* Minneapolis: University of Minnesota Press.

Myerhoff, Barbara. 1982. "Life History among the Elderly: Performance, Visibility and Re-Membering." In *A Crack in the Mirror: Reflexive Perspectives in Anthropology*, edited by Jay Ruby, 99–117. Philadelphia: University of Pennsylvania Press.

Nadasdy, Paul. 2007. "The Gift in the Animal: The Ontology of Hunting and Human-Animal Sociality." *American Ethnologist* 34 (1): 25–43. https://doi.org/10.1525/ae.2007.34.1.25.

Nadasdy, Paul. 2017. *Sovereignty's Entailments: First Nation State Formation in the Yukon.* Toronto: University of Toronto Press.

Nader, Laura. 1972. "Up the Anthropologist: Perspectives Gained from Studying Up." In *Reinventing Anthropology*, edited by Dell Hymes, 284–311. New York: Pantheon Books.

Napolitano, Valentina, and David Pratten. 2007. "Michel de Certeau: Ethnography and the Challenge of Plurality." *Social Anthropology* 15 (1): 1–12. https://doi.org/10.1111/j.1469-8676.2007.00005.x.

National Aboriginal Housing Committee. 1993. *First Our Lands, Now Our Homes...A Response to the Urban and Rural Native Housing Crisis Created by Canada's Federal Budget Cutbacks.* Brief presented to the Royal Commission on Aboriginal Peoples, June 3, 1993.

National Indian & Inuit Community Health Representatives Organization (NIICHRO). 2010. *Voices of Community Health Representatives.* Kahnawake, QC.

National Inquiry into Missing and Murdered Indigenous Women and Girls. 2019. *Reclaiming Power and Place: The Final Report of the National Inquiry into Missing and Murdered Indigenous Women and Girls.* https://www.mmiwg-ffada.ca/final-report/.

Nelson, Alondra. 2012. "Reconciliation Projects: From Kinship to Justice." In *Genetics and the Unsettled Past: The Collison of DNA, Race, and History*, edited by Keith Wailoo, Alondra Nelson, and Catherine Lee, 20–31. New Brunswick, NJ: Rutgers University Press.

New Democratic Party Task Force on Northern Health Issues. 1989. *First Come, Last Served: Native Health in Northern Ontario.* New Democratic Party.

Ngũgĩ wa Thiong'o. 2009. *Something Torn and New: An African Renaissance.* New York: Basic Civitas Books.

Nielsen, Marianne O., and Karen Jarratt-Snider, eds. 2023. *Indigenous Justice and Gender.* Tucson: University of Arizona Press.

Oldani, Michael J. 2009. "Uncanny Scripts: Understanding Pharmaceutical Emplotment in the Aboriginal Context." *Transcultural Psychiatry* 46 (1): 131–56. https://doi.org/10.1177/1363461509102291.

Ontario Federation of Indigenous Friendship Centres. 2015. *"We Are Li'l Beavers": Reflecting on a Program That Created Safe and Culturally-Grounded Spaces for Indigenous Children and Youth.* Toronto: Ontario Federation of Indigenous Friendship Centres.

Ontario Native Women's Association (ONWA). 1989. *Breaking Free: A Proposal for Change to Aboriginal Family Violence.* Thunder Bay: Ontario Native Women's Association.

Ontario Women's Justice Network. n.d. "Understanding Matrimonial Property Rights on Reserves." Accessed June 1, 2024. http://owjn.org/2014/12/understanding-matrimonial-property-rights-on-reserves/.

Orsini, Michael. 2010. "The Journalist and the Angry White Mob: Reflections from the Field." In *This Is an Honour Song: Twenty Years since the Blockades*, edited by Leanne Simpson and Kiera L. Ladner, 249–60. Winnipeg: ARP Books.

O'Sullivan, Dominic. 2018. "Māori, the State and Self-Determination in the Neoliberal Age." In *The Neoliberal State, Recognition and Indigenous Rights: New Paternalism to New Imaginings*, edited by Deirdre Howard-Wagner, Maria Bargh, and Isabel Altamirano-Jiménez, 241–55. Canberra: Australian National University Press.

Paine, Robert, ed. 1977. *The White Arctic: Anthropological Essays on Tutelage and Ethnicity.* Toronto: University of Toronto Press.

Pasternak, Shiri. 2015. "How Capitalism Will Save Colonialism: The Privatization of Reserve Lands in Canada." *Antipode* 47 (1): 179–96. https://doi.org/10.1111/anti.12094.

Peters, Evelyn J. 2001. "Developing Federal Policy for First Nations People in Urban Areas: 1945–1975." *Canadian Journal of Native Studies* 21 (1): 57–96.

Petryna, Adriana. 2002. *Life Exposed: Biological Citizens after Chernobyl*. Princeton, NJ: Princeton University Press.

Pettipas, Katherine. 1994. *Severing the Ties that Bind: Government Repression of Indigenous Religious Ceremonies on the Prairies*. Winnipeg: University of Manitoba Press.

Pheasant-Neganigwane, Karen. 2020. *Powwow: A Celebration through Song and Dance*. Victoria, BC: Orca Book Publishers.

Pierre, Marlene. 1994. Interview on *Distant Voices*. Aired June 23, 1994, on TV Ontario. Transcript TVO. Last accessed June 1, 2024. https://www.tvo.org/transcript/533403/marlene-pierre.

Pierre, Marlene. 2011. "Ms. Marlene Pierre (Advisor, Robinson Superior Treaty Women's Council) at the Status of Women Committee." Statement, January 14, 2011. https://openparliament.ca/committees/status-of-women/40-3/48/marlene-pierre-1/only/.

Povinelli, Elizabeth A. 1998. "The State of Shame: Australian Multiculturalism and the Crisis of Indigenous Citizenship." *Critical Inquiry* 24 (2): 575–610. https://www.jstor.org/stable/1344180.

Povinelli, Elizabeth A. 2002. *The Cunning of Recognition: Indigenous Alterities and the Making of Australian Multiculturalism*. Durham, NC: Duke University Press.

Proulx, Craig. 2003. *Reclaiming Aboriginal Justice, Identity and Community*. Saskatoon, SK: Purich Publishing Ltd.

Rabinow, Paul, and Nikolas Rose. 2006. "Biopower Today." *BioSocieties*, no. 1, 195–217. https://doi.org/10.1017/S1745855206040014.

Razack, Sherene H. 2015. *Dying from Improvement: Inquests and Inquiries into Indigenous Deaths in Custody*. Toronto: University of Toronto Press.

Reasons, Charles E. 1975. "Native Offenders and Correctional Policy." *Crime and / et Justice* 4 (4): 255–67.

Redfield, Peter. 2005. "Doctors, Borders, and Life in Crisis." *Cultural Anthropology* 20 (3): 328–61. https://doi.org/10.1525/can.2005.20.3.328.

Régnier, Michel, dir. 1967. *Indian Memento*. National Film Board. https://www.nfb.ca/film/indian_memento/.

Reid, Andrea J., Lauren E. Eckert, John-Francis Lane, Nathan Young, Scott G. Hinch, Chris T. Darimont, Steven J. Cooke, Natalie C. Ban, and Albert Marshall. 2021. "'Two-Eyed Seeing': An Indigenous Framework to Transform Fisheries Research and Management." *Fish and Fisheries* 22 (2): 243–61. https://doi.org/10.1111/faf.12516.

Reimer, Gwen. 2010a. *The Indian Residential Schools Settlement Agreement's Common Experience Payment and Healing: A Qualitative Study Exploring Impacts on Recipients*. Ottawa: Aboriginal Healing Foundation.

Reimer, Gwen. 2010b. *"Mapping Progress" on Community Healing since Implementation of the Settlement Agreement*. Ottawa: Aboriginal Healing Foundation.

Rifkin, Mark. 2017. "Indigenizing Agamben: Rethinking Sovereignty in Light of the 'Peculiar' Status of Native Peoples." In *Sovereign Acts: Contesting Colonialism Across Indigenous Nations and Latinx America*, edited by Frances Negrón-Muntaner, 296–335. Tuscon: University of Arizona Press.

Robinson, Dylan, and Keavy Martin, eds. 2016. *Arts of Engagement: Taking Aesthetic Action in and beyond the Truth and Reconciliation Commission of Canada*. Waterloo, ON: Wilfrid Laurier University Press.

Roher, Sophie I.G., Ziwa Yu, Debbie H. Martin, and Anita C. Benoit. 2021. "How Is *Etuaptmumk*/Two-Eyed Seeing Characterized in Indigenous Health Research? A Scoping Review." *PLOS ONE* 16 (7): e0254612. https://doi.org/10.1371%2Fjournal.pone.0254612.

Rouse, Carolyn M. 2021. "Necropolitics versus Biopolitics: Spatialization, White Privilege, and Visibility during a

Pandemic." *Cultural Anthropology* 36 (3): 360–67. https://doi.org/10.14506/ca36.3.03.

Royal Commission on Aboriginal Peoples (RCAP). 1993. *The Path to Healing: Report of the National Round Table on Aboriginal Health and Social Issues*. Ottawa: Ministry of Supply and Services Canada.

Rutherford, Scott. 2010. "Canada's Other Red Scare: The Anicinabe Park Occupation and Indigenous Decolonization." In *The Hidden 1970s: Histories of Radicalism*, edited by Dan Berger, 77–94. New Brunswick, NJ: Rutgers University Press.

Rutherford, Scott. 2017. "'We Have Bigotry All Right—but No Alabamas': Racism and Aboriginal Protest in Canada during the 1960s." *American Indian Quarterly* 41 (2): 158–79. https://doi.org/10.1353/aiq.2017.a663049.

Sabiston, Leslie James. 2021. "Fetal Alcohol Spectrum Disorder and the Fear of Indigenous (dis)Order: New Medico-Legal Alliances for Capturing and Managing Indigenous Life in Canada." PhD diss., Columbia University. https://doi.org/10.7916/d8-g3z4-9x21.

Samson, Colin. 2009. "A Colonial Double-Bind: Social and Historical Contexts of Innu Mental Health." In *Healing Traditions: The Mental Health of Aboriginal Peoples in Canada,* edited by Laurence J. Kirmayer and Gail Guthrie Valaskakis, 109–39. Vancouver: UBC Press.

Shewell, Hugh E.Q. 2004. *"Enough to Keep Them Alive": Indian Welfare in Canada, 1873–1965*. Toronto: University of Toronto Press.

Simard, Norman. 1997."Pedahbun Goes West." *Toronto Native Times*, September 1977, 11–14.

Simpson, Audra. 2008. "Commentary: The 'Problem' of Mental Health in Native North America: Liberalism, Multiculturalism, and the (Non)Efficacy of Tears." *Ethos* 36 (3): 376–79. https://www.jstor.org/stable/20486583.

Simpson, Audra. 2011. "Settlement's Secret." *Cultural Anthropology* 26 (2): 205–17. https://doi.org/10.1111/j.1548-1360.2011.01095.x.

Simpson, Audra. 2014. *Mohawk Interruptus: Political Life across the Borders of Settler States*. Durham, NC: Duke University Press.

Simpson, Leanne Betasamosake. 2017. *As We Have Always Done: Indigenous Freedom through Radical Resurgence*. Winnipeg: University of Manitoba Press.

Simpson, Leanne Betasamosake. 2018. "Centring Resurgence: Taking on Colonial Gender Violence in Indigenous Nation Building." In *Keetsahnak / Our Missing and Murdered Indigenous Sisters*, edited by Kim Anderson, Maria Campbell, and Christi Belcourt, 215–39. Edmonton: University of Alberta Press.

Smith, Paul Chaat, and Robert Allen Warrior. 1996. *Like a Hurricane: The American Indian Movement from Alcatraz to Wounded Knee*. New York: New Press.

Snelgrove, Corey, Rita Kaur Dhamoon, and Jeff Corntassel. 2014. "Unsettling Settler Colonialism: The Discourse and Politics of Settlers, and Solidarity with Indigenous Nations." *Decolonization: Indigeneity, Education & Society* 3 (2): 1–32. https://jps.library.utoronto.ca/index.php/des/article/view/21166.

Snyder, Emily, Val Napoleon, and John Borrows. 2015. "Gender and Violence: Drawing on Indigenous Legal Resources." *University of British Columbia Law Review* 48 (2): 593–654. https://hdl.handle.net/1807/128524.

Sparling, Gordon, dir. 1965. *The Queen in Canada, 1964*. National Film Board. https://www.nfb.ca/film/queen_in_canada_1964/.

Spice, Anne. 2018. "Fighting Invasive Infrastructures: Indigenous Relations against Pipelines." *Environment and Society: Advances in Research*, no. 9, 40–56. https://www.jstor.org/stable/26879577.

Spice, Anne. 2024. "Queer Re(generations). Disrupting Apocalypse Time." In *Unsettling Queer Anthropology: Foundations, Reorientations, and Departures*, edited by Margot Weiss, 266–82. Durham, NC: Duke University Press.

Starblanket, Gina, and Dallas Hunt. 2020. *Storying Violence: Unravelling Colonial Narratives in the Stanley Trial*. Winnipeg: ARP Books.

Starblanket, Gina, and Heidi Kiiwetinepinesiik Stark. 2018. "Towards a Relational Paradigm –Four Points for Consideration: Knowledge, Gender, Land, and Modernity." In *Resurgence and Reconciliation: Indigenous-Settler Relations and Earth Teachings*, edited by

Michael Asch, John Borrows, and James Tully, 175–207. Toronto: University of Toronto Press.

Stark, Heidi Kiiwetinepinesiik. 2023. "Introduction: Generating a Critical Resurgence Together." In *Indigenous Resurgence in an Age of Reconciliation*, edited by Heidi Kiiwetinepinesiik Stark, Aimée Craft, and Hōkūlani K. Aiku, 3–20. Toronto: University of Toronto Press.

Stark, Heidi Kiiwetinepinesiik, Aimée Craft, and Hōkūlani K. Aikau, eds. 2023. *Indigenous Resurgence in an Age of Reconciliation*. Toronto: University of Toronto Press.

Stefanovich, Olivia. 2022. "Residential School Survivors, Indigenous Leaders Say Queen Should Apologize Next." *CBC News*, May 16, 2022. https://www.cbc.ca/news/politics/royal-visit-queen-reconciliation-apology-reparations-1.6454190.

Stevenson, Lisa. 2012. "The Psychic Life of Biopolitics: Survival, Cooperation, and Inuit Community." *American Ethnologist* 39 (3): 592–613. https://doi.org/10.1111/j.1548-1425.2012.01383.x.

Stevenson, Lisa. 2014. *Life Beside Itself: Imagining Care in the Canadian Arctic*. Berkeley: University of California Press.

Stewart, Jane. 1998. "Statement of Reconciliation." In "Address by the Honourable Jane Stewart Minister of Indian Affairs and Northern Development on the Occasion of the Unveiling of *Gathering Strength – Canada's Aboriginal Action Plan*." Delivered January 7, 1998, Ottawa. https://www.rcaanc-cirnac.gc.ca/eng/1100100015725/1571590271585#sec2.

Stoler, Ann Laura. 1995. *Race and the Education of Desire: Foucault's History of Sexuality and the Colonial Order of Things*. Durham, NC: Duke University Press.

Strakosch, Elizabeth. 2015. *Neoliberal Indigenous Policy: Settler Colonialism and the "Post-welfare" State*. London: Palgrave Macmillan.

Stringer, Rebecca. 2007. "A Nightmare of the Neocolonial Kind: Politics of Suffering in Howard's Northern Territory Intervention." *Borderlands* 6 (2).

Sundar, Nandini. 2004. "Toward an Anthropology of Culpability." *American Ethnologist* 31 (2): 145–63. https://www.jstor.org/stable/3805420.

Suzack, Cheryl. 2005. "Law Stories as Life Stories: Jeannette Lavell, Yvonne Bédard, and Halfbreed." In *Tracing the Autobiographical*, edited by Marlene Kadar, Susanna Egan, Jeanne Perreault, and Linda Warley, 72–86. Waterloo, ON: Wilfrid Laurier University Press.

Sylvester, Joe. 1982. Interview by Jocelyn Keeshig. August 11. Tape IH-OT.13, transcript, Indian History Film Project, Canadian Plains Research Centre, University of Regina. Regina, SK. https://hdl.handle.net/10294/1912.

Tait, Caroline L. 2009. "Disruptions in Nature, Disruptions in Society: Aboriginal Peoples of Canada and the "Making" of Fetal Alcohol Syndrome." In *Healing Tradition: The Mental Health of Aboriginal Peoples in Canada*, edited by Laurence J. Kirmayer and Gail Guthrie Valaskakis, 196–218. Vancouver: UBC Press.

Talaga, Tanya. 2017. *Seven Fallen Feathers: Racism, Death, and Hard Truths in a Northern City*. Toronto: House of Anansi Press.

Talbot, Robert J. 2009. *Negotiating the Numbered Treaties: An Intellectual and Political Biography of Alexander Morris*. Saskatoon, SK: Purich Publishing.

TallBear, Kim. 2016. "Dear Indigenous Studies, It's Not Me, It's You: Why I Left and What Needs to Change." In *Critical Indigenous Studies: Engagements in First World Locations*, edited by Aileen Moreton-Robinson, 69–82. Tucson: University of Arizona Press.

Tanner, Adrian. 2009. "The Origins of Northern Aboriginal Social Pathologies and the Quebec Cree Healing Movement." In *Healing Traditions: The Mental Health of Aboriginal Peoples in Canada*, edited by Laurence J. Kirmayer and Gail Guthrie Valaskakis, 249–71. Vancouver: UBC Press.

Taylor, Janelle S. 2003. "Confronting 'Culture' in Medicine's 'Culture of No Culture.'" *Academic Medicine* 78 (6): 555–59. https://doi.org/10.1097/00001888-200306000-00003.

Taylor, Janelle S. 2008. "On Recognition, Caring and Dementia." *Medical Anthropology Quarterly* 22 (4): 313–35. https://doi.org/10.1111/j.1548-1387.2008.00036.x.

Thatcher, Margaret. 1987. "Interview for *Women's Own*." By Douglas Keay. Margaret Thatcher Foundation, Thatcher Archive, THCR 5/2/262, COI transcript, https://www.margaretthatcher.org/document/106689.

Thomas, Eva, dir. 2023. *Redlights*. Eva Thomas Inc. https://gat.ca/portfolio/redlights/.

Thunder Bay Indigenous Friendship Centre. n.d. "Our History." Accessed June 1, 2024. https://tbifc.ca/aboutus/history.

Ticktin, Miriam I. 2011. *Casualties of Care: Immigration and the Politics of Humanitarianism in France*. Berkeley: University of California Press.

Timpson, Joyce, Ethel Turtle, Sally Kakegamic, Donna Roundhead, Louise Sinclair, Grace Matewapit, Joel Chapman. 1987. "Spouse Abuse in the Sioux Lookout Zone." In *Family Violence: A Native Perspective: Proceedings of the Canadian Psychiatric Association Section on Native Mental Health, September 19–21, 1987, at London, Ontario*, 36–61. Ottawa: Canadian Psychiatric Association.

Treaty #3 Achievers Project Committee. 2000. *Celebration of Anishinaabe Achievers of the Treaty #3 Nation*. N.p.

Troutman, John. 2007. "The Citizenship of Dance: Politics of Music among the Lakota, 1900–1924." In *Beyond Red Power: American Indian Politics and Activism since 1900*, edited by Daniel M. Cobb and Loretta Fowler, 91–108. Santa Fe, NM: School for Advanced Research Press.

Truth and Reconciliation Commission of Canada. 2015. *Honouring the Truth, Reconciling for the Future: Summary of the Final Report of the Truth and Reconciliation Commission of Canada*. Winnipeg: Truth and Reconciliation Commission of Canada. https://nctr.ca/records/reports/#trc-reports.

Tuck, Eve, and K. Wayne Yang. 2012. "Decolonization Is Not a Metaphor." *Decolonization: Indigeneity, Education & Society* 1 (1): 1–40. https://jps.library.utoronto.ca/index.php/des/article/view/18630.

Turner, Dale. 2006. *This Is Not a Peace Pipe: Towards a Critical Indigenous Philosophy.* Toronto: University of Toronto Press.

Turpel, Mary Ellen. 1991. "Home / Land." *Canadian Journal of Family Law* 10 (1): 17–40.

Valaskakis, Gail Guthrie. 2005. "Rights and Warriors: Media Memories and Oka." In *Indian Country: Essays on Contemporary Native Culture,* 35–66. Waterloo, ON: Wilfrid Laurier University Press.

Van Krieken, Robert. 2004. "Rethinking Cultural Genocide: Aboriginal Child Removal and Settler-Colonial State Formation." *Oceania* 75 (2): 125–51. https://www.jstor.org/stable/40331967.

Van Styvendale, Nancy, J.D. McDougall, Robert Henry, and Robert Alexander Innes, eds. 2021. *The Arts of Indigenous Health and Well-Being.* Winnipeg: University of Manitoba Press.

Vennum, Thomas. 2009. *The Ojibwa Dance Drum: Its History and Construction.* St. Paul: Minnesota Historical Society Press.

Vizenor, Gerald. 1994. *Manifest Manners: Narratives on Postindian Survivance.* Lincoln: University of Nebraska Press.

Waldram, James B. 1997. *The Way of the Pipe: Aboriginal Spirituality and Symbolic Healing in Canadian Prisons.* Peterborough, ON: Broadview Press.

Waldram, James B. 2004. *Revenge of the Windigo: The Construction of the Mind and Mental Health of North American Aboriginal Peoples.* Toronto: University of Toronto Press.

Waldram, James B., ed. 2008. *Aboriginal Healing in Canada: Studies in Therapeutic Meaning and Practice.* Ottawa: Aboriginal Healing Foundation.

Waldram, James B., D. Ann Herring, and T. Kue Young. 2006. *Aboriginal Health in Canada: Historical, Cultural, and Epidemiological Perspectives.* 2nd ed. Toronto: University of Toronto Press.

Warin, Megan, Emma Kowal, and Maurizio Meloni. 2020. "Indigenous Knowledge in a Postgenomic Landscape: The Politics of Epigenetic Hope and Reparation in Australia." *Science, Technology, and Human Values* 45 (1): 87–111. https://doi.org/10.1177/0162243919831077.

Watts, Vanessa. 2013. "Indigenous Place-Thought and Agency amongst Humans and Non-humans (First Woman and Sky Woman Go on a European World Tour!)." *Decolonization: Indigeneity, Education & Society* 2 (1): 20–34. https://jps.library.utoronto.ca/index.php/des/article/view/19145.

Watts, Vanessa. 2016. "Smudge This: Assimilation, State-Favoured Communities and the Denial of Indigenous Spiritual Lives." *International Journal of Child, Youth and Family Studies* 7 (1): 148–70. https://doi.org/10.18357/ijcyfs.71201615676.

Watts, Vanessa. 2020. "Growling Ontologies: Indigeneity, Becoming-Souls and Settler Colonial Inaccessibility." In *Colonialism and Animality: Anti-Colonial Perspectives in Critical Animal Studies*, edited by Kelly Struthers Montford and Chloë Taylor, 115–28. London: Taylor and Francis Group.

Weaver, Sally. 1993. "First Nations Women and Government Policy, 1970-1992: Discrimination and Conflict." In *Changing Patterns: Women in Canada*, edited by Sandra D. Burt, Lorraine Code, and Lindsay Dorney, 92–150. Toronto: McClelland & Stewart.

Weibel-Orlando, Joan. 1999. *Indian Country, L.A.: Maintaining Ethic Community in Complex Society*. Chicago: University of Illinois Press.

Weibel-Orlando, Joan. 2009. "Telling Paula Starr: Native American Woman as Urban Indian Icon." In *Keeping the Campfires Going: Native Women's Activism in Urban Communities*, edited by Susan Applegate Krouse and Heather A. Howard, 163–88. Lincoln: University of Nebraska Press.

Wiebe, Sarah Marie. 2014. "Beyond Biopolitics? Ecologies of Indigenous Citizenship." In *Routledge Handbook of Global Citizenship Studies*, edited by Engin F. Isin and Peter Nyers, 535–44. Abingdon: Routledge.

Willow, Anna J. 2011. "Conceiving Kakipitatapitmok: The Political Landscape of Anishinaabe Anticlearcutting Activism." *American Anthropologist* 113 (2): 262–76. https://doi.org/10.1111/j.1548-1433.2011.01329.x.

Willow, Anna J. 2012. *Strong Hearts Native Lands: Anti-Clearcutting Activism at Grassy Narrows First Nation.* Winnipeg: University of Manitoba Press.

Wilson, Alex. 2018. "Skirting the Issues. Indigenous Myths, Misses, and Misogyny." In *Keetsahnak / Our Missing and Murdered Indigenous Sisters*, edited by Kim Anderson, Maria Campbell, and Christi Belcourt, 161–74. Edmonton: University of Alberta Press.

Wilson, Brianna. 2023. "AIM Patrol, Minneapolis." *MNOpedia*, last modified May 16, 2023. https://www.mnopedia.org/group/aim-patrol-minneapolis.

Wilson, Richard Ashby. 2003. "Anthropological Studies of National Reconciliation Processes." *Anthropological Theory* 3 (3): 367–87. https://doi.org/10.1177/14634996030033007.

Wilson, Shawn. 2008. *Research Is Ceremony: Indigenous Research Methods.* Halifax: Fernwood Publishing.

Windspeaker. 1990. "Ontario Study Finds Eight of 10 Native Women Abused." February 2, 1990, 2.

Wolfe, Patrick. 2006. "Settler Colonialism and the Elimination of the Native." *Journal of Genocide Research* 8 (4): 387–409. https://doi.org/10.1080/14623520601056240.

Womack, Craig S. 2009. "Beth Brant and the Aesthetics of Sex." In *Art as Performance, Story as Criticism: Reflections on Native Literary Aesthetics*, 366–86. Norman: University of Oklahoma Press.

Women's Earth Alliance, and Native Youth Sexual Health Network. 2016. *Violence on the Land, Violence on Our Bodies: Building an Indigenous Response to Environmental Violence.* http://land-bodydefense.org/uploads/files/VLVBReportToolkit_2017.pdf.

Wright, Peter, and Andrew Treacher, eds. 1982. *The Problem of Medical Knowledge: Examining the Social Construction of Medicine.* Edinburgh: Edinburgh University Press.

Younging, Gregory, Jonathan Dewar, and Mike DeGagné, eds. 2009. *Response, Responsibility, and Renewal: Canada's Truth and Reconciliation Journey.* Ottawa: Aboriginal Healing Foundation.

Index

Aboriginal Healing and Wellness Strategy (AHWS), 126, 132–34, 135–39, 145, 208n13
Aboriginal Healing Foundation (AHF), 132, 141–43, 152, 159, 161, 162–63, 208n7, 210n38, 211n39
Aboriginal Health Access Centres (AHACs), 133–38
academic work, and re-membering, 32–33
Addiction Research Foundation (ARF), 53, 55, 58, 61–63, 75. *See also* Waystation (Kenora hostel)
Adelson, Naomi, 184n5

adoption and foster placement, 19–20, 90, 115–16. *See also* child welfare system
Agamben, Giorgio, 190n47
agency, Indigenous, 4–5, 12, 16, 24, 30–32, 172
aging, 37–38
alcohol and alcohol abuse
family violence and, 56, 108
Giizhiiganang (Don Morrison) and, 45, 46–47, 56, 58–59, 64–66, 70, 71–74
Kenora Waystation, rehabilitation, and Anishinaabe re-membering, 55, 56, 58–59, 60–63, 75, 77, 83–84, 195n51

Lake of the Woods Powwow
Club as sobriety celebration, 66, 67–69
Pedahbun Lodge (Toronto),
96–97, 200n37
racialized criminalization and
prohibition, 45–46, 55–56,
57, 194n23, 194nn29–30
settler colonialism and, 52–53,
57–58
Alcoholics Anonymous (AA), 58,
59, 64–65, 70, 71–73, 83, 96,
197n80
Alfred, Taiaiake, 192n61
alter-politics, 38–39, 167, 168–69, 172.
See also anti-politics
American Indian Movement (AIM),
76, 80–82, 198n2. See also
Red Power movement
Anderson, Grace, 25
Anderson, Kim, 7, 49, 184n5
Life Stages and Native Women, 22
Anderson, Warwick, 2, 190n46
Anduhyaun (Indigenous women's
centre), 108–09, 203n14
Anicinabe Park, occupation of,
79–80, 81–82, 89, 198n4
Anishinaabe (Treaty 3)
introduction, 41–42
Alcoholics Anonymous (AA)
and, 64–65, 70, 72–73, 83,
197n80
Anicinabe Park, occupation of,
79–80, 81–82, 89, 198n4
assertiveness against settler
state, 51–52
family violence and, 56
Grandfather Drum, 46, 49,
66–67, 70, 77, 192nn4–5,
196n60, 197n84

interrelationship between livelihoods, territory, humans,
and other-than-humans,
53, 193n15
Kenora march (1965), 50–51,
52–53, 54–55, 193n12
Lake of the Woods Powwow
Club, 66, 67–70, 91–92,
196n64, 200n31
masculinity and, 71, 74
Native Healers Program, 91–92
Ne-Chee Friendship Centre, 69,
81, 82, 139, 148
Ne-Chee Street Patrol, 69, 77,
82–86, 106, 140, 199n15
Paypom Treaty, 195n41
racialized prohibition against,
45–46, 55–56, 194n23
re-membering and, 48–49,
54–55, 61, 69, 73, 88
residential schools and, 193n16
in Second World War, 192n2
transportation services, demand
for, 80, 138, 143, 209n20
Treaty 3 (1873), 51
Waystation (Kenora hostel),
55, 56, 58–59, 60–63, 75, 77,
83–84, 195n51
While People Sleep (Grand
Council Treaty #3, 1973), 76,
78–79, 80, 121, 198n1, 198n4
white opposition and violence
against, 57–58, 75, 79–80
See also ceremony;
Giizhiiganang (Don
Morrison)
Anishinabequek (Indigenous
women's organization),
108–09, 202n6, 203n13,
203n18

Anishnawbe Health Toronto, 97, 145–46, 147
anonymous care, 92, 200n33
antibiopolitics, 188n37
anti-politics, 38–39, 167, 168, 171. *See also* alter-politics
Aotearoa New Zealand, 3–4, 29, 38
apologies, public, 6, 159
Armstrong, Jeannette
    Slash, 201n44
Armstrong, Tina, 133, 134
Assembly of First Nations (AFN), 130, 156, 160–61, 188n33, 210nn35–36
Asubpeeschoseewagong (Grassy Narrows) First Nation, 194n31, 197n84
Australia, 2, 3–4, 29, 175, 185n10, 199n21

Baker, William Bineshi, Sr., 192n5
Band Councils, 52, 77, 103, 117, 187n29, 205n36
Banks, Dennis, 81
Bartlett, Cheryl, 173
Beaucage, Josephine (née Commanda), 87–88
Bédard, Yvonne, 99
Beendigen (Indigenous women's shelter), 109–10, 148, 203n13
Belcourt, Christi, 184n5
Bill C-31, 111–12, 204n26
Bill S-2 (Family Homes on Reserves and Matrimonial Rights or Interest Act), 205n37
biocitizenship, 31
biomedical knowledge and health care
    anti-Indigenous racism and, 184n3
    and biopolitics and necropolitics, 4
    definition, 186n19
    Indigenous advocacy for, 12–13
    Indigenous healing practices and, 14–15, 91–92, 134–35
    vs. Indigenous health and healing, 6–7
    medical pluralism and, 14–15
    subjectification and, 24, 188n38
    Two-Eyed Seeing (Etuaptmumk) and, 173
biopolitics
    introduction, 4–5, 9–10, 15–16, 120, 190n47
    anonymous care and, 92, 200n33
    antibiopolitics, 188n37
    as mode of liberal governance, 16, 18, 32, 36, 49
    necropolitics and, 4, 36–37, 57–58
    subjectification and, 23–25, 188n32, 193n10
biopolitics, Indigenized
    introduction, 12, 30–32, 37–38, 172–73, 177
    agency and, 4–5, 12, 16, 24, 30–32, 172
    alter-politics and, 38–39, 167, 168–69, 172
    and biologization of Indigenous suffering and healing, 175–76
    divergent understandings of healing and, 131–32
    family violence and, 102, 113, 116, 120–22
    gender and, 77–78
    healing and, 164
    individuation and, 78–79, 123–24, 143–44, 152–55

Ne-Chee Street Patrol and, 83–86, 106
neoliberalism and, 124–25, 126–27, 132, 143–44, 170–71
prison visitation and, 86–91, 106
recognition politics and, 95
re-membering and, 32, 75–76, 92
settler colonialism and, 165–66
Two-Eyed Seeing (Etuaptmumk) and, 173–75
See also re-membering
biopower, 16, 20–21, 102, 120, 164, 186n22, 190n47
Bird, Kathy, 135
Bitter Wind (film), 60–61, 195n40
Black civil rights movement, 50–51, 94
Blackfoot Hospital, 20
blood quantum, 112
Bombay, Amy, 162
Borrows, John, 193n9, 195n54
Boushie, Colten, 191n59
Brant, Beth (Degonwadonti)
A Gathering of Spirit, 99–100, 201n45
Brave Heart, Maria Yellow Horse, 102
Breaking Free (ONWA report, 1989). *See* Ontario Native Women's Association
breastfeeding, 23
Brighter Futures (initiative), 150
British Columbia, 14, 184n3
Burnett, Kristin, 184n5
bus services, 209n20. *See also* transportation services
Butler, Judith, 23, 188n36

Calder v. Attorney-General of British Columbia (1973), 158
Cameron, Adolphus, 71–73, 197n80, 197n83

Cameron, Anita, 133–35
Campbell, Maria, 23, 184n5
Halfbreed, 98–99
Canada Prenatal Nutrition Program, 150
Canadian Charter of Rights and Freedoms, 111, 204n25
Canadian Institutes of Health Research, 211n6, 212n7
Cannon, Martin, 112
Cariou, Warren, 11
Carlick, Alice, 27
Carr, E. Summerson, 167–68
Cecilia Jeffrey residential school, 56, 67–68, 79, 196n66, 200n31
ceremony
Alcoholics Anonymous (AA) and, 72–73
dismemberment and suppression, 17, 53–54, 187nn23–25, 193n18
Grandfather Drum, 46, 49, 66–67, 70, 77, 192nn4–5, 196n60, 197n84
Lake of the Woods Powwow Club, 66, 67–70, 91–92, 196n64, 200n31
powwows, 66–67, 196n60, 196n63
Chacaby, Maya Ode'amik, 106
Chartrand, Paul, 209n30
Cheeseman, Corene, 139
Child, Brenda, 14
child-rearing, 22–23
child services, 148–52
child welfare system, 130, 151, 155, 164–65, 170, 185n11, 199n26, 203n12. *See also* adoption and foster placement
Chrisjohn, Roland, 156–57, 210n33

254 Index

Christianity
   dismemberment and suppression by, 17, 54, 187n23, 187n25, 193n18
   family violence and, 110, 118
   residential schools and, 19
   tactical engagement with, 13, 14, 186n15, 190n48
Circle of the Sun (film), 60
citizenship
   biocitizenship, 31
   ecological citizenship, 31–32
   Indigenous Peoples, transition from wardship to, 21, 27, 188n34, 189n43
civil rights movement, Black, 50–51, 94
colonialism. *See* settler colonialism
colonial middle figures, 25–26, 189n39
colonial violence, 77–78, 102, 112–13, 204n28. *See also* family violence; lateral violence
"Combahee River Collective Statement" (1977), 205n30
Committee of Concerned Citizens in Kenora, 198n4
Community Action Program for Children, 150
community health representatives (CHRs), 26–27, 114, 189n40
Copenace, Charles, 80, 81, 82, 84, 86, 139, 140
Copenace, Rosalyn, 119
Copenace, Sam, 63, 82, 86
Corntassel, Jeff, 35
Coulthard, Glen Sean, 34–35, 39, 95, 192n61, 198n2
Couture, Joseph, 144, 156, 157, 184n5, 210n32

crafts, traditional, 28, 87–88, 106, 142–43
Crey, Ernie, 199n26
criminal justice system (criminalization)
   alcohol abuse and, 55–56, 57, 194n23
   family violence and, 106, 122–23, 206n44
   individuating approach to, 155
   residential school internment and, 185n11
   settler colonialism in, 130
   While People Sleep (Grand Council Treaty #3, 1973), 80
   See also legal systems; prisons

Davis, Bill, 110–11
day schools, 22. *See also* education; residential schools
de Certeau, Michel, 11–12
decolonization, 7, 170
DeGagné, Mike, 141–42, 159
Degonwadonti (Beth Brant)
   A Gathering of Spirit, 99–100, 201n45
de la Cadena, Marisol, 186n16
Derrickson v. Derrickson (1986), 116
dibenindizowin, 106
Dietrich, René
   Biopolitics, Geopolitics, Life (with Knopf), 211n3
difference, 168
disciplinary power, 16–17, 19–21, 47, 57, 172, 186n22
dismemberment
   of Anishinaabe (Treaty 3), 75
   of ceremony, 17, 53–54, 187nn23–25, 193n18

child development paradigm
and, 151–52
Copenace family's experience,
86
family violence and, 116–17,
118–19, 122
gender and, 98–99, 110–12, 116–17
hospitals and, 91
Indian Residential Schools
Settlement Agreement and,
161–62
Marlene Pierre's family
experience, 106–07
settler state interventions and,
4, 18–20
social services and, 22, 93–94
See also child welfare system;
residential schools; settler
colonialism
Dog Lake, 105
Don Jail (Toronto), 89–91, 92
drum. *See* Grandfather Drum
Dubec, Bernice, 203n13
Dumont, Jim, 200n37
Duran, Eduardo, 102

Echaquan, Joyce, 184n3
ecological citizenship, 31–32
education, 22, 188n35, 200n34.
See also residential schools
El-Haj, Nadi, 191n55
enfranchisement, 19, 187n29
epigenetics, 175–76, 208n5
Episkenew, Jo-Ann, 184n5
epistemology, 14, 18, 33, 39, 135,
186n20
equality discourse, 19, 22, 49–50, 52,
57, 93–94
Erasmus, Georges, 209n30
ethnography, 34, 35–36, 169, 171–72

Etuaptmumk (Two-Eyed Seeing),
173–75
everyday, 34
extension of knowledge, 186n16

Family Homes on Reserves and
Matrimonial Rights or
Interest Act (Bill S-2),
205n37
family violence (spousal violence)
introduction, 42
Aboriginal Healing and
Wellness Strategy (AHWS)
and, 138–39
alcohol abuse and, 56, 108
Beendigen (Indigenous women's
shelter), 109–10, 148, 203n13
biopolitics and, 113, 116, 120–22
vs. colonial violence, 112–13,
204n28
complicity of Indigenous
leaders, 97–98, 110–11,
119–20, 201n41, 206n38
court-mandated abuser participation in treatment, 206n43
criminalization, 106, 122–23,
206n44
family healing approach, 42,
102–03, 104–05, 106, 115,
122, 123–24, 130
Indigenous legal resurgence
and, 101, 103, 113–14, 117–18,
120, 123, 124, 126–27, 133, 169
interim occupancy orders,
205n34
lack of access to resources,
121–22, 206n40
lack of attention to, 77–78
matrimonial property rights
and, 117, 123, 205n37

Ontario Native Women's
    Association (ONWA) on,
    112–23
scale of, 114–15, 205n31, 205n33
white liberal feminism and, 103,
    106, 112–13, 115, 117, 118–19,
    122–23
Fanon, Frantz, 47–48
feminism
    Indigenous, 39, 48, 98, 107
    white liberal, 103, 106, 112–13, 115,
        117, 118–19, 122–23, 205n30
fetal alcohol spectrum disorder
    (FASD), 165, 172, 175
Fisher, Charlie, 63
Fiske, Jo-Anne, 119
Flanagan, Tom
    Beyond the Indian Act, 6
floating signifiers, 5
Fontaine, Phil, 129–30, 131, 145, 155,
    160, 207nn1–2
Fort Alexander Residential School,
    129
foster placement and adoption,
    19–20, 90, 115–16. See also
    child welfare system
Foucault, Michel
    on biopolitics, 15–16, 36, 83, 102
    on biopower, 16, 102, 190n47
    on disciplinary power, 16–17,
        186n22
    Eurocentric blind spots of, 31
    on power/knowledge, 171
    on subjectification, 23–24,
        188n32, 193n10
    See also biopolitics; biopower;
        disciplinary power;
        subjectification
Fournier, Suzanne, 199n26
freedom, 105–06

Friedland, Hadley, 118, 206n39
Friendship Centres
    background and purpose,
        28–29, 93, 189n43
    family violence and, 98
    Hamilton Regional Indian
        Centre, 139
    Indigenous women and, 22, 77,
        109, 203n13
    Li'l Beavers children's program,
        148–49, 151–52
    Native Canadian Centre
        (Toronto), 87, 96, 199n23,
        203n14
    Ne-Chee Friendship Centre
        (Kenora), 69, 81, 82, 139, 148
    Ontario Federation of
        Indigenous Friendship
        Centres, 8, 108, 110, 149, 150
    service provision and, 93, 95
    in Sudbury, 150
    in Thunder Bay, 107–08, 203n13
    Winnipeg Indian and Métis
        Friendship Centre, 29

Garman, Al, 142
Garneau, David, 33, 190n52
A Gathering of Spirit (Degonwadonti
    (Beth Brant)), 99–100,
    201n45
Gathering Strength policy (1998), 141,
    152, 158–59, 208n7
gender
    Grandfather Drum and, 77,
        197n84
    Indian Act's gender discrimina-
        tion and Bill C-31, 111–12
    and Indigenous-managed
        health and social services,
        77–78

Index   257

Red Power movement and,
    81–82, 199n25
settler colonialism and, 48,
    98–99
White Paper (1969) and, 98
See also family violence;
    masculinities; women
genetics. See epigenetics
genocide, 4, 36
geopolitics, 20, 99, 100, 103, 113–14,
    123, 126–27
George, Dudley, 191n58
Giizhiiganang (Don Morrison)
    background, 45, 56
    at Cecilia Jeffrey residential
        school, 56, 196n66
    counselling roles at
        Waystation and elsewhere,
        56, 58, 63
    gendered abuse and, 77
    Lake of the Woods Powwow
        Club and, 66, 67–70
    re-membering and Alcoholics
        Anonymous, 64–66, 70,
        72–73
    re-membering and relational
        subjectivity, 46–47, 70,
        71–72, 73–74
    repairing family relationships,
        58–60, 195n38
    Waakebiness (Grandfather
        Drum), 46, 66–67, 70
Gilbeau, Audrey, 203n13
Gladue legal system, 172. See also
    legal systems
Globe and Mail (newspaper), 125,
    207n47
Gone, Joseph P., 175–76, 184n5
Gradual Civilization Act (1857),
    187n27

Gradual Enfranchisement Act (1869),
    187n29
Grand Council Treaty #3
    While People Sleep (1973), 76,
    78–79, 80, 121, 198n1, 198n4
Grande, Sandy, 32, 37
Grandfather Drum, 46, 49, 66–67,
    70, 77, 192nn4–5, 196n60,
    197n84
Grandmothers Group, 142
Greenland, Winnie, 27
Greyhound, 209n20. See also
    transportation services
grounded normativity, 192n61
Gunner, Alex, 119
Gzowski, Peter, 193n12

Hage, Ghassan, 38, 167, 169
Hakenson, Len, 56
Hamilton Regional Indian Centre,
    139
Harper, Stephen (Harper
    government), 159, 162–63
Harper, Vern, 89, 90, 92, 97, 199n25,
    200n37
Harris, Aroha, 27
Harris, Mike (Harris government),
    126, 139, 148
Head Start model, 149, 209n26
healing. See biomedical knowledge
    and health care; Indigenous
    health and healing
Health Canada, 141–42, 162
health sovereignty, 20, 30
Henry, Robert, 184n5
Herman, Judith, 210n32
Hester, Joe, 145, 146, 147
Hill, Daniel G., 193n12
historical trauma, 102, 146
HIV/AIDS activism, 30

Hokowhitu, Brendan, 38, 174–75
homelessness, 79, 144–45, 147
Homemakers' Clubs, 27–28, 189n42
hospitals
    Indian hospital system, 20–21, 25, 91, 188n31, 200n34
    Native Healers Program at Lake of the Woods Hospital (Kenora), 91–92
housing programs, Indigenous, 147–48, 203n15
Howard, Heather, 28, 87, 88
humanitarianism, settler, 78–79, 159–60
Hunt, Nancy Rose, 25
Hunt/Tłaliłila'ogwa, Sarah, 34

incarceration. *See* prisons
Independent Assessment Process, 162, 163, 210n37
Indian Act
    ceremony, suppression of, 17, 187n24
    children apprehension and, 19
    gendered discrimination, challenges to, 99, 111–12
    Indigenous knowledge of, 204n21
    Marlene Pierre and, 106
    racialized prohibition and, 57
    White Paper (1969) and, 94, 98
    women's activism and, 110, 117, 119, 201n42
Indian and Northern Affairs Canada (INAC), 162, 210n38
Indian hospital system, 20–21, 25, 91, 188n31, 200n34
Indian Memento (film), 60
Indian Men's Lodge and Indian Women's Lodge, 201n38

Indian Residential Schools Resolution Canada, 210n35
Indian Residential Schools Settlement Agreement, 130, 152, 160–62, 185n9, 210n38
Indian Self-Government in Canada (Penner report), 202n3
Indigenous feminism, 39, 48, 98, 107
Indigenous health and healing
    introduction, 2–3, 9–10, 41–43, 176–77
    analysis limitations, 43–44
    author's background with, 8–9
    biomedical health care, tactical engagement with, 11, 12–15, 186n18
    colonial middle figures, 25–26, 189n39
    community health representatives (CHRs), 26–27, 114, 189n40
    decolonization and, 7
    Fontaine on, 129–30
    healing, as metaphor, 184n4
    healing, use of term, 185n13
    health histories, 29
    health sovereignty, 20
    Indian hospital system, 20–21, 25, 91, 188n31, 200n34
    justice and, 7, 17, 168–69
    literature on, 29–30
    malleability of, 5–9
    medical pluralism and, 14–15
    methodology and scope, 39–41
    nursing and, 21–22
    as paradox, 1–2, 5, 167–68
    settler colonialism and, 4, 7–8
    See also biopolitics, Indigenized; re-membering

Indigenous Peoples
  child-rearing, 22–23
  citizenship and, 21, 27, 188n34, 189n43
  enfranchisement, 19, 187n29
  Homemakers' Clubs, 27–28
  housing programs, 147–48, 203n15
  liberationist politics, 76–77, 177
  masculinities, 48–49, 71, 74, 81–82, 121
  mid-century subjugation, 19–20, 22, 49–50, 52, 137
  professionals and paraprofessionals, 207n4
  purposeful deprivations, 36–37, 191n56
  resurgence politics, 11, 30, 32, 33–36, 48, 97, 112–13
  social spaces for, 68–69, 107–08, 139–40, 190n52
  subjectification and, 24–25
  tactical engagement with colonialism, 11–14, 35–36, 75–76, 78–79, 89, 131–32, 169–71
  Treaty Rights, 50, 53, 93, 97
  "turning away" from colonialism, 34–35, 95, 177
  urban Indigenous life, 28–29, 77–78, 93, 95–96, 98
  See also alcohol and alcohol abuse; Anishinaabe (Treaty 3); biopolitics, Indigenized; ceremony; child welfare system; dismemberment; family violence; Indigenous health and healing; legal systems, Indigenous; Red Power movement; relational subjectification; re-membering; residential schools; women
Indigenous philosophy, 43–44, 174–75
Indigenous rights, 50, 94. See also Treaty Rights
Indigenous studies, 189n44
individuation
  critique of, 78–79
  Indian Residential Schools Settlement Agreement and, 160–62
  as Indigenous biopolitical tactic, 143–44, 153–54
  individual embodiment of colonialism trope, 164–66
  neoliberalism and, 153–54, 207n3
  vs. re-membering, 148
  residential school Survivors and, 154–59
  settler colonialism and, 18, 151–52
Innes, Robert Alexander, 49, 184n5, 191n59
"integration" discourse, 28–29, 45, 52, 93–94
intergenerational relations, 23, 26–27, 69, 142–43
intergenerational transmission, 73, 175–76
Inuit, 2, 16–17, 25, 41, 200n33
Ipperwash Provincial Park, 191n58
Israel, 191n55

Jacob, Michelle M., 184n5
Jamieson, Kathleen
  Indian Women and the Law in Canada, 204n29
Janovicek, Nancy, 203n13
Jeffries, Marshall, 32, 190n48

Johnston, Basil, 195n54
justice, and healing, 7, 17, 168–69.
    See also legal systems

Kanehsatà:ke Resistance (Oka
    Crisis), 145, 153, 209n21
Keebuck, Elisabeth, 105
Keebuck, Jack, 105
Keebuck, Margaret, 105, 106
Kelly, Fred, 50, 52, 53, 56
Kelly, Peter, 56, 79
Kelm, Mary-Ellen, 14, 184n5
Kenora (ON)
    Anicinabe Park, occupation of,
        79–80, 81–82, 89, 198n4
    Anishinaabe march (1965),
        50–51, 52–53, 54–55, 193n12
    Lake of the Woods Hospital,
        91–92
    Ne-Chee Friendship Centre, 69,
        81, 82, 139, 148
    Ne-Chee Street Patrol, 69, 77,
        82–86, 106, 140, 199n15
    racialized prohibition against
        Anishinaabe, 45–46, 55–56,
        194n23
    Waasegiizhig
        Nanaandawe'iyewigamig
        (health centre), 133–35, 138
    Waystation (hostel), 55, 56,
        58–59, 60–63, 75, 77, 83–84,
        195n51
    While People Sleep (Grand
        Council Treaty #3, 1973), 76,
        78–79, 80, 121, 198n1, 198n4
    white opposition and violence
        against Anishinaabe, 57–58,
        75, 79–80
Kenora Native Women's Association,
    85

Kenora Social Planning Council,
    198n4
Kettle and Stony Point First Nation,
    191n58
Kimiksana, Alice, 27
Kinew, Kathi Avery, 54
Kingston Penitentiary, 87–88
Kirmayer, Laurence, 175–76, 184n5
Kleinman, Arthur, 186n19
Knopf, Kerstin
    Biopolitics, Geopolitics, Life
        (with Dietrich), 211n3
Kowal, Emma, 175, 208n5
Kyriakides, Theodoros, 11–12

Labrador, Charlie, 173
Ladner, Kiera, 29, 34
Lady Willingdon Hospital (Six
    Nations), 20
Lake of the Woods Hospital
    (Kenora), 91–92
Lake of the Woods Powwow Club,
    66, 67–70, 91–92, 196n64,
    200n31
Lakota, 15
land defenders' movement, 37, 211n2
language learning, Indigenous, 35
lateral violence, 49, 70, 77–78, 113, 163,
    169, 187n26. *See also* colonial
    violence; family violence
Lavell, Jeannette Corbiere, 98–99
Lawrence, Bonita, 19, 184n5
legal systems, Indigenous
    healing interdependent with,
        7, 17
    Ontario Native Women's
        Association on healing
        and legal resurgence, 101,
        103, 113–14, 117–18, 120, 124,
        126–27, 133, 169

legal systems, settler colonial
dismemberment by, 116
Gladue legal system, 172
residential school Survivors,
litigation by, 157–58, 160,
208n7
See also criminal justice system;
prisons
Letander, Mary Equay (née Henry),
1–2, 114
Li, Tania, 36–37
liberalism
biopolitics and, 16, 18, 32, 36, 49
and Indigenous health and
healing, 168
residential schools and, 19,
188n30
settler colonialism and, 18–19,
36–37, 49–50, 52, 57, 171–72,
187n28
white liberal feminism, 77, 103,
106, 112–13, 115, 117, 118–19,
122–23, 205n30
White Paper (1969) and, 94
See also neoliberalism
liberationist politics, 76–77, 177
Li'l Beavers (children's program),
148–49, 151–52
Lindsay, Irene, 142
Liquor Control Board of Ontario,
194n29
Little Grand Rapids First Nation,
185n11
Los Angeles, 201n38
Lovelace, Sandra, 204n26
Lux, Maureen, 20, 25

MacLeod, Linda, 117
Mandamin, Josephine, 206n44
Manitoba, 135

Māori, 38, 208n12
Maracle, Lee
Bobbi Lee Indian Rebel, 201n44
Maracle, Sylvia, 8–9, 109, 149, 150
Marshall, Albert, 173, 174
Marshall, Murdena, 173, 174
Martin, Keavy, 184n5
Marxism, 38, 39
masculinities, Indigenous, 48–49, 71,
74, 81–82, 121
Mason, Jim, 89, 90, 92
matrimonial property rights, 117, 123,
205n37
Matthews, Maureen, 8, 23, 26, 185n11
McCallum, Mary Jane Logan, 21, 27,
189n39
McCarty, Teresa, 32
McDougall, J.D., 184n5
McGuinty, Dalton, 132, 133, 136, 137
McKay, Ian, 18
McKay, Wally, 97, 123
McMurty, Roy, 204n23
McNab, Shirley, 27
medical pluralism, 14–15
medicine. *See* biomedical knowledge
and health care
Meech Lake Accord, 153
Meloni, Maurizio, 208n5
Memegwesiwag (semi-human spirit
entities), 23
mental health, 6, 124, 142, 146–47,
149–50
Mercer, G.W., 60, 194n23
Métis, 11, 23, 41, 99
Michon, Xavier, 107, 109
middle figures, colonial, 25–26,
189n39
Midewiwin ceremonies, 54, 196n60
Million, Dian, 7, 18, 30, 33, 185n10
Mills, Aaron, 33

Minneapolis–Saint Paul, 80–81
Minwaashin Lodge (Ottawa), 139, 142–43
Miskimmin, Susanne, 209n26
Missing and Murdered Indigenous Women and Girls, 37, 155, 168–69, 209n16
missionaries. *See* Christianity
Mitchell, Loren, 117
Mohanty, Chandra, 205n30
Molema, Arie, 210n37
Morgensen, Scott, 30
Morin, Yvonne, 27
Morrison, Ada (née Crow), 56, 58, 59, 60, 65, 66, 69, 196n66
Morrison, Albert, 65
Morrison, Don. *See* Giizhiiganang
Morrison, Joseph, 54, 56, 58–60, 65, 69, 80, 82, 195n38, 196n66
Mosionier, Beatrice
  In Search of April Raintree, 201n44
Mulroney, Brian (Mulroney government), 125, 153
multiculturalism, 34, 42, 94–95
Murray, Jill (pseudonym), 152
Myerhoff, Barbara, 66

National Action Committee on the Status of Women, 205n35
National Indian Brotherhood, 22, 98, 99, 188n33
National Inquiry into Missing and Murdered Indigenous Women and Girls, 209n16
National Native Alcohol and Drug Addictions Program, 210n31
National Post (newspaper), 6
National Roundtable on Health and Social Issues, 153–55
Native Alcohol Abuse Program, 96

Native Alliance for Red Power, 198n2. *See also* Red Power movement
Native Canadian Centre (Toronto), 87, 96, 199n23, 203n14
Native Canadian Centre's Ladies' Auxiliary, 86–88, 96, 106
Native Healers Program, 91–92
Native People of Thunder Bay Development Corporation, 148, 203n15
Native Sons, 89–90, 200n27
Native Women's Association of Canada, 170, 202n6
Naylor report (2017), 212n7
Ne-Chee Friendship Centre, 69, 81, 82, 139, 148
Ne-Chee Street Patrol, 69, 77, 82–86, 106, 140, 199n15
Nechi Institute, 153
necropolitics, 4, 36–37, 57–58
Nelson, Alondra, 211n5
neoliberalism
  introduction, 5, 42–43
  Aboriginal Healing and Wellness Strategy (AHWS) and self-determination rhetoric, 132–39
  child services and, 148–52
  colonialism as etiology of Indigenous suffering and, 147
  Indian Residential Schools Settlement Agreement and, 160–62
  Indigenous biopolitical tactics and, 124–25, 126–27, 132, 143–44, 170–71
  individuation and, 153–54, 207n3

mental health discourse and,
    146–47
public services and, 143
reconciliation politics and, 2–3,
    140–41, 150
relational subjectification and,
    140, 151–52
vs. re-membering, 130, 137,
    139–40, 154
resilience and, 124–25
scarcity and, 155
settler colonialism and, 136–39
vilification and, 144–45
See also individuation;
    liberalism
Network Environments for
    Indigenous Health
    Research, 173, 211n6
New Zealand. *See* Aotearoa New
    Zealand
Ngũgĩ wa Thiong'o, 10, 48, 186n14
Nishnawbe Aski Nation, 97, 188n35,
    204n23
North American Indian Club, 87
Nunavut, 16, 200n33
nursing, Indigenous, 21–22

Obonsawin, Roger, 200n37
Occaneechi, 32
Oglala Sioux, 76
Ojibway Warriors Society, 76, 80
Ojibwe Jingle Dress Dance, 14–15
Ojibwe Unity Conference and
    powwow, 80
Oka Crisis (Kanehsatà:ke
    Resistance), 145, 153, 209n21
Old Guy from Naicatchewinin,
    46–47, 52, 54, 65, 67, 69–70,
    193n6
O'Neil, John, 153–54

Ontario
    Aboriginal Healing and
        Wellness Strategy (AHWS),
        126, 132–34, 135–39, 145,
        208n13
    Indigenous population, 41
    Indigenous relations and
        provincial politics, 125–26,
        207n48
Ontario Federation of Indigenous
    Friendship Centres, 8, 108,
    110, 149, 150
Ontario Native Women's Association
    (ONWA)
    on alcohol abuse and family
        violence, 108
    and artificial individuation of
        collective matters, 123–25
    biopolitical approach to family
        violence, 102, 113, 116,
        120–22
    Breaking Free (1989), 101, 102–04,
        113–14, 123, 124, 125, 126–27,
        130, 138, 145, 163, 202n1,
        206n38, 207n47
    comparison to Waasegiizhig
        Nanaandawe'iyewigamig,
        133–34
    on court-mandated abuser
        participation in treatment,
        206n43
    family healing approach, 42,
        102–03, 104–05, 106, 115, 122,
        123–24, 130
    on family violence, 112–23
    geopolitical approach to
        Indigenous legal resurgence
        and healing, 101, 103, 113–14,
        117–18, 120, 123, 124, 126–27,
        133, 169

on Indigenous leaders'
    complicity, 110–11, 119–20,
    206n38
Marlene Pierre on, 170
neoliberal embrace of
    Indigenous biopolitical
    tactics and, 124–25, 126–27,
    170–71
research by, 114, 204n29
vs. white liberal feminism,
    106, 112–13, 115, 117, 118–19,
    122–23
Ontario Northlands, 209n20
Ontario Women's Directorate,
    204n29
ontology, 14, 18, 33, 39, 135, 186n20
Ottawa
    Inuit population, 41
    Minwaashin Lodge, 139,
        142–43
    Wabano Centre for Aboriginal
        Health, 6, 152
Ottawa Citizen (newspaper), 125,
    207n47

Paine, Robert, 2
Palestinians, 191n55
paradox, 2, 167–68
Pauingassi First Nation, 185n11
Paul v. Paul (1986), 116
Paypom Treaty, 195n41
Pedahbun Lodge (Toronto), 96–97,
    200n37
Penner report (*Indian
    Self-Government in Canada*),
    202n3
Pheasant-Neganigwane, Karen,
    196n63
Piche, Cindy, 68–69
Pierre, Cyril, 105, 106

Pierre, Marlene
    on Aboriginal Healing and
        Wellness Strategy, 126
    activism and volunteer work,
        107–08, 202n6
    and Anishinabequek (women's
        organization) and
        Beendigen (women's
        shelter), 108–10, 148
    on *Breaking Free* (ONWA), 125
    family background, 105, 106–07
    on family healing, 104–05
    on family violence, 119
    Fighting Inertia, 202n4
    on freedom, 105–06
    on gendered exclusion by
        Indigenous leaders, 110–11
    on Indigenous women's and
        children's lives, 170–71
pipelines, 37
political dismemberment. *See*
    dismemberment
Porter, Tom, 197n87
postcolonial theory, 3
Poundmaker's Lodge, 153
power
    biopower, 16, 20–21, 102, 120, 164,
        186n22, 190n47
    disciplinary power, 16–17, 19–21,
        47, 57, 172, 186n22
    sovereign power, 15–16, 17, 20–21,
        24, 37
    tactics and, 12
    See also biopolitics; necropolitics
powwows
    about, 66–67, 196n63
    Grandfather Drum and, 196n60
    Lake of the Woods Powwow
        Club, 66, 67–70, 91–92,
        196n64, 200n31

Ojibwe Unity Conference and powwow, 80
Presbyterian Fellowship Centre, 79–80
primitive accumulation, 39, 192n60
prisons
    child welfare system and, 199n26
    Indigenous representation, 206n42
    visiting Indigenous inmates, 86–88, 89–91, 92, 106, 200n29
protection, 81
Proulx, Craig, 184n5

The Queen in Canada, 1964 (film), 61
queer perspectives, 30, 34, 39, 211n2. *See also* Two-Spirit people

Rabinow, Paul, 102
racism, anti-Indigenous, 51, 145, 184n3
reciprocity and reciprocal recognition
    Coulthard on, 35, 157, 192n61
    Indigenous-only social spaces and, 190n52
    re-membering and, 25, 35, 90–91, 92, 137, 141
recognition politics, 26, 34–35, 94, 95, 97
reconciliation politics
    about, 2–3
    colonialism as embodied past event and, 164
    Indigenized biopolitics and, 91
    liberalism and, 36
    neoliberalism and, 2–3, 140–41, 150
    public apologies and, 6, 158–59
    resurgence and, 30, 35
    settler colonialism and, 158–60, 163
reconciliation project, 211n5
Red and White Committee, 198n4
Redmond, Millie (née White), 87, 199n24
Red Power movement
    about, 38–39, 198n2
    family violence and, 112–13
    gender politics and, 77, 199n25
    influence of and participation in, 87, 89, 96
    masculinity and, 81–82
    occupation tactics, 76
Reform Party, 145
Reid, Andrea J., 174
relationality, 18, 32, 75–76, 192n61
relational subjectification
    Anishinaabe protestors (1965) and, 55
    community health representatives (CHRs) and, 26
    Homemakers' Clubs and, 28
    identifying and supporting, 169
    Indigenized biopolitics and, 21
    Indigenous medical paraprofessionals and, 25
    Li'l Beavers and, 148, 151–52
    Ne-Chee Street Patrol and, 83
    neoliberalism and, 140, 151–52
    re-membering and, 61
relational subjectivity, 46–47, 69, 106, 115, 140
relief payments, 52
re-membering
    introduction, 3, 10–11, 25, 32–34, 35–36, 47–48, 75–76, 168, 176–77

academic work and, 32–33
Alcoholics Anonymous (AA)
   and, 72–73
Anishinaabe and, 48–49, 54–55,
   61, 63, 69, 73, 88
challenges and constraints, 86
Giizhiiganang (Don Morrison)
   and, 46–47, 64–66, 70, 71–72,
   73–74
vs. Indian Residential Schools
   Settlement Agreement,
   160–62
Indigenous housing programs
   and, 147–48
intergenerational, 69
Jeffries on, 32, 190n48
Li'l Beavers children's program
   and, 148–49
Minwaashin Lodge (Ottawa)
   and, 142–43
Native Healers Program and,
   91–92
vs. neoliberalism, 130, 137,
   139–40, 154
Pedahbun Lodge (Toronto) and,
   96–97, 200n37
prison visitation and, 86–88,
   89–91
reconciliation politics and, 141
relational subjectivity (subjectification) and, 24, 46–47, 61,
   69, 106
settler colonial opposition to,
   92–93
trauma discourse, critiques of,
   and, 157
research methods, 169, 171–72, 211n4.
   See also ethnography
residential schools
   introduction, 8, 19, 152–53

Cecilia Jeffrey residential
   school, 56, 67–68, 79,
   196n66, 200n31
closure of, 22
family violence and, 115
Fontaine on, 129–30, 207nn1–2
Fort Alexander Residential
   School, 129
Independent Assessment Process, 162, 163, 210n37
Indian Residential Schools
   Resolution Canada, 210n38
Indian Residential Schools
   Settlement Agreement, 130,
   152, 160–62, 185n9, 210n38
individual traumatized Survivor
   approach, 154–59
litigation by Survivors, 157–58,
   160, 208n7
Minister Stewart's "Statement
   of Reconciliation," 158–59
Queen Elizabeth II, call for
   apology from, 6
re-membering to counter, 47
as synecdoche for colonialism,
   30, 131, 152–53
in Treaty 3 territory, 193n16
undocumented deaths and
   unmarked graves, 68
See also education
resilience, 124–25
responsibilization, 144
resurgence politics, 11, 30, 32, 33–36,
   48, 97, 112–13. *See also* legal
   systems, Indigenous
Robinson, Dylan, 184n5
Robinson, Viola, 209n30
Roher, Sophie I.G., 174
Rose, Nikolas, 102
Rouse, Carolyn, 188n37

Royal Commission on Aboriginal
Peoples (RCAP), 131, 141, 152,
153–55, 208n7, 209n30
Rural and Native Housing Program,
147
Rush, Ella, 87
Rutherford, Scott, 193n12

Sabiston, Les, 165, 172, 175
Saunders, Leslie, 89–90, 91, 146–47
scarcity, 155
scholarship, and re-membering,
32–33
Scott, Ian, 125, 207n46
Second World War, 45, 192n2
self-determination
Band membership and, 112
healing as prerequisite, 7
multiculturalism and, 94
neoliberal self-management
and, 132–39
ONWA on Indigenous legal
resurgence and, 103, 117
United Nations Declaration on
the Rights of Indigenous
Peoples on, 208n8
well-being and, 29
settler colonialism
introduction, 3–4, 184nn1–2
Aboriginal Healing
Foundation's termination
and, 162–63
Anishinaabe assertiveness
against, 51–52
colonial middle figures, 25–26,
189n39
colonial violence, 77–78, 102,
112–13, 204n28
divergent understandings of,
130–31

as etiology of Indigenous
suffering, 42–43, 116, 124–25,
130, 132, 145, 147
individuated embodiment
trope, 157–58, 164–66
liberalism and, 18–19, 36–37,
49–50, 52, 57, 171–72, 187n28
neoliberalism and, 136–39
opposition to Indigenous
re-membering, 92–93,
95–96
residential schools as
synecdoche for, 30, 131,
152–53
tactical engagement with, 11–14,
35–36, 75–76, 78–79, 89,
131–32, 169–71
"turning away" from, 34–35, 95,
177
White Paper (1969) and, 94
See also dismemberment;
hospitals; neoliberalism;
residential schools
settler humanitarianism, 78–79,
159–60
Seymour, Peter, 50, 53
Sherman, Linda, 121
Shewell, Hugh, 52
Shirt, Eric, 153–54
Shirt, Pauline, 200n37
Siksika, 13–14, 20
Sillett, Mary, 209n30
Simpson, Leanne Betasamosake, 43
Sinclair, Murray, 162
Sioux, 46, 192n4
Six Nations, 20
Skead, Clifford, 63, 73
Skead, Doug, 64–65, 66, 72, 196n66
Skead, Madeline, 63, 64–65, 66, 72,
134, 196n66, 198n3

Slipperjack, Ruby
   Honour the Sun, 201n44
Smith, Gilbert, 73
Smith, Mary Alice, 195n38
Smith, Paul Chaat, 80–81
Smith Clinic (Thunder Bay), 70, 71
social dismemberment. *See* dismemberment
social history, 169
social spaces, alternate/Indigenous-only, 68–69, 107–08, 139–40, 190n52. *See also* Friendship Centres; Waystation (Kenora hostel)
Solomon, Art, 200n37
sovereign power, 15–16, 17, 20–21, 24, 37
sovereignty, Indigenous. *See* legal systems, Indigenous
Spice, Anne, 37, 211n2
spousal violence. *See* family violence
Stanley, Gerald, 191n59
Starblanket, Gina, 36
Stark, Heidi Kiiwetinepinesiik, 36
starlight tours, 191n56
Stevenson, Lisa, 2, 16–17, 200n33
Stewart, Jane, 158–59, 160
street patrols
   AIM Patrol (Minneapolis-Saint Paul), 80–81
   Ne-Chee Street Patrol, 69, 77, 82–86, 106, 140, 199n15
   in Toronto, 145–46
subjectification, 23–25, 26, 29, 188n32, 193n10. *See also* relational subjectification
Sudbury (ON), 144–45, 150
suicide prevention, 16–17, 24, 200n33
Sundance ceremony, 17, 60, 187n24

Sundar, Nandini, 140
Suzack, Cheryl, 99
Sylvester, Joe, 93, 96, 97
syncretism, 14

tactics, 11–12, 35–36, 75–76, 78–79, 89, 131–32, 169–71
TallBear, Kim, 189n44
Thatcher, Margaret, 130, 207n3
Thunder Bay (ON)
   about, 202n8, 202n11
   Beendigen (Indigenous women's shelter), 109–10, 148, 203n13
   Smith Clinic, 70, 71
   Thunder Bay Friendship Centre, 107–08, 203n13
Toronto
   Anduhyaun (Indigenous women's centre), 108–09, 203n14
   Anishnawbe Health Toronto, 97, 145–46, 147
   Native Canadian Centre, 87, 96, 199n23, 203n14
   Native Canadian Centre's Ladies' Auxiliary, 86–88, 96, 106
   Pedahbun Lodge, 96–97, 200n37
   prison visitation, 86–88, 89–91, 92
   street patrol, 145–46
Torrie, Allan, 56, 71, 89, 91
transportation services, 80, 138, 143, 209n20
trauma
   biologization of Indigenous suffering and trauma, 175–76
   historical trauma, 102, 146

residential school Survivors and, 155–57, 159, 160–62, 185n9, 210n32
Treaty 3 (1873), 51. *See also* Anishinaabe (Treaty 3)
Treaty Rights, 50, 53, 93, 97. *See also* Indigenous rights
Troutman, John, 15
Troy, Castille, 139
Trudeau, Pierre (Trudeau government), 94
Truth and Reconciliation Commission (TRC), 131, 161–62, 164–65, 185n11, 188n30, 210n37
Tully, James, 193n9
Turner, Dale, 94
Turpel, Mary Ellen, 116
Two-Eyed Seeing (Etuaptmumk), 173–75
Two-Spirit people, 30, 34, 39, 48, 71, 201n44

Union of Ontario Indians, 125
United Nations Declaration on the Rights of Indigenous Peoples, 208n8
United Nations Human Rights Committee, 204n26
urban Indigenous life, 28–29, 77–78, 93, 95–96, 98. *See also* Friendship Centres; housing programs; Kenora; Ottawa; street patrols; Sudbury; Thunder Bay; Toronto
Urban Native Housing Program, 148

Valaskakis, Gail, 184n5
Van Styvendale, Nancy, 184n5
Vennum, Thomas, 192n5
victimhood, 152–53, 155, 156
vilification, 144–45
violence. *See* colonial violence; family violence; lateral violence

Waasegiizhig Nanaandawe'iyewigamig (Kenora health centre), 133–35, 138
Wabano Centre for Aboriginal Health (Ottawa), 6, 152
Waldram, James, 184nn4–5, 200n29
Warin, Megan, 175, 208n5
Warrior, Robert Allen, 80–81
Waystation (Kenora hostel), 55, 56, 58–59, 60–63, 75, 77, 83–84, 195n51
Welfare Planning Council (Winnipeg), 28
Wet'suwet'en, 37
While People Sleep (Grand Council Treaty #3, 1973), 76, 78–79, 80, 121, 198n1, 198n4
White, Andy, 68
White, Tommy, 73
White Paper (1969), 94, 98, 112, 119
Wiebe, Sarah Marie, 31–32
Williamson, Beverly (Bev), 63, 68–69
Windigo, 17, 187n26, 206n39
Windspeaker (newspaper), 125, 207n47
Winnipeg, 28, 29, 70, 76, 84
Winnipeg Indian and Métis Friendship Centre, 29

women, Indigenous
  in academy, 32
  activism against political
    dismemberment, 78,
    98–100, 101–02, 108–10,
    201n42
  Anduhyaun (women's centre),
    108–09, 203n14
  Anishinabequek (women's
    organization), 108–09,
    202n6, 203n13, 203n18
  Beendigen (women's shelter),
    109–10, 148, 203n13
  Bill C-31 and, 111–12
  child-rearing, 22–23
  exclusion by Indigenous leaders,
    110–11
  Friendship Centres and, 22, 77,
    109, 203n13
  A Gathering of Spirit
    (Degonwadonti (Beth
    Brant)) and, 99–100, 201n45
  Grandfather Drum and, 77,
    197n84
  Grandmothers Group, 142
  Homemakers' Clubs, 27–28,
    189n42
  *Indian Women and the Law in
    Canada* (Jamieson), 204n29
  matrimonial property rights on
    reserves, 117, 123, 205n37
  Minwaashin Lodge (Ottawa),
    139, 142–43
  Missing and Murdered
    Indigenous Women and
    Girls, 37, 155, 168–69, 209n16
  missionaries, tactical
    engagement with, 13–14
  nursing and, 21–22
  settler colonialism and, 48,
    98–99
  White Paper (1969) and, 98
  See also family violence;
    Ontario Native Women's
    Association
Women's Institutes, 27, 189n41
World War II, 45, 192n2

Yawney, Carol, 62